T0339987

Macro-Social Marketing Insights

Macro-social marketing is an approach to solving wicked problems. Wicked problems include obesity, environmental degradation, smoking cessation, fast fashion, gambling, and drug and alcohol abuse. As such, wicked problems are those problems that are so complex and multifaceted, it is difficult to define the exact problem, its contributing factors, and paths to a solution. Increasingly, governments, NGOs, and community groups are seeking to solve these types of problems. In doing so, the issues with pursuing macro-level change are beginning to emerge. Issues stem from the interconnected nature of stakeholders involved with a wicked problem—where one change may create a negative ripple effect of both intended and unintended consequences.

Macro-social marketing, then, provides a holistic and systemic approach to both studying and solving wicked problems. Within the chapters of this book, macro-social marketing approaches to analysing and defining wicked problems, to identifying stakeholders and potential ripple effects, and to implementing macro-level change are presented. In this emerging area of academia, the theories, models, and approaches outlined in this book are cutting edge and provide a critical approach from top researchers in the area. Both practical and theoretical aspects are presented as well as caveats on such societal and/or country-wide change. A must-have for social marketing academics and those interested in macro-level change at a practical or theoretical level.

Ann-Marie Kennedy is a senior lecturer in marketing at the University of Canterbury. She specialises in macro-social marketing and sustainability.

Routledge Interpretive Marketing Research

Recent years have witnessed an 'interpretive turn' in marketing and consumer research. Methodologies from the humanities are taking their place alongside those drawn from the traditional social sciences.

Qualitative and literary modes of marketing discourse are growing in popularity. Art and aesthetics are increasingly firing the marketing imagination.

This series brings together the most innovative work in the burgeoning interpretive marketing research tradition. It ranges across the methodological spectrum from grounded theory to personal introspection, covers all aspects of the postmodern marketing 'mix', from advertising to product development, and embraces marketing's principal sub-disciplines.

Taste, Consumption, and Markets
An Interdisciplinary Volume
Edited by Zeynep Arsel and Jonathan Bean

Consumption, Psychology and Practice Theories
A Hermeneutic Perspective
Tony Wilson

Gifts, Romance, And Consumer Culture
Edited by Yuko Minowa and Russell W. Belk

Food and Experiential Marketing
Pleasure, Wellbeing and Consumption
Edited by Wided Batat

Macro-Social Marketing Insights
Systems Thinking for Wicked Problems
Edited by Ann-Marie Kennedy

For more information about this series, please visit: www.routledge.com/Routledge-Interpretive-Marketing-Research/book-series/SE0484

Macro-Social Marketing Insights

Systems Thinking for Wicked Problems

Edited by Ann-Marie Kennedy

Routledge
Taylor & Francis Group

NEW YORK AND LONDON

First published 2020
by Routledge
605 Third Avenue, New York, NY 10017

and by Routledge
2 Park Square, Milton Park, Abingdon, Oxon, OX14 4RN

First issued in paperback 2021

Routledge is an imprint of the Taylor & Francis Group, an informa business

© 2020 Taylor & Francis

The right of Ann-Marie Kennedy to be identified as the author
of the editorial material, and of the authors for their individual
chapters, has been asserted in accordance with sections 77 and 78
of the Copyright, Designs and Patents Act 1988.

All rights reserved. No part of this book may be reprinted
or reproduced or utilised in any form or by any electronic,
mechanical, or other means, now known or hereafter invented,
including photocopying and recording, or in any information
storage or retrieval system, without permission in writing from
the publishers.

Trademark notice: Product or corporate names may be
trademarks or registered trademarks, and are used only for
identification and explanation without intent to infringe.

Library of Congress Cataloging-in-Publication Data
A catalog record for this book has been requested

ISBN 13: 978-0-367-78547-5 (pbk)
ISBN 13: 978-1-138-32208-0 (hbk)

Typeset in Sabon
by Apex CoVantage, LLC

Contents

Figures

Tables

1 Macro-Social Marketing Overview

Ann-Marie Kennedy

Introduction

Social marketing is evolving from a strictly individual-based approach to behaviour change. Traditionally the individual was assumed to be in control of their behaviour, and thus pure exchange and persuasion were considered "de rigueur." Ultimately, however, difficulty in identifying sustainable change from interventions, unintended consequences, victim blaming, and created stigmas has led to an acknowledgement that a person may not be in complete control of their own behaviour—as is the case with wicked problems.

Wicked problems are complex, multi-layered issues, such as obesity, which have multiple causes, perpetuating factors, and solutions. Each intervention also has the potential for positive and negative unintended consequences, making intervention planning difficult (Kennedy & Parsons, 2014). They require a holistic, systemic approach to create change and a recognition of the embeddedness of an individual in their social context. Macro-social marketing considers social change in a holistic manner and is especially pertinent with wicked problems. Macro-level social marketing proposes that such issues should be approached holistically, at multiple levels concurrently—micro, meso and macro. As such, *"macro-social marketing seeks to use social marketing techniques in a holistic way to effect systemic change, as opposed to individual level change"* (Kennedy, 2016, p. 354).

Since the first mentions of the words "macro-social marketing" by Domegan (2008), the area has blossomed with theoretical and methodological development. Multi-level perspective (MLP) theory, behavioural ecology, institutional theory, and mechanism, action, structure (MAS) theory (Layton, 2015) are among those theories that have been applied to solving wicked problems through macro-level social marketing. While these seem broad, authors have one thing in common—they all apply a systems perspective to the area. So consistent is this view that Domegan has coined the term *systems social marketing* (SSM) (Domegan & Layton, 2015) as the overall approach to macro-level social marketing. This book sets out to showcase the latest thinking in macro-social marketing. But first, this chapter will provide an overview of the field thus far. The major theoretical developments in macro-social marketing for wicked problems will first be explored, followed by the current methodologies to approach macro-level change. Lastly, an overview of the book's chapters is provided and linked to aid the reader.

Social Ecology

Applying social ecology to social marketing, Collins, Tapp, and Pressley (2010) were some of the first to apply systems-related theory to holistically address wicked problems. While not directly referring to wicked problems, they noted the complexity of problems such as obesity. Ultimately, the application of systems thinking called for social marketers to address the broader social context of an issue rather than focusing on individuals (Stokols, 1994). Individuals do not always have the ability to change perpetuating factors contributing to their obesity or addiction, etc. (Hastings, MacFayden, & Anderson, 2000), and this can create stigma and victim blaming (Green, 1984). As a response, Collins et al. (2010) applied social ecology theory.

Social ecology looks at the context or system surrounding an individual throughout their life—all the social influences in their environment (Bronfenbrenner, 1977). For instance, at the micro level, a person's family and friends are seen to influence them. At the meso level, the influences include their school, community, church, and workplace (to name a few), while at the exosystem level, influences can arise from their political, legal, and economic contexts, along with the media. The final macrosystem level is the culture and belief system which shapes the other levels (Bronfenbrenner, 1994).

Using this theory and the work of Gregson et al. (2001), Stokols (1994), and Dresler-Hawke and Veer (2006) in the area, they present their social ecology framework. The framework explains what information needs to be collected at each level and suggests research methods to achieve that. The information should then be theorised as either facilitating the desired behaviour change (positive) or obstructing it (negative). For each combination of positives and negatives, the authors provide social marketers with specific questions to explore what levels and aspects marketers should seek to influence.

Brennan, Previte, and Fry (2016) specifically apply the behavioural ecological model to wicked problems. They advocate it as a relational approach to change versus persuasion for individual change, which assumes rationality (Spotswood & Tapp, 2013). Their discussion of customer myopia explains that social marketers have focused on people as customers, ignoring the influence of social context on their behaviour (Smith, Drumwright, & Gentile, 2010). They suggest social marketers must partner with multiple organisations at multiple levels of the social system to ensure long-term change. They combine systems thinking with behavioural ecology, furthering the original hierarchical model to one in which the individual is embedded within the ecological layers. Layers are interrelated and intertwined, causing ripple effects from interventions. Social marketers are then encouraged to look at the way subsystems relate and interact with one another, especially addressing the actors within the subsystems.

Population Health Views

Taking a population health perspective to change, Hoek and Jones (2011) also advocate that environmental factors in an individual's life need to be addressed to support change—rejecting the myth of individual responsibility. They suggest that uniting upstream and downstream interventions and partnering with public health specialists would drive more effective change for wicked problems. They see social marketing as a continuum from downstream to upstream interventions instead of as separate forms of interventions. The type of interventions is dictated by a policy maker's amount of enthusiasm for them. Hoek and Jones (2011) adeptly debate the myth of individual responsibility and the need for contextual and environmental intervention for behaviour change in areas such as obesity, excessive alcohol consumption, and smoking.

Also taking a population health view, Koch and Orazi (2017) consider the epidemic life cycle of soft drink and tobacco consumption. They propose that both commercial marketing and socio-economic factors drive wicked consumer behaviour (such as consumption of high calorie food and drinks), which leads to wicked health problems such as non-communicable diseases (e.g., diabetes, cardiovascular disease). Their framework uses consumption data to uncover the unfurling cycle of use of these products and the stages at which intervention can occur. Specifically, they

> contend that the rise, stagnation and decline of tobacco and soft drink consumption follow a systematic pattern akin to an epidemic life cycle, whose outbreak is induced by the marketing activities of global manufacturers and reduced or enhanced by the timing and intensity of upstream interventions informed by medical research. The epidemic life cycle of wicked consumption behaviors follows four stages.
>
> (p. 362)

These stages are 1) epidemic breakout; 2) epidemic multiplication; 3) epidemic intervention and host reaction; and 4) epidemic extinction or co-existence.

Systems Views

In a review of the evolution of systems social marketing, Brychkov and Domegan (2017) take an historical approach to the literature and periodise the integration of systems thinking with social marketing. They identify three periods: 1) 1950s–early 1970s, with initial use of systems in marketing; 2) late 1970s–1990s, with the beginnings of use of systems thinking in social marketing; and 3) 2000s–present, with "*[d]eep integration of social marketing and systems science*" (p. 79). As such, articles which use systems directly for social marketing for theory development are reviewed here, which take place from 2000 onwards, though such work clusters after 2010.

Systems thinking was applied by Kennedy and Parsons (2012) to the case of Canadian anti-smoking campaigns from 1985–2009. The Canadian government undertook a systematic approach to behaviour change that focused on the micro (individual), meso (organisational), and macro (structural) levels all at once, with several interventions. Their interventions took a systemic approach to block tobacco companies from successfully marketing tobacco products while also considering structural and individual support for change, limiting facilitating factors. Through de-marketing, in the form of increasing taxes on tobacco products to control price; limiting the places and retail display options; banning advertising and promotion; and limiting product development, availability, and packaging, the Canadian government led the way in tobacco control policy that most countries now follow.

Domegan and colleagues have championed further application of systems thinking to social marketing. Their 2016 article (Domegan et al., 2016) defines a system as being "*made up of structures, actors, behaviours, motivations, values, activities and actions that have social, cultural, political and psychological characteristics*" (p. 1125). Their approach to systems is based largely on Layton's work and theory in the area of systems. However, unlike previous studies, they concern themselves less with interventions, and more with causation of a wicked problem. They use interactive management (IM – Warfield, 1974) to research "*interactions among the parts of the system, the connections, the pathways and what to work on*" (p. 1127) and discover failures in social mechanisms (from Layton's Mechanisms, Action, Structure (MAS) theory – Layton, 2015).

Following Domegan and Layton's (2015) contention that social mechanisms, strategic action fields, and value co-creation (from MAS theory – Layton, 2015) can explain the causal dynamics of social marketing interventions, Layton's MAS theory (Layton, 2015) was used by Kennedy (2016) in her theoretical conceptualisation of macro-social marketing. Using the case of fast fashion, Kennedy combines MAS theory and institutional theory to provide an explanation of the process of macro-level change. As such, a system includes both economic-task norms (e.g., that define expectations and boundaries for behaviour for businesses and marketers) as well as cultural-moral institutional norms (which provide meaning systems, symbolic meaning, and constitutive rules). Strategic action fields, such as social marketing interventions, can then be used to influence and change norms perpetuating a wicked problem. Interventions need to be undertaken at multiple levels in an iterative process over a longer period of time for norms to gradually change.

Using an alternative systems theory—MLP theory—Kemper and Ballantine (2017) take a different theoretical view of macro-level social marketing. Focusing on obesity, they propose a theoretical framework that explains how social marketing can be used to replace, reduce, or eliminate facilitators of a wicked problem. These social marketing interventions would be directed to challengers or incumbents to bring about change. Such change comes with promoting niche solutions and sabotaging regimes that perpetuate the wicked problem. Interventions include creating adaptive capacity and landscape pressures as well as undertaking up-, mid-, and downstream social marketing.

Cherrier and Gurrieri (2014) provide a qualitative study using Giddens' structuration theory. They uncover the institutions surrounding alcohol consumption and suggest interventions through down-, mid-, and upstream social marketing concurrently. They provide a framework of the social marketing system of interaction which suggests that institutional orders at the upstream/macro level might surround the themes of signification, domination, and legitimation. Through interpretive schemes, resources, and norms, individuals were able to use communication, sanctions, and their own power to abstain from alcohol for a month.

Methodological Developments

Beyond theoretical developments in the area, there have also been methodological developments in macro-level and systems social marketing. Domegan et al. (2016) provide a methodology for systems thinking social marketing for wicked problems based on interactive management (IM) software. They use their study on issues occurring within a European marine ecosystem to map out the barriers to change as collected using their IM method. The IM software allows groups of stakeholders to map their thoughts and potential actions for change even with diverse and contradictory people. It uses trigger questions to develop discussion and then voting to create structural barrier maps and ways of overcoming those barriers. Duane, Domegan, McHugh, and Devaney (2016) also use IM methodology to extend the area. They consider the case of obesity and use IM to map the structural barriers and influences for long-term behaviour change. Specifically, they map the complex webs and chains of exchange surrounding the behavioural change reality programme

"Operation Transformation" in Ireland. Their map allows social marketers to identify key areas for intervention to plan strategy.

Kennedy, Kapitan, Bajaj, Bakonyi, and Sands (2017) extend Camillus' (2008) work by incorporating systems theory from Layton (2014) to provide a framework for identifying wicked problem actors, system structure, and intervention points. Using the case of fast fashion, they propose that the social mechanisms that drive system actors first need to be identified as exchange, specialisation, scale and strategic choice, uncertainty reduction, or systems transition. Once these drivers have been identified, the role of the actor should be defined as either an Incumbent, Challenger, or Governance unit, and their shared narratives used to understand the total system dynamics and areas for change.

Moving on from qualitative case studies, Domegan, McHugh, Biroscak, Bryant, and Calis (2017) apply non-linear causal modelling in the forms of fuzzy cognitive mapping, collective intelligence, and systems dynamics modelling to wicked problem dynamics mapping. They find that these forms of modelling allow for practical mapping of wicked problems when their data is collected through participatory measures allowing for strategic planning of multi-level social marketing interventions. Most recently, McHugh, Domegan, and Duane (2018) provide a participatory method to map system actors and plan for their involvement in macro and systemic change research programmes. Their seven protocols for stakeholder participation include 1) analysing boundaries of relevant systems, 2) creating a working party, 3) identifying stakeholders, 4) classifying stakeholders, 5) identifying stakeholder levels of interest and influence in the wicked problem, 6) selection and recruiting of stakeholders, and 7) creating a stakeholder engagement strategy.

Kennedy (2017) provides a methodology for approaching macrosocial marketing using systems thinking and theory. She first sets out to explore the difference between systems thinking versus specific systems theories. In doing so, she reviews social marketing literature's use of either, finding that many more articles use systems thinking without explicitly applying systems theories. After this discussion, Kennedy (2017) conceptualises the philosophy behind macro-level social marketing thinking and research before outlining a new methodology for its research. The methodology

> combines soft-systems methodology (Checkland and Scholes, 1990), interactive management methodology (Duane et al., 2016), the socio-ecological framework (Collins, Tapp, and Pressley, 2010), structuration theory (Giddens, 1979), total systems intervention methodology (Flood and Jackson, 1991), and chrematistics methodology (Kadirov, Varey, and Wolfenden, 2016).
>
> (p. 350)

This creates a four-step methodology which is made up of: 1) understanding the situation; 2) modelling the system; 3) debating the model; and 4) taking action.

Lastly, based on creating intervention programmes for wicked problems, Fry, Previte, and Brennan (2017) provide criteria to use in macrolevel social change in their indicators for social change framework. They go beyond Andreasen's (2002) traditional benchmark criteria for social marketing to incorporate behavioural ecology and a systems perspective.

Book Overview

The area of macro-level social marketing and systems social marketing for wicked problems is clearly heating up. Presented in this volume then are the latest thoughts on the area from many of its key authors.

- For those new to the area, Chapter 2 provides an overview of systems theory and its journey into mainstream marketing. Here Ben Wooliscroft aids readers who are unfamiliar with systems theory by providing a very accessible explanation of a complex and potentially confusing area. This chapter is essential reading to understand the following chapters and provides the base set of theories for macro-social and systems social marketing.

- Sommer Kapitan undertakes an analysis of the uptake of renewable energy in the Pacific and Caribbean Islands. She applies Kennedy et al.'s (2017) framework for macro-social marketing in Chapter 3 and identifies the social structures and conditions which drive and maintain unsustainable energy sources. According to the theory, the narratives of stakeholders relating to the wicked problem, their roles, and the social mechanisms they use are identified. Finally, specific macro-social marketing interventions are discussed, based on different critical action fields. She shows how a complex wicked problem such as renewable energy adoption can be broken down and targets for change identified.

- Explaining another of the key theories in macro-level social marketing in Chapter 4, Ekant Veer, Maja Golf-Papez, and Kseniia Zahrai, discuss the socio-ecological model. This theory also takes a holistic view of a person's behaviour within their environment and suggests areas of change. They review variants of the socio-ecological model and compare and contrast theory, reflecting on how indigenous beliefs and values are incorporated into the model.

- In Chapter 5, Joya Kemper and Paul Ballantine expand on their original use of MLP theory to look at how social marketers can create landscape pressure and drive change. Specifically, they suggest appropriate communication messages using both framing and narratives to create societal need for change, using obesity as a case study.

- Developing theory further in the area, Davide Orazi, Matthias Koch, and Srishti Varma look at systems of wicked consumption in Chapter 6. They discuss how one can define wicked consumption and their etiology. They broaden theory in the area by considering the tensions between stakeholders in interconnecting systems of wicked consumption and areas for intervention through disruption of wicked product diffusion.

- In Chapter 7, Christine Domegan and Patricia McHugh argue very convincingly for the need for stakeholder participation in macro-social marketing. By reflecting on co-creation of systemic interventions, they explore the value bases of holistic social marketing and the importance of co-discovering, designing, and delivering those values through the system.

- In Chapter 8, Jeff French explores the contribution of social marketing to social and economic policy. He uniquely applies social marketing to economic as well as ideological and philosophical drivers of policy, social progress, and wealth creation. He extends theory in the area also through a systems map combining up-, mid-, and downstream social marketing.

- Looking at alternative research methods for macro-social marketing, Anne Hamby, Meghan Pierce, and Kim Daniloski consider the use of human-centred design for co-creating social change in Chapter 9. This acknowledges the need for participation and co-creation of interventions that social marketing increasingly advocates, building on the messages from Chapter 7.

- Josephine Previte and Liam Pomfret explore the use of collaboration for social marketing in Chapter 10, as a means to achieve system-wide change. Undertaking an analysis of existing macro-social marketing literature, they create a typology of use of collaborative systems thinking. This combines service dominant logic, marketing systems theory, shared value, and the logics of collaborative consumers to provide a holistic approach to social change including all stakeholders.

- Looking at an often neglected and potentially contested area for social marketing, Lynne Eagle, Stephan Dahl, and David Low explore the ethical dimensions of social marketing in Chapter 11. While much is often made of the good wishes of social marketers, it is important to consider the unintended negative micro-level consequences of macro-level social marketing interventions. They do this using clear examples of how unintended negative effects might occur, along with their possible solutions.

- Moving into an even more macro view of the potential negatives of macro-level social marketing, Natalia Szablewska and Krzysztof Kubacki consider social engineering and its links with macro-social marketing in Chapter 12. While there are arguments from some that macro-level social marketing is essentially part of social engineering and is neither inherently 'good' or 'bad', the authors explore this premise and provide a solution to 'bad' social engineering with a human-rights based approach to using social engineering tools for the 'social good'.

- Djavlonbek Kadirov further explores the links between macro-social marketing and government in Chapter 13 on chrematistics. This final chapter applies his chrematistics framework to warmth rationing and brings macro-social marketing back to its roots of wicked problems caused by dysfunctional marketing systems. Addressing the profit-driven basis of the marketing system, the chapter shows how social marketers can analyse marketing system design issues and power structures to identify areas for intervention.

Overall, this book explains the key theories and concepts in macro-social marketing for those new to the area. It then moves on to explore and extend theory in the area for those already initiated into the macro-social marketing and wicked problems sphere. For practitioners, the book also provides practical methods and examples for undertaking social marketing at a macro level or for addressing wicked problems. Lastly, the book considers the unintended consequences of holistic system-wide change and the influence of government and society on the macro-social marketing process of change. It is hoped that the thoughts explored in this book provide areas for future research in the academic arena, extend the social marketer's tool belt, and provide food for thought for those interested in macro-level social change and solving wicked problems.

References

Andreasen, A. R. (2002). Marketing social marketing in the social change marketplace. *Journal of Public Policy and Marketing*, 21(1), 3–13.

Brennan, L., Previte, J., & Fry, M. L. (2016). Social marketing's consumer myopia: Applying a behavioural ecological model to address wicked problems. *Journal of Social Marketing*, 6(3), 219–239.

Bronfenbrenner, U. (1977). Toward an experimental ecology of human development. *American Psychologist*, 32(7), 513–531.

Bronfenbrenner, U. (1994). Ecological models of human development. In *International encyclopedia of education* (vol. 3, 2nd ed.). Oxford: Elsevier.

Brychkov, D., & Domegan, C. (2017). Social marketing and systems science: Past, present and future. *Journal of Social Marketing*, 7(1), 74–93.

Camillus, J. C. (2008). Strategy as a wicked problem. *Harvard Business Review*, 86(5), 98.

Checkland, P., & Scholes, J. (1990). *Soft systems methodology in action*. New York, NY: Wiley.

Cherrier, H., & Gurrieri, L. (2014). Framing social marketing as a system of interaction: A neo-institutional approach to alcohol abstinence. *Journal of Marketing Management*, 30(7–8), 607–633.

Collins, K., Tapp, A., & Pressley, A. (2010). Social marketing and social influences: Using social ecology as a theoretical framework. *Journal of Marketing Management, 26*(13–14), 1181–1200.

Domegan, C., & Layton, R. A. (2015, April). *Social marketing and marketing systems: Towards a coherent theory of change.* Paper presented at the World Social Marketing Conference, Sydney, Australia.

Domegan, C., McHugh, P., Biroscak, B. J., Bryant, C., & Calis, T. (2017). Non-linear causal modelling in social marketing for wicked problems. *Journal of Social Marketing, 7*(3), 305–329.

Domegan, C., McHugh, P., Devaney, M., Duane, S., Hogan, M., Broome, B. J., . . . Piwowarczyk, J. (2016). Systems-thinking social marketing: Conceptual extensions and empirical investigations. *Journal of Marketing Management, 32*(11–12), 1123–1144.

Domegan, C. T. (2008). Social marketing: Implications for contemporary marketing practices classification scheme. *Journal of Business and Industrial Marketing, 23*(2), 135–141.

Dresler-Hawke, E., & Veer, E. (2006). Making healthy eating messages more effective: Combining integrated marketing communication with the behaviour ecological model. *International Journal of Consumer Studies, 30*(4), 318–326.

Duane, S., Domegan, C., McHugh, P., & Devaney, M. (2016). From restricted to complex exchange and beyond: Social marketing's change agenda. *Journal of Marketing Management, 32*(9–10), 856–876.

Flood, R. L., & Jackson, M. C. (1991). *Critical systems thinking.* Chichester, UK: John Wiley.

Fry, M. L., Previte, J., & Brennan, L. (2017). Social change design: Disrupting the benchmark template. *Journal of Social Marketing, 7*(2), 119–134.

Giddens, A. (1979). *Central problems in social theory: Action, structure, and contradiction in social analysis* (vol. 241). California: University of California Press.

Green, L. W. (1984). Modifying and developing health behaviour. *Annual Review Public Health, 5,* 215–236.

Gregson, J., Foerester, S., Orr, R., Jones, L., Benedict, J., Clarke, B., . . . Zotz, K. (2001). System, environmental, and policy changes: Using the social- ecological model as a framework for evaluating nutrition education and social marketing programs with low-income audiences. *Journal of Nutrition Education, 33,* S4–S15.

Hastings, G. B., Macfayden, L., & Anderson, S. (2000). Whose behaviour is it anyway? *Social Marketing Quarterly, 6*(2), 46–58.

Hoek, J., & Jones, S. C. (2011). Regulation, public health and social marketing: A behaviour change trinity. *Journal of Social Marketing, 1*(1), 32–44.

Kadirov, D., Varey, R. J., & Wolfenden, S. (2016). Investigating chrematistics in marketing systems: A research framework. *Journal of Macromarketing, 36*(1), 54–67.

Kemper, J. A., & Ballantine, P. W. (2017). Socio-technical transitions and institutional change: Addressing obesity through macro-social marketing. *Journal of Macromarketing, 37*(4), 381–392.

Kennedy, A. M. (2016). Macro-social marketing. *Journal of Macromarketing, 36*(3), 354–365.

Kennedy, A. M. (2017). Macro-social marketing research: Philosophy, methodology and methods. *Journal of Macromarketing, 37*(4), 347–355.

Kennedy, A. M., Kapitan, S., Bajaj, N., Bakonyi, A., & Sands, S. (2017). Uncovering wicked problem's system structure: Seeing the forest for the trees. *Journal of Social Marketing, 7*(1), 51–73.

Kennedy, A. M., & Parsons, A. (2012). Macro-social marketing and social engineering: A systems approach. *Journal of Social Marketing, 2*(1), 37–51.

Kennedy, A. M., & Parsons, A. (2014). Social engineering and social marketing: Why is one "good" and the other "bad"? *Journal of Social Marketing, 4*(3), 198–209.

Koch, M., & Orazi, D. C. (2017). No rest for the wicked: The epidemic life cycle of wicked consumer behavior. *Journal of Macromarketing, 37*(4), 356–368.

Layton, R. (2014), "Formation, growth, and adaptive change in marketing systems", *Journal of Macromarketing*, Vol. 35 No. 3, pp. 302–319.

Layton, R. A. (2015). Formation, growth, and adaptive change in marketing systems. *Journal of Macromarketing, 35*(3), 302–319.

McHugh, P., Domegan, C., & Duane, S. (2018). Protocols for stakeholder participation in social marketing systems. *Social Marketing Quarterly, 24*(3), 164–193.

Smith, N. C., Drumwright, M. E., & Gentile, M. C. (2010). The new marketing myopia. *Journal of Public Policy and Marketing, 29*(1), 4–11.

Spotswood, F., & Tapp, A. (2013). Beyond persuasion: A cultural perspective on behavior. *Journal of Social Marketing, 3*(3), 275–294.

Stokols, D. (1994). Translating social ecological theory into guidelines for health promotion. *American Journal of Health Promotion, 10*(4), 282–298.

Warfield, J. N. (1974). *Structuring complex systems*. Columbus, OH: Battelle Memorial Institute.

2 Systems and Macro-Social Marketing
Researching Wicked Problems

Ben Wooliscroft

Systems

Systems are all around us, but the study of systems is restricted to a subset of research. Systems research is more difficult, involves more variables, many more interactions, and presents less certainty than more common reductionist research, which considers a small part of the system in isolation.

Layton (2007) defined a marketing system as:

> a network of individuals, groups and/or entities, embedded in a social matrix, linked directly or indirectly through sequential or shared participation in economic exchange, which jointly and/or collectively creates economic value with and for customers, through the offer of assortments of goods, services, experiences and ideas, that emerge in response to or anticipation of customer demand.
>
> (Layton, 2007, p. 230)

The nature and attributes of systems in general is considered before moving on to the specific case of marketing, social marketing, and macro-social marketing.

Systems can be closed or open. Closed systems do not interact with objects, people, or inputs from outside the system. The idea of closed systems is very useful as a thought experiment, but closed systems are rare. Using the closed system as a thought experiment is in itself a type of reductionism. Even the earth, sometimes thought of as a closed system, receives considerable energy from the sun and radiates heat and light out into space. The earth is not a closed system but an isolated system.

Outside of a few specific cases, systems are open, or as Alderson (1957) names them, ecological, systems interacting with other systems or embedded in a wider system. It is this attribute of systems that can be most challenging; where does the system end? How can we as researchers, policy makers, or citizens work out where the influence on our focal system comes from?

Von Bertalanffy (1968) wrote the seminal General Systems Theory, an attempt to provide a philosophy of science that applies to all disciplines. It is centred on open systems that interact with their environment: receiving inputs, processing these inputs, exporting outputs to the environment, and exchanging information and energy with the environment.

Building on von Bertalanffy (1968), in a study of management systems Katz and Kahn (1966) give nine characteristics of complex, open, and behavioural systems (with examples from a manufacturing firm provided):

1. The importation of energy —electricity, raw materials, labour
2. The throughput—manufacturing or other transformation within the system
3. The output—the finished goods, services, or experiences that the firm produces. There are likely to be externalities as well.
4. Systems as cycles of events—examples of the cycles in a firm include budget cycles, sales cycles, planning cycles, and daily/weekly cycles
5. Negative entropy—systems import more energy than they export, due to necessary inefficiencies
6. Information input, negative feedback, and the coding process—information flows into the firm in the form of sales, warranties, returns, etc. That information feeds into the strategy, budgeting, and other planning cycles.
7. Steady state and dynamic homeostasis—equilibria shift over time as other items in the environment change
8. Differentiation—it is normal for firms to move to different places in the landscape of offers relative to other firms
9. Equifinality—there is more than one way to get to a destination (strategic goal) and those ways are effected by the interaction with other systems.

Associated with complex systems is the problem of non-linearity. In spite of non-linearity being incredibly widespread and the norm in the world, it is not convenient for scientists and researchers to deal with non-linear systems, and much research assumes linearity. Non-linearity brings with it the potential for chaos (Gleick, 1987) and self-organised critical states (Buchanan, 2000), both of which lead to unpredictability. Marketing systems, and macro-social marketing systems, are indeed wicked problems (Churchman, 1967).

Chaos theory demonstrates that unless you have perfect measurement, not present in the physical sciences let alone social sciences, a non-linear system can be in a chaotic state—deterministic but with unpredictable feedback loops. Associated with the butterfly effect, a tiny change in inputs can lead to a major change in outputs when a system is in a chaotic state. This is uncomfortable for researchers, policy makers, and citizens alike.

In the related case of self-organised criticality, a non-linear system exhibits the sand pile effect (Bak, Tang, & Wiesenfeld, 1987). In this case the same input to a system—dropping a single grain of sand on a sand pile—can have vastly different outcomes—small through large slumps in the sand pile. The distribution of the outcomes has a power law with many small slumps in the sand pile and very few large slumps, all for exactly the same input—one grain of sand dropped from the same height at the same place. This applies to social marketing messages where one delivery of a message may lead to a large change in behaviour, while another may have almost no effect. This difference in outcome is not necessarily the result of a difference in the quality of the message delivery.

There is a phase transition between a 'stable' non-linear system and a self-organised critical state, then a further phase transition between that and a chaotic state for the system (Campbell-Hunt, 2007). Unfortunately, the complexity of social science systems means that it is currently impossible to know when we are in one of these states. We do know that we have the pre-requisites for these states.

Marketing, macromarketing, and social sciences must deal with DOCAS (Dynamic Open Complex Adaptive Systems). That is further complicated by the opportunity to define systems differently; is the transport system an automobile scheduling system, a mobility system, an economic system, a social system, etc.? All answers can be correct, and that starting point will lead to defining, conceptualising, and modelling the system differently, which will in turn lead to different 'solutions' to system problems.

Marketing as a Synthetic Discipline

Marketing has always been a synthetic discipline, a blending of theories, methods, and concepts from a variety of other disciplines around the central phenomena of the market. Alderson and Cox in "Towards a theory of marketing" (1948) demonstrate the synthetic nature of marketing, with the inclusion of theory from, among others, economics, psychology, sociology, and geography.

What is the centre of the discipline—the phenomena that anchors the system? In the case of marketing, it is the market and exchange (Alderson, 1957; Bagozzi, 1975, 1978).

Marketing as the Study of Systems

The history of marketing theory is full of systems ideas, even though the current state of marketing theory is dominated by reductionist research and theory. An overview of the foci of marketing systems thinking is presented here.

The earliest writing identified with marketing as a discipline describes how the systems involved in getting goods from production to market are—or should be—the positive or normative dichotomy from Hunt (1977) and the three dichotomies model. Marketing was concerned with getting goods from where they were produced to market, distribution systems.

Very early marketing authors addressed the system centred on different types of goods and how those goods should be transported, stored, retailed, etc. (Parlin, 1912; Copeland, 1923; Bucklin, 1963). This approach remains with us through the treatment of high and low involvement goods in Assael's (2004) model of different buyer behaviour for different product categories (or more accurately different consumer involvement levels).

Other authors considered where goods should be sold, where factories should be sited, where customers will go to purchase, etc. A focus on the geographic at the centre of the system. Reilly's (1929) Law of Retail Gravitation is in many ways the starting point for this geographically based systems perspective. The importance of considering the interactions between where customers are and where production and distribution are based has not decreased through time, with the notable exception of digital products, but has frequently left the purview of marketing departments in business schools. The geographic approach to marketing systems modelled the relationship between customers and firms in a rich manner, providing useful insights that are used to this day, particularly in locating retail outlets for maximum impact (e.g. Walmart, Starbucks, etc.).

Early marketing academic researchers considered what marketing practitioners did—their functions—and catalogued them. This approach to studying the system with the marketer at the centre has led to the 4Ps (Product, Place, Price, Promotion—McCarthy, 1960), and many other lists of functions. What has been less successful is the generation of theory regarding the interaction between the functions of the marketer. We do have the theory of penetration pricing that suggests links between distribution (place), price and promotion, and related pricing strategies, but little else in the way of a systematic understanding of interactions. Studying the Ps individually has been much easier than combining them, and post-1959 research productivity became more important than research impact.

A group of scholars focused on the institutions required for efficient market operation (Alderson, 2006a). They defended the channel as a creator of utility at a time when middlemen were looked down on for providing no additional value. Duddy and Revzan (1947, p. 14) highlighted the breadth of institutions involved in value creation including, "*management using authoritarian and persuasive techniques, by government regulations, and by social convention and custom*". The elements of the system impacting on the market phenomena was widened with this view.

The height of systems research in marketing belongs to a small group of scholars headed by Wroe Alderson (2006b, 1957, 1965, 1968), a genius who brought together findings from many disciplines to consider the phenomena of the market (Wooliscroft, 2006). Alderson was a dominant figure in the discipline of marketing during his life, holding presidency of the American Marketing Association (AMA) and winning every prize worth winning in the discipline. He counted among his friends Stanley J. Shapiro (Alderson & Shapiro, 1963; Alderson, Terpstra, & Shapiro, 1965; Shapiro, 1963), Kenneth Boulding (1956), Russell Ackoff and Emery (1972, 1978), C. West Churchman (1968, 1971, 1979), and other leading systems thinkers. It was a colleague, George Fisk (1967), who wrote the first (and arguably only) marketing systems introductory textbook: *Marketing Systems: An Introductory Analysis*. When asked to prepare a second edition, Fisk declined, and the introduction to marketing textbook market was dominated by Kotler (1967), and McCarthy (1960).

Alderson's (1957, 1965) books are managerial texts that start with a discussion of the philosophy of science and why systems/functionalism is the best paradigm for studying marketing phenomena. His (1965) *Dynamic Marketing Behavior* includes descriptions of different subsystems as he assembles one of the most comprehensive theories of marketing to date, and he left the discipline with 150 falsifiable propositions to test his theories at the time of his death. Those propositions have received little attention, and apart from a formalisation (Hunt, Muncy, & Ray, 2006), a number of comparisons to other theories (Priem, Rasheed, & Amirani, 2006; Hunt & Arnett, 2006), and a call to keep teaching Aldersonian marketing (Wilkinson & Young, 2006), his systems view of marketing and market phenomena has been largely forgotten by mainstream marketing.

Marketing Moves Away From Systems

In 1959 two major reports were published into business education in the U.S., the Ford Foundation (Gordon & Howell, 1959) and Carnegie Corporation (Pierson, 1959) reports into business education in the U.S.—and with it the rest of the English speaking world. The attendant, and very well resourced, re-education of business faculty saw a major shift in the way business was researched, communicated, and educated—a shift to reductionist science. This shift to publish or perish, where academics are required to publish articles to keep their jobs or receive promotion, led to reductionist science as the dominant framework for research, leaving systems research by the wayside. Systems research takes longer, requires collecting many more variables, and provides less certainty about the result.

Post-Ford Foundation and Carnegie Corporation reports the Managerial—how do we do marketing better—and Buyer Behaviour—how do we get people to buy more—approaches to marketing emerged. They deal with, and they still dominate marketing research and education, how to sell things and how to get people to buy things in turn. In recent decades Buyer Behaviour has widened into the study of consumption that includes post-purchase, but research is still dominated by the stages of the purchase decision model up to purchase and not beyond. There is a preponderance of experiments in mainstream marketing research, or questionnaire driven research that is analysed with highly technical models.

Science, as we understand it today, is a result of the reductionist revolution. By breaking down wholes and systems to dyads, answers are available, often with many decimal places. Leading research papers and textbooks feature theories about:

- A/the brand and the consumer(s)
- A firm and a consumer
- A consumer in relation to other consumers
- A firm in relation to other firms, and
- The social message and the consumer

What is missing in mainstream marketing textbooks and thought is theories and models that consider a multitude of firms and a multitude of consumers (and non-consumers—Wooliscroft, 2013) at the same time. Or, multiple social messages from multiple social agencies to multiple publics.

Recently business has been fascinated with big data, gathering lots of data from a system and automatically looking for predictions. This approach is subject to spurious correlations, predicted relationships that may have no basis in reality, such as lip stick use in Africa and the price of grain in the USA. It flattens the system to lots of data and one variable of interest (generally who will buy) and is anti-systems in its approach. A rich interactive system is flattened into a series of correlations, those with the highest values. Decisions are driven from these black box results, which will change the system through feedback loops (Wooliscroft, 2011).

Marketing Rediscovering Systems

Systems have in recent decades become more prominent in marketing thought, though often without the systems nature being explicitly recognised.

With his "Invitation to participate in affairs of the Journal of Macromarketing", Fisk (1981) built on the work of the Macromarketing Seminars before and launched the Journal. That journal remains the home of systems thinking in the marketing discipline. The journal is the publisher of a series of papers by Roger Layton that place systems at the very centre of (macro)marketing thought (Layton, 2007, 2009, 2011, 2014, 2017; Layton & Duffy, 2018). Figure 2.1 is Layton's latest model of marketing systems; it shows the many influences on and interactions in the formation and growth of a marketing system. While this model is based around the exchange of goods and services, it is equally applicable to ideas—macro-social marketing messages—and the market for their acceptance and communication/sharing.

Layton and Duffy (2018) show how markets evolve to fill the needs of society and those in it. Where there is a deficit, or a surplus, markets will emerge to fill the deficit and reduce/eliminate the surplus. This is a natural human phenomena. Layton and Duffy (2018) also demonstrate that past decisions influence what choices we have available to us as a society today. In a social example, past investment in public transport or active transport (walking and cycling) allows the choice of mode to move through our cities. However, when a city has been dominated by automobiles, and roads have been designed for cars, other choices are not readily available and significant investment is required to make those choices available again. Mode of transport is but one example of a market decision with many influences and with associated path dependencies.

Macromarketing is considered at a different level—aggregates—with a different intent—societal (and ecological) wellbeing. The findings from macromarketing may not be useful for a business aiming to increase sales or profit, but they were never designed to be. Business can learn from the investigation of aggregate systems and value creation.

Bagozzi built on Alderson (1957, 1965) to make explicit the social system in which the exchange and value creation is embedded. Clearly that system is embedded in wider systems, and exchange being at the centre of marketing leads to a systems perspective being required for rich study of the phenomena in the discipline. This conceptualisation has led to Vargo and Lusch (2007) and the service dominant logic, a managerial interpretation of the systems of meaning creation around exchange.

Surprisingly brands, a concept at the very heart of marketing, has had a near constant definition for the best part of a century. It is only recently that a conceptualisation of brands as a system of meaning has been published (Conejo & Wooliscroft, 2015). Meaning is created by different groups, not just customers, through feedback loops, and conflict, shared meaning, and contested meanings emerge (see Figure 2.2). Of course this system of meaning is also present in social marketing messages. The brand in Figure 2.2 can be replaced by the social marketing campaign or message, with the recognition that its meaning is negotiated by recipients, stakeholders, senders, and competing message senders, all within the context of the environment.

Relationship marketing and CRM recognise that the bond between brand/firm and customer are weaker than in the past—the system has

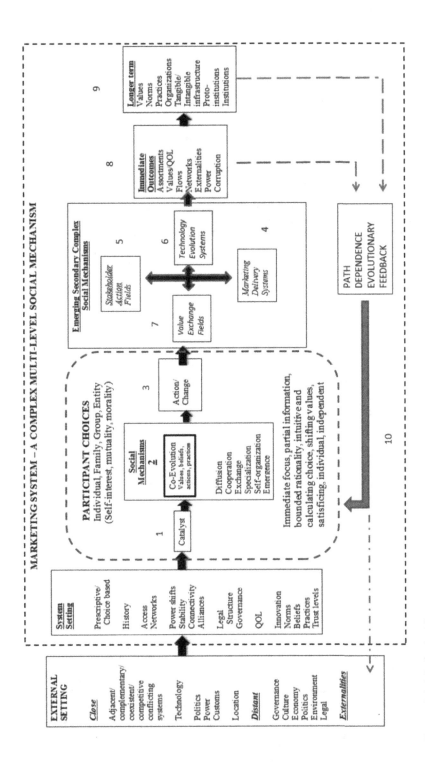

Figure 2.1 Marketing System

Source: (Layton & Duffy, 2018)

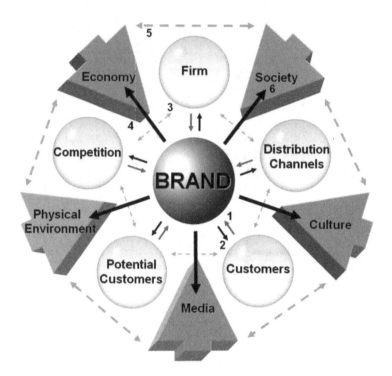

Figure 2.2 Brand System
Source: (Conejo & Wooliscroft, 2015)

changed—and that firms want to do something to strengthen those bonds. But rather than consider the whole system, they focus on the link between firm/brand and consumer while assuming ceteris paribus for the rest of the system.

Technological disruption of marketing systems

There has been repeated angst over the impact of new communication and distribution technologies on the marketing discipline and system. Among the first challenges was catalogue shopping, which was seen as a threat to bricks and mortar shops. Later the telephone was going to revolutionise the way firms and (potential) customers communicated.

The advent of movies and television did revolutionise communication between firms and (potential) customers. The earliest years of television and movies featured—largely through novelty—extremely effective advertising. Now that advertising is all-pervading, the effectiveness of mass communication has decreased and firms once more seek more targeted messages through social media, targeted and adaptable internet advertising, etc.

Online shopping has shifted some custom as consumers chase cheaper deals or wider selections, but bricks and mortar shops are far from closing, and Amazon, amongst other online retailers, has opened bricks and mortar shops to satisfy the needs of their potential consumers.

The technology/media may change, but the market system is charged with matching heterogeneous demand and supply, that has not fundamentally changed.

Researching Through the Lens of Systems

There are different levels of systems research, from systems informing a conceptual model, through empirical models that describe a system, to a dynamic model with the ability to simulate changes to the system. The idea of running computer simulations is not new (c.f. Brink, 1963). Wroe Alderson ran simulations with industry representatives and punch card driven computers in the 1950s to model changes to the pharmacy market (Wooliscroft, 2006).

"All models are wrong; some models are useful" (Box, Hunter, & Hunter, 2005, p. 440). Box's quote reminds us of the danger and promise of abstractions. The higher the level of the systems model, towards dynamic modelling, the more useful it can be. The opportunity to inform a situation with competing simulations reminds us of the variability of potential outcomes. But there are many useful systems informed research opportunities before the dynamic systems model.

The first step in systems informed research is a conceptual model that is founded in a systems world view reflecting the presence of multiple interactions and feedback loops. Examples include branding (Conejo & Wooliscroft, 2015), markets and their formation (Layton, 2007, 2009, 2011, 2014, 2017; Layton & Duffy, 2018), cultures of consumption (Stephenson et al., 2015), and many others. It is relatively easy to draw a conceptual model that abstracts a system. They are always wrong, incomplete, etc. but very useful to broaden the consideration of impacts on the focal phenomena and to lead to insights.

The second stage involves the description of a system, generally in a static state. Tools for this include social network analysis (Scott, 2005; Wasserman & Faust, 1994), which has been applied to the system/network of editorships and editorial boards in marketing journals (Rosenstreich & Wooliscroft, 2006), scientific collaborations (Barabási et al., 2002), and the impact of social activity on travel mode (Carrasco, Hogan, Wellmand, & Miller, 2008).

These widely used tools are extremely useful for describing the snapshot of a system at a given time, but do not give insights into changes over time. Regression and structural equation modeling provide a system of interactions with a focal output but lack the feedback loops that true systems require. There are other tools that can be used to map systems in a pre-dynamic manner depending on your software platform.

The highest level of systems integration into research is dynamic model creation and simulation. Vensim and Stella are among the leading programmes that offer the opportunity to model and simulate dynamic systems. Many teaching in business schools today will have used simulations like Markstrat in the past, multi-player simulations run in discrete cycles. Most of the students of today have extensive experience with simulations in the form of online or console based immersive video games. Simulation is now normal; being aware of it is not.

World Climate, an interactive simulation, gives participants the opportunity to negotiate on behalf of different countries in a large-scale comprehensive Stella model of climate change for the earth (www. climateinteractive.org/programmes/world-climate/). The opportunity for multiple people to come together representing different countries or regions, make policy choices, and have the simulation run in real time is a very stimulating experience. Participants are seldom unmoved by the competing goals of different countries as they try to look after their own people and economy while 'solving' climate change together. It provides a United Nations-style experience.

A dynamic system model is very flexible and can be used to test different distributions of response to a change in one variable. The output can be set to a normal, bimodal, poisson, quadratic, etc. distribution and switched between different distributions with relative ease. The model also allows for sensitivity testing through running a very large number of simulations to find which variable(s) have the most impact on the focal variable. In this way the major targets for policy intervention can be identified. Uncertainty analysis, or risk analysis, is a further step that allows researchers to quantify the likelihood of specific outcomes (typically extreme outcomes).

Sterman (2000) provides business modelers with a textbook on the application of dynamic systems modeling in the context of business. The book takes the reader through the steps of developing models and points to resources that will aid the development. There are libraries of dynamic system models that can be copied, adapted, or extended to suit an analogous situation. Macro-social marketing deals with changes in attitude and behaviour, as does much business modeling.

Macro-Social Marketing Research

Macro-social marketing presents researchers with complex situations/ systems that will benefit from true systems research. There are clear benefits to using dynamic system simulations in macro-social marketing studies. To provide a useful model, we have to answer a number of questions:

- What is the problem we seek to understand and solve/resolve?
- What is the central phenomena being studied or sought; behaviour change, attitudechange, or policy change?
- What are the bounds of the system?
- Who should/could change? Firms, advertising, citizens, or customers?

These choices will impact on what our model will look like and what policy recommendations it might lead to.

Considering, for example, body image, there is no sense in restricting a system to a country in a world where influence comes from advertising, movies, television, etc. from any number of countries, in print, online, social media, and broadcast. In this example the system input—the images that are charged with influencing body image—cannot be separated into a geographic system. Much of the input is beyond the control of those in the focal system—the only choice is whether this audience chooses to access the images, or be influenced by them.

There is similarly little choice deciding that the image producers should stop production; they are frequently out of the jurisdiction of the citizens being effected and protected by free speech, etc. Which elements can we change to get the outcome we seek, if that is possible at all? Wicked problems like this require systems thinking if we are to understand and influence their impact on society and its members.

Depending on how a dynamic system model is designed and what it includes, the model will present different opportunities for interventions. Specifying what is included in the model in a social science situation is typically undertaken through the use of a panel of experts, in combination with the available data, to specify which variables and interactions should be included in the model. This mapping stage gives us a preliminary or working model.

Do we consider a sugar tax macro-social marketing? We should if we consider price to be one of the attributes that marketing can use to change the outcome of the system. Can we use brand community, tribes, market mavens, etc. to proselytise for our goal? Associated with this might be CRM (citizen relationship management) and relationship marketing. The marketing discipline has many theories and tools that it can apply to social systems, which ones we choose to include in our models will impact on what policy recommendations we generate from our research.

References

Ackoff, R., & Emery, F. E. (Eds.). (1972). *On purposeful systems*. Chicago: Aldine Atherton.

Ackoff, R. L. (1978). *The art of problem solving*. New York, NY: John Wiley & Sons, Inc.

Alderson, W. (1957). *Marketing behavior and executive action: A functionalist approach to marketing.* Homewood, IL: Richard D. Irwin Inc.

Alderson, W. (1965). *Dynamic marketing behavior: A functionalist theory of marketing.* Homewood, IL: Richard D. Irwin Inc.

Alderson, W. (1968). The analytical framework for marketing. In J. Kernan & M. Sommers (Eds.), *Perspectives in marketing theory* (pp. 69–82). New York, NY: Appleton-Century-Crofts.

Alderson, W. (2006a). Information flows in heterogeneous markets. In B. Wooliscroft, R. D. Tamilia, & S. J. Shapiro (Eds.), *A twenty-first-century guide to Aldersonian marketing thought* (pp. 217–227). New York, NY: Springer.

Alderson, W. (2006b). *The analytical framework for marketing* (pp. 67–80). New York, NY: Springer.

Alderson, W., & Cox, R. (1948, October). Towards a theory of marketing. *Journal of Marketing, 13,* 137–152.

Alderson, W., & Shapiro, S. J. (1963). *Marketing and the computer: An overview, marketing and the computer* (pp. 2–13). Englewood Cliffs, NJ: Prentice-Hall Inc.

Alderson, W., Terpstra, V., & Shapiro, S. J. (Eds.). (1965). *Patents and progress: The sources and impact of advancing technology.* Homewood, IL: Richard D. Irwin Inc.

Assael, H. (2004). *Consumer Behavior: A Strategic Approach, Hunghton Mifflin Company,* Boston, MA.

Bagozzi, R. P. (1975). Marketing as exchange. *Journal of Marketing, 39*(4), 32–39.

Bagozzi, R. P. (1978). Marketing as exchange: A theory of transactions in the marketplace. *American Behavioral Scientist, 21*(4), 535–556.

Bak, P., Tang, C., & Wiesenfeld, K. (1987). Self-organized criticality: An explanation of the 1/f noise. *Physical Review Letters, 59*(4), 381.

Barabási, A., Jeong, H., Neda, Z., Ravasz, E., Schubert, A., & Vicsek, T. (2002). Evolution of the social network of scientific collaborations. *Physica A: Statistical Mechanics and Its Applications, 311*(3–4), 590–614.

Boulding, K. E. (1956, April). General systems theory – The skeleton of science. *Management Science, 2,* 197–208.

Box, G. E., Hunter, J. S., & Hunter, W. G. (2005). *Statistics for experimenters: Design, innovation, and discovery* (vol. 2). New York, NY: Wiley-Interscience.

Brink, E. L. (1963). Analog computers in the simulation of marketing systems. In W. Alderson & S. J. Shapiro (Eds.), *Marketing and the computer* (pp. 248–259). Englewood Cliffs, NJ: Prentice Hall, Inc.

Buchanan, M. (2000). *Ubiquity: The science of history or why the world is simpler than we think.* London: Phoenix.

Bucklin, L. P. (1963). Retail strategy and the classification of consumer goods. *Journal of Marketing, 27*(1), 50–55.

Campbell-Hunt, C. (2007). Complexity in practice. *Human Relations, 60*(5), 793–823.

Carrasco, J. A., Hogan, B., Wellmand, B., & Miller, E. J. (2008). Collecting social network data to study social activity-travel behavior: An egocentric approach. *Environment and Planning B, 35*(6), 961–980.

Churchman, C. W. (1967). Guest editorial: Wicked problems. *Management Science, 14*(4), B141–B142.

Churchman, C. W. (1968). *The systems approach*. New York, NY: Dell Publishing Co., Inc.

Churchman, C. W. (1971). *The design of inquiring systems: Basic concepts of systems and organization*. New York, NY: Basic Books, Inc.

Churchman, C. W. (1979). *The systems approach and its enemies*. New York, NY: Basic Books, Inc.

Conejo, F. J., & Wooliscroft, B. (2015). Brands defined as semiotic marketing systems. *Journal of Macromarketing, 35*(3), 287–301.

Copeland, M. (1923). Relation of consumers' buying habits to marketing methods. *Harvard Business Review, 1*(3), 282–289.

Duddy, E. A., & Revzan, D. A. (1947). *Marketing: An institutional approach*. New York, NY: McGraw-Hill Book Co.

Fisk, G. (1967). *Marketing systems an introductory analysis*. New York, NY: Harper & Row, Publishers.

Fisk, G. (1981, Spring). An invitation to participate in affairs of the Journal of Macromarketing. *Journal of Macromarketing, 1*, 3–6.

Gleick, J. (1987). *Chaos*. London: Minerva.

Gordon, R. A., & Howell, J. E. (1959). *Higher education for business*. New York, NY: Columbia University Press.

Hunt, S. D. (1977). The three dichotomies model of marketing: An elaboration of issues. In C. C. Slater (Ed.), *Macro-marketing: Distributive processes from a social perspective, business research division* (pp. 52–56). Boulder, CO: University of Colorado.

Hunt, S. D., & Arnett, D. B. (2006). Toward a general theory of marketing: Resource-advantage theory as an extension of Alderson. In B. Wooliscroft, R. Tamilia, & S. J. Shapiro (Eds.), *A twenty-first century guide to Aldersonian marketing thought* (pp. 453–472). New York, NY: Springer.

Hunt, S. D., Muncy, J. A., & Ray, N. M. (2006). Alderson's general theory of marketing: A formalization. In B. Wooliscroft, R. Tamilia, & S. J. Shapiro (Eds.), *A twenty-first century guide to Aldersonian marketing thought* (pp. 359–371). New York, NY: Springer.

Katz, D., & Kahn, R. L. (1966). *The social psychology of organizations*. New York, NY: John Wiley & Sons, Inc.

Kotler, P. (1967). *Marketing management: Analysis, planning, implementation, and control*. Englewood Cliffs, NJ: Prentice Hall, Inc.

Layton, R. (2007). Marketing systems: A core macromarketing concept. *Journal of Macromarketing, 27*(3), 227–242.

Layton, R. (2017). Can macromarketing learn from 40,000 years of history? *Journal of Macromarketing, 37*(3), 334–335.

Layton, R., & Duffy, S. M. (2018). Path dependency in marketing systems – Where history matters and the future casts a shadow. *Journal of Macromarketing, 38*(4), 400–414.

Layton, R. A. (2009). On economic growth, marketing systems, and the quality of life. *Journal of Macromarketing, 29*(4), 349–362.

Layton, R. A. (2011). Towards a theory of marketing systems. *European Journal of Marketing, 45*(1–2), 259–276.

Layton, R. A. (2014). Formation, growth, and adaptive change in marketing systems. *Journal of Macromarketing, 35*(3), 302–319.

McCarthy, E. J. (1960). *Basic marketing: A managerial approach*. Homewood, IL: Richard D. Irwin Inc.

Parlin, C. C. (1912). *Department store lines*. Philadelphia, PA: University of Pennsylvania Press.

Pierson, F. C. (1959). *The education of American businessmen: A study of university-college programs in business administration*. New York, NY: McGraw-Hill Book Company, Inc.

Priem, R. L., Rasheed, A. M. A., & Amirani, S. (2006). Alderson's transvection and Porter's value system: A comparison of two independently developed theories. In B. Wooliscroft, R. D. Tamilia, & S. J. Shapiro (Eds.), *A twenty-first-century guide to Aldersonian marketing thought* (pp. 379–406). New York, NY: Springer.

Reilly, W. J. (1929). *Methods for the study of retail relationships*. Austin: University of Texas.

Rosenstreich, D., & Wooliscroft, B. (2006). Sociometric status in the top 37 marketing journals using social network analysis. In M. Layton, R. Layton, & B. Wooliscroft (Eds.), *Macromarketing 2006 seminar proceedings: Macromarketing the future of marketing?* (pp. 567–581). Dunedin, New Zealand: Macromarketing Society, Marketing Department, University of Otago.

Scott, J. (2005). *Social network analysis: A handbook* (2nd ed.). London: Sage Publications.

Shapiro, S. J. (1963). Decision making, survival and the organized behavior system: A case study of the Ontario hog producer organization. In W. Decker (Ed.), *Emerging concepts in marketing* (pp. 438–442). Chicago: American Marketing Association.

Stephenson, J., Barton, B., Carrington, G., Doering, A., Ford, R., Hopkins, D., . . . Wooliscroft, B. (2015). The energy cultures framework: Exploring the role of norms, practices and material culture in shaping energy behaviour in New Zealand. *Energy Research & Social Science, 7*, 117–123.

Sterman, J. (2000). *Business dynamics: Systems thinking and modelling for a complex world*. Boston, MA: Irwin McGraw Hill.

Vargo, S., & Lusch, R. (2007). Service-dominant logic: Continuing the evolution. *Journal of the Academy of Marketing Science, 36*(1), 1–10.

von Bertalanffy, L. (1968). *General systems theory: Foundations, development, applications*. New York, NY: George Braziller.

Wasserman, S., & Faust, K. (1994). *Social network analysis: Methods and applications*. Cambridge: Cambridge University Press.

Wilkinson, I., & Young, L. (2006). To teach or not to teach Alderson? there is no question. In B. Wooliscroft, R. D. Tamilia, & S. J. Shapiro (Eds.), *A twenty-first-century guide to Aldersonian marketing thought* (pp. 529–539). New York, NY: Springer.

Wooliscroft, B. (2006). Wroe Alderson a life. In B. Wooliscroft, R. D. Tamilia, & S. J. Shapiro (Eds.), *A twenty-first-century guide to Aldersonian marketing thought* (pp. 3–32). New York, NY: Springer.

Wooliscroft, B. (2011). Marketing theory as history. *Marketing Theory, 11*(4), 499–501.

Wooliscroft, B. (2013). Rehumanizing marketing (and consumer behavior). In R. J. Varey & M. Pirson (Eds.), *Humanizing marketing, humanism in business* (pp. 53–58). New York, NY: Palgrave Macmillan.

3 Macro-Social Marketing as a Tool to Increase the Share of Renewable Energy in Developing Island Nations

Sommer Kapitan

The image is striking: White sand, sun, wind, and crystal clear waters in a remote locale. Yet the tropical island states of the Caribbean and South Pacific produce and consume surprisingly little renewable energies.

Higher energy prices and climate change are a reality for the 66 million people of the Caribbean and the South Pacific that form the U.N.-protected small island developing states (UN DESA, 2017; Prism, 2018). Residents of these island states pay dearly for their imported, fossil fuel-based electricity. The price is sometimes upwards of 40 U.S. cents per kilowatt hour, versus the 12 U.S. cents/kw Americans pay and the 15 pence or 21 U.S. cents/kw UK residents pay (Ince, 2013; Ince, Vredenburg, & Liu, 2016; NPR, 2011; CompareMySolar, 2012). They pay this as climate change is witnessed first-hand on these island nations. Rising seas and temperatures threaten shorelines and coral reef habitats as stronger and more frequent storms hit these islands. Yet the sun shines and warm breezes ripple through the palm trees of these scenic islands, a stark reminder of the potential for solar- and wind-based renewable energies. How has this wicked entanglement occurred in the energy sectors powering more than 66 million people's lives (UN DESA, 2017; PRISM, 2018)? And, how can scholars, policy makers, institutions, and consumers together seek to address its solution?

Tackling the problem of renewable energy adoption in small island developing states involves a market orientation to determine the system and institutions in which the emerging problem is embedded. What underlies the existence of a market for renewable energies in these economies? This chapter will consider the social conditions and social structures surrounding energy use, consumer acceptance and demand, investor support, regulatory frameworks, and international and governmental policies (i.e., Martinot, Chauery, Lew, Moreira, & Wamukonya, 2002).

Many of the world's most pressing issues stem from interrelated, multifaceted constellations of problems. These problems pit the needs and wants of different stakeholders against one another (Rittel & Weber, 1973). Social marketers tend to focus their lenses on achieving behaviour change among a stakeholder group or a level of a problem. This approach is a valid path to achieving some behaviour change. Yet such a micro-focused approach tends to view the system in which the problem is embedded as a facet of the problem, rather than a key facilitator. Such approaches can encourage micro-level, shorter term behavioural target change. Yet macro-social marketing questions the impact of social marketing campaigns that fail to address the systemic root causes of pressing social issues. This is especially the case for problems that are wicked and complex in nature, such as increasing the share of renewable energies in developing nations. Macro-social marketing is a tool and an approach for social marketers to use to first assess wicked problems, and then plan strategically for their improvement. Doing so involves adoption of a macromarketing orientation to a large scale social marketing problem.

This chapter seeks to expand on and deepen uptake of the framework for macro-social marketing (i.e., Kennedy, 2016; Kennedy, Kapitan, Bejaj, Bakonyi, & Sands, 2017). The goal is to explore the deployment of macro-social marketing as a theory-based tool to solve pressing issues faced by marketing systems. The wicked question of renewable energy adoption in small island developing states is one of these issues ripe for macro-social marketing interventions. Uptake of renewables thus forms the context of this market-based investigation of energy security and independence in key parts of the developing world.

This chapter will first examine what macro-social marketing is, and outline the process and market orientation of the approach. Next, following the steps of Figure 3.1 and Table 3.1 for the macro-social marketing process, the focal system will be described, including the context and stakeholders. Then social mechanisms, roles, critical action fields, and narratives will be determined for the key stakeholders. Finally, as shown in Table 3.3, macro-social marketing is employed to determine key points of potential strategic intervention for social marketers and scholars.

Macro-Social Marketing: A Process

Macro-social marketing uses systems thinking, systems theory, and a framework drawn from Camillus (2008) and Kennedy et al. (2017) for responding to wicked problems with strategy formation. Figure 3.1 illustrates this process. In macro-social marketing, social marketers and scholars chart the involved stakeholders, their functions and social mechanisms (Layton, 2014), the actions taken, and the interactions between actors with conflicting shared narrative views. Then strategy is developed and refined based on these analyses to provide points of intervention.

Social marketing is *"the capacity to bring about behaviour change"* (Hastings & Domegan, 2017, p. 6). Applying marketing insights beyond the commercial marketplace and into social systems is a clear goal in modern social marketing, in order *"to make all our lives better, improve social cohesion and even save the planet"* (Hastings & Domegan, 2017, p. 6). Most social marketing problems are wicked problems (McAuley,

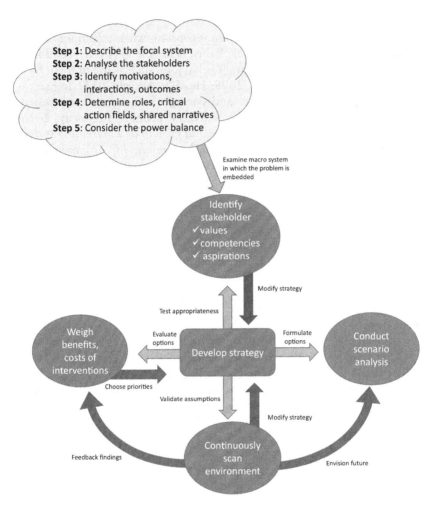

Figure 3.1 Macro-Social Marketing for Solving Wicked Problems

2014). Yet the social marketing literature has just begun to point towards an approach for social marketers to use to assess wicked problems in order to plan strategically for their improvement. Stakeholder involvement that forms a shared narrative for the problem and joint commitment to action are considered key to approaching wicked problems (Conklin, 2006; Kreuter, De Rosa, Howze, & Baldwin, 2004). Information sharing, consultation, and active participation as part of stakeholder engagement for wicked problems is further advocated in French and Gordon's strategic social marketing text (2015). Broadening the theoretical understanding of how social marketing at a macro level may bring about system-wide change for a wicked problem, Kennedy (2016) posits that systems theory and institutional theory can be applied in a framework of macro-social marketing.

Macro-social marketing is a tool appropriate when traditional linear thinking, which focuses on causal chains, is unable to effectively address the complexities that sustain a target behaviour, such as use of fossil fuels (Kreuter et al., 2004; Camillus, 2008; Head & Alford, 2015). In macro-social marketing, systems theory and systems thinking are used to map out the social system perpetuating a wicked problem (Kennedy, 2016; Kennedy et al., 2017). "*The formation and growth of a marketing system reflects the social, cultural, political and economic life of communities [and] the physical environment*" (Layton, 2014, p. 4). This macro-level marketing orientation allows social marketers to consider all the inputs to a problem in which key changes to behaviour are sought.

This definition is key to considering how the macro, system-level perspective creates a tableau against which the various actors, activities, inputs, and outputs are arranged. To understand the strategic implications of any behaviour change or social marketing action, macro-social marketing asks practitioners to first identify the individuals, groups, or entities which make up the system (Kennedy et al., 2017). Once the focal system is understood, macro-social marketing seeks to analyse the social mechanisms, critical action fields, and participant interactions within the system (see Figure 3.1). This presents social marketers with a snapshot of the system, so that the structures, functions, and outcomes of a system can be better illuminated (Kennedy et al., 2017; Layton, 2014).

This systems analysis becomes more dynamic when macro-social marketers examine each entity within the focal system. Entities are then assessed to understand their roles and relative power, along with the narratives they share regarding the wicked problem.

Key entities are reconceptualised as incumbents who benefit from the system, challengers who benefit less from the system and might agitate for change, or governance units which respond to both and can maintain or change the system. This reframing of entities gives social marketers a tool for informed strategic options (Kennedy et al., 2017). The roles, relative power balance, and willingness of entities to participate in behaviour change efforts are key to strategising in macro-social marketing. The advantages or disadvantages each entity derives from the current system maintaining the problem are potential strategic turning points. A key arena for macro-social marketing thus stems from the shared narratives that support each entity's ideology. Narratives can help to uncover interactions, motivations, influences, and value propositions (Normann, 2001). Of crucial importance to enacting strategic behaviour change is capturing these evolving and dynamic narratives.

The analysis of the case for encouraging greater uptake of renewables in the small island developing states of the Caribbean and Pacific begins, as in Figure 3.1 and Table 3.1, with an analysis of the focal system.

Table 3.1 How to Use Macro-Social Marketing to Strategise Wicked Problems

Step	Main Task	Insights Into This Task
1. Describe the focal system.	Identify the system and institutions in which an emerging problem is embedded.	• Consider: What is the system about, and what drives it? What is the market orientation? What are the social conditions and social structures that allow the problem to flourish? Look at the micro, meso, and macro levels. • Remember that informal (i.e., norms, taboos, sanctions, and community groups) and formal institutions (i.e., banks, governments, regulatory frameworks, and international agencies) can be key to the creation and maintenance of the system that supports a wicked problem.
2. Analyse the stakeholders.	Identify the individuals, groups, or entities which make up the system, or whatever level of aggregation a social marketing is examining.	• Consider the stakeholders most involved in or affected by the wicked problem's creation, maintenance, or destruction. • Begin by describing the origins, the present status and nature, and the future goals of these stakeholders. • What key challenges exist to each stakeholders' continued thriving? What key opportunities exist to spur each stakeholder group's success?
3. Identify the entities' motivations to behave as they do, how they interact with one another, and the outcomes of these interactions in the social system.	Determine the relevant social mechanisms involved from each stakeholder.	• Some social mechanisms drive the maintenance and replication of a wicked problem through co-evolved means in the social network in which a wicked problem is embedded. So first, *analyse the behaviours, beliefs, and practices of the* key stakeholder groups. • Co-operative social mechanisms facilitate development of a shared narrative that sustains or challenges the wicked problem. How do the stakeholders *cooperate, exchange, and signal to one another* within their groups or entities? What are their *specialisations*, how do they *reduce uncertainty*, how do they *organise* and what route forward do they see for transitioning the system in which they operate?

(Continued)

Table 3.1 (Continued)

Step	Main Task	Insights Into This Task
4. Determine roles, critical action fields, and shared narratives in the system.	Categorise the stakeholder groups as incumbents, challengers, and governance units.	• Incumbents (Layton, 2014) are the entities that benefit from the current structure of a system. • Challengers benefit less from the current structure and functioning of a system (Layton, 2014). They might seek to create instability in the system to effect change that will yield further benefits. • Governance units are the entities that respond to both incumbents and challengers. These governing bodies are the ultimate force responsible for maintaining the status quo or regulating change. • Determine the narratives that most drive each group. Look for overlap, intersectionality, or how each narrative may feed off each other and weave together to tell the story.
5. Consider the relative power of each entity.	Consider each entity's role and how that influences the efficacy of their actions.	• What is the balance of power among the incumbents, challengers, and governance units? • Create a power balance figure (see Fig. 3.2) to help visualize the push and pull of levers of power involved in the wicked problem.

Sources: Layton, 2014; Martinot et al., 2002; Kennedy et al., 2017

Step 1. Analysing the Focal System: The Case for Renewables in Small Island Developing States

By the industrial revolution, a shift in energy reliance moved clean agrarian economies with renewable resources (solar, wind, water, muscle) to fossilised sources such as coal, gas, and oil (Menegaki & Tsagarakis, 2015). Yet the world's economy is shifting to a cleaner services basis of harnessing energy from self-renewing resources. This includes wind, sunlight, heat from inside the earth, and even plants and flowing water (i.e., Bull, 2001).

Wind, solar, biomass, hydrofuel, and geothermal energies exist in a range of technological development, commercialisation, and acceptance. The growth of renewable energies has been continual and stable in developed economies. European economies' needs are still mostly covered by fossil-fuel produced energy (Mengaki & Tsagarakis, 2015). Yet marketing for 'green' and sustainable energies has helped to drive social acceptance (i.e., Wustenhagen, Wolsink, & Burer, 2007). For instance, 25%–35% of Germany's electricity is generated from renewable resources (Wasserman, Reeg, & Nienhaus, 2015). The majority of Italians express positive views about wind energy. Yet Italians still prefer offshore locations for wind-farms due to aesthetic concerns of wind turbine height and proximity to houses and coastlines (Vecchiato, 2014). Social acceptance is therefore a key part of a marketplace's readiness for renewable resource technology (Wustenhagen et al., 2007).

The case for uptake of renewable energies is more complicated for developing nations in the Caribbean and Pacific. Limited resources mean less investment and ability to afford implementation of existing renewable technologies. Developing economies are thus more dependent on donor aid and smaller subsidies (Martinot et al., 2002). The need is also higher among these nations for skills and knowledge transfer around renewable energy technology. Why and how are small island development states importing fuel, paying a fortune, and not thinking about renewables (Ince, 2013; Ince et al., 2016)? A need exists for more coherent international policy, governmental support, investment, and social acceptance for renewable energy technology.

How Have Marketing Systems Curated Conditions for Renewables?

Marketing systems (Layton, 2014) have created the conditions for consumption energy resources. Market factors include energy product characteristics, financing, suppliers and distributors, regulatory frameworks, social conditions, pricing, environmental and related costs, and consumer knowledge and demand for sustainable development in energy. What underlies that marketing system becomes of key importance for social marketers seeking a macro view. How have marketing systems been involved in curating conditions for acceptance and further penetration of renewable resources?

Social marketing at the micro level focuses on the need to create conditions for social acceptance of renewable energy technologies (Menegaki, 2012). Social marketing should thus focus first on identifying, creating, communicating, delivering, and monitoring consumers' values and trends. Convincing consumers to avoid waste in their household usage is also a step towards greater acceptance of renewables. Marketing around social norms for electricity savings helps to change the social structure and institutional environment around energy consumption (Thogerson & Gronhoj, 2010). Green power marketing also gives sustainable electricity grid providers a competitive advantage in the marketplace. Transparent, detailed marketing information on the electricity generation mix, along with a preference for domestically produced energy, contribute to willingness to pay (Kaenzig, Heinzle, & Wustenhagen, 2013)

Island ecosystems in the Pacific and Caribbean are unique. Yet most of these islands are overwhelmingly dependent on fossil fuels to power their electricity grids and transportation. Most of these islands are also dependent on costly import of oil and gas shipped via tanker over long distances. And most of these islands face shoreline erosion, coral bleaching, and more frequent and damaging storms that are driven in part by the world's reliance on non-renewable fossil fuel resources.

How can macro-social marketing help unfurl the interrelated, complex needs and competing interests of renewable energy adoption in the developing island states of the world? This chapter follows the next steps of the macro-social marketing process (see Table 3.1) to examine the stakeholders most involved in and affected by the problem's creation, maintenance, or destruction. Who are the players and what are their stakes? What are the narratives that drive their behaviour in the marketplace for renewable energy adoption?

Steps 2–4. Stakeholders in Renewable Energy Adoption

Micro Level: Domestic Consumers and Tourists

Domestic consumers in remote island states in the Pacific and the Caribbean exist in a "*micro-scale context*" consisting of "*their very smallness and compressed societal nature, their openness and external dependence*" (Connell & Conway, 2000, p. 53). Substantial emigration to nearby large metropolitan countries has forged international linkages. Remittances from migrants in Tonga and Samoa, for instance, have helped raise the standard of living of families living on the home islands (Brown & Ahlburg, 1999). Islanders tend to see emigration or employment overseas "*as a means of escaping limited domestic economic opportunities and maximising their household development options*" (Connell & Conway, 2000, p. 72). Yet islanders' strong tie to the land and climate and their willingness to look to the future characterises their approach to the concept of renewable energy.

Narrative 1: Access to Affordable, Reliable Energy.
Achievement of Energy Independence. Less Dependence on
External Intervention and External Energy Sources.

Residents of the small island developing states generally have lower income with little commercial power in loosely organised marketplaces heavily dependent on imports. As a result, Caribbean and Pacific consumers command relatively little influence over the adoption of electricity and fuel standards in their microstates. Some live with little access to utilities such as electricity and internet. Some live in larger towns with uninterrupted access to energy. But all live in closer harmony with their environments. Energy security and the desire for energy independence also loom larger for island residents (REEEP, 2014, 2012).

Changes in community and lifestyle could be widespread with the adoption of renewable energies based on smaller, more modular systems. Millions in the developing world lack access to electricity and/or cooking fuel, leading to a lack of medical services, a lack of education, thirst, hunger, and environmental depletion (Bull, 2001). Wind turbines, solar panels, and modular biomass gasifiers would instil sweeping change even adopted village by village and home by home. Such renewable systems have a clear appeal for island consumers. Modular renewable systems in particular would contribute electrical capacity and greatly reduce the costs to consumers of using electricity.

Narrative 2: Clean, Green Destination that Matches the
Sparkling Island Backdrop of Many Small Island Developing
States. Persistent, Pervasive Support for a Clean Environment.
Future-Focused.

Tourism is an economic imperative and major export for the small island developing states. Navigating the needs of tourists, especially those seeking an ethical, clean green destination, is a key motivation to pursue renewable resources for some of these developing island states. Costa Rica actively pursued tourist dollars as it adopted more renewable resources (Espinoza & Vredenburg, 2010). Many island states have some investment, though small, in renewable energy resources. Though St. Lucia, for instance, still imports fossil fuels and has a 98% electrification rate on its tourist-drawing landscapes, the island relies extensively on solar water heating for use in domestic and hotel sectors (REEEP, 2012; Ince, 2013).

Non-renewable energy production is less visible, and takes place mostly underground, further removed from consumer consciousness. Renewable resources are likely to be localised with more visible elements such as solar panels and wind turbines. Renewable energies are thus likely to be more prevalent in consumers' minds. It remains unclear how visibility or aesthetic concerns impact consumers in the Caribbean and South Pacific. Would visible signals of renewable infrastructure help these consumers view the renewable energy investment as part of a clean, green locale (i.e., Espinoza & Vredenburg, 2010)? Would visible signals of renewable energy spur clean, green brand association for tourists? Or, might the presence of turbines and solar panel farms serve to scar the pristine palm trees, green hills, and white-sand landscapes most prized by islanders and the tourists who flock to these islands?

Meso- Level: Suppliers, Private Sector Investors, Direct Marketers

The locus of power looms large for electric utilities who have a stake in maintaining their traditional, petroleum-based energy sources. The influence of electric utilities, for instance, is a negative variable in the adoption of renewable energies among 34 island jurisdictions in the Caribbean (Ince et al., 2016). Yet changing investment patterns and increased entrepreneurial activity with institutional support might tip the balance towards uptake of more renewable resources.

Narrative 1: More Entrepreneurial Opportunity Given the Modular, Smaller-Scale Development of Renewable Technologies. Informal Institutions, the Presence of Green Culture, and Social Norms and Collaboration Can Turbocharge Investment in Renewables.

Development of renewable energies can flourish in areas with cultures of entrepreneurship and ecology. Collective social capital underpins the development and social acceptance of renewable energy technology. For instance, the founding of sustainable energy industries in California, France, and Germany are driven first by natural capital resources (i.e., wind and land) and economic capital (i.e., monetary investment). But these renewable industries require widespread deployment of social capital via institutional environments to thrive (Russo, 2003; Jobert, Laborgne, & Mimler, 2007). Institutional support in the form of public subsidies, tax credits, and statutory support for prices for electricity generated from wind resulted in widely varied adoption of wind energy in California (Russo, 2003). Informal institutions still play a large, and even positive role in the adoption of renewable energies in the 34 far-flung island jurisdictions assessed by Ince et al. (2016). Economist North (1990) points to the role of institutions as drivers of behaviour, both informal institutions (i.e., taboos, sanctions, and customs) and formal institutions (i.e., constitutions, laws, and property rights).

Narrative 2: Changing Investment Patterns Elicit Increased Decision Making and Participation from a Wider Variety of Stakeholders.

Commercial markets for renewable energy are expanding in developing nations. This is shifting investment patterns away from traditional government and international donor sources to greater reliance on private firms and banks (Martinot et al., 2002). The small, modular nature of many renewable technologies is expected to spur growth of entrepreneurial ventures that manufacture, service, and sell renewable energy in developing economies (Bull, 2001).

Entrepreneurs who are willing to invest in disruptive, renewable energy technologies are already among the biggest drivers in increasing share of the renewable sector in developed economies. Direct marketing actions of these entrepreneurs is a key strategic action field (Wasserman et al., 2015). They act as intermediates in deregulated, liberalised marketplaces. Direct marketers choose the best market strategies (i.e., premium pricing vs. green power pricing), develop technical services such as monitoring day-ahead forecasts based on weather predictions and sun availability, and schedule communications to spread value among the renewable energy supply chain to end-consumers (Wasserman et al., 2015). Such entrepreneurs, hand in hand with civil servants, rely on institutional support. They seek to foster a collaborative climate to pursue renewable energy development (Agterbosch, Glasbergen, & Vermuelen, 2007).

Narrative 3: Are Conditions Right on my Island for This Renewable Technology? Renewable Technology Must be Adapted to Local Climates, Needs, and Geographies. Knowledge Transfer Around the Installation, Use, and Repair of Renewable Energy Technologies is Key. Renewable Energy Maintenance Funds Are Lacking.

Populations of the small island developing states often take from existing ideas for renewable energy development, but seldom research or make their own renewable technologies as suited to the individual environmental needs. This means that technologies used are not always the best suited for local conditions. Consider both the immediate and long-term impact after wind turbines set up in Barbados in the 1980s rusted in the salt water, showing high signs of corrosion (Ince, 2013).

The project failed within a year as a result. To this day this warning story discourages policy makers in Barbados from investing in renewable resources.

A more appropriate, modular, and quickly adaptable renewable technology in the small island developing states is the use of solar panels to heat water (REEEP, 2012). Though such solar heating of domestic and commercial hotel water has had some success in the islands, larger contributions to the power grid have been overall negligible (REEEP, 2014, 2012). And importantly, even after solar panels are installed, they can fall into disrepair when maintenance funds are low and knowledge transfer around the use and repair of such technologies is limited.

Macro Level: Governments, Trade, International Agencies

Foreign direct investment is beginning to play a larger role in bringing more renewable energies into developing states, including the islands of the Pacific and Caribbean. However, support for renewable energies in the international marketplace, vulnerability to climate change, and international agreements together bear weight to be considered in the push for renewable energy adoption among small developing island nations.

Narrative 1: Vulnerability to Climate Change, Damaging Storms, and Shoreline Erosion.

Consider the startling case of soil erosion in Kiribati, a string of 33 small islands and atolls straddling the equator that sits just 2–3 meters above sea level. Half of its population has fled from the rising sea to its main island of South Tarawa. The main island now has one of the highest population densities in the world, reminiscent of Tokyo or Hong Kong (Siddle, 2014). Residents in Tarawa are fleeing subsistence on the outer islands of Kiribati, trying to train as nurses and builders so they can emigrate (Rytz, 2018). The nation is slowly sinking amid rising sea levels, with the sea devouring unprotected tracts of land. Kiribati is defenceless during storm surges that flood past barrier and sea walls and spoil underground storage of fresh water supplies (Rytz, 2018).

No island is immune to climate change, and no island resident has remained unaffected by storms. Climate change with its rising ocean temperatures is driving more turbulent storms, eroding shorelines, bleaching coral reefs, and killing fish. Climate change thus should form a clear set of motivations for small island developing states to consider renewable energies. A series of unimaginably destructive hurricanes and cyclones in recent years, including Hurricanes Irma and Maria in 2017, caused severe damage across the Caribbean. A year later, parts of Puerto Rico were still without power, homes, and transportation links, while rates of social isolation, loss of livelihood, and depression led to a spike in suicides.

The role of extensive cyclones in the South Pacific have also taken their toll. Vanuatu, an archipelago of 82 small islands, was hit with 7 severe tropical cyclones (category 3 and higher, with wind speeds ranging from 130 km/hour to 280 km/hour) in just a 3-year period from 2015 to 2018. Significant damage from these storms causes problems with water supplies, sanitation, food supply, electricity, transportation, shelter, communications, security, medical care, and mosquito control. Climate change is thus a powerful force for governments considering ways to mitigate the effects of dependence on fossil fuels.

Narrative 2: Governments Seek Access to Modern, Quality Environmentally Friendly Services.

The diffusion rate of eco-innovative technologies in the energy sector varies considerably among countries, mainly due to the lack of attractive policies to leverage the decision making process in favour of renewables (i.e., Toka, Iakovou, Vlachos, Tsolakis, & Grigoriadou, 2014). Diffusion of renewable energy can be enhanced by budgetary policy interventions on initial investment start-up costs for creating renewable infrastructure, direct access to biomass materials, and imposed oil taxes. Such incentives could contribute significantly in accelerating the adoption of renewables such as biomass heating systems, besides reaching timely national targets on carbon emissions reduction (Toka et al., 2014). This prescription from the literature on increasing diffusion of renewables in small island developing states is showing to work in practice as well as in theory. But many forces must come together to allow governments to gain access to new renewable energy technologies.

Narrative 3: There is a Will to Increase Uptake of Renewables. But Financial Backing and International Support are Highly Necessary for Governments to Make Up More of their Energy Balance with Renewable Resources.

Governments can lead efforts, but it is clear that they are less effective in isolation and seek the support of international parties and coalitions including direct foreign investment. International agencies help provide knowledge, lobbying, and access to grants. For instance, the Alliance Of Small Island States works on behalf of 44 island and low-lying nations that comprise 5% of the world's population to address the U.N. assembly with issues particular to the islands.

But funding tends to come in ebbs and flows for small island developing states. From 2009 to 2014, the Australian government funded the Pacific Climate Change Science programme to investigate capacity building and adaptation planning of renewable energies in the South Pacific. Yet funding and interest waned after 2014. The 2015 Paris accords have 179 signatory countries aimed at reducing carbon emissions in a more flexible, self-regulatory environment. The Paris accords set aside funding for developing countries to cut emissions and cope with shoreline erosion and storms. Yet in 2017, the United States officially pulled support from the Paris accords. For a small island developing state, uncertainty with such projects is high. Funding fluctuates, policies change, and competing needs mean the world's attention and financial backing can be drawn to other populations and problems. Working with international agencies and international efforts is thus a path forward for governments seeking to increase their share of renewable energy to power their grid. Yet it cannot function as the only solution for such small-island policy makers.

Step 5: Power Balance

The last consideration in the macro-social marketing process is to weigh each entity's role, relative power, and how that influences the efficacy of their actions. This consideration of stakeholder power balance is necessary to determine which areas to strategise from, as in Figure 3.1. Table 3.2 assigns each stakeholder in renewable energy adoption to roles as challengers, incumbents, and governance units.

In many market-based systems, the incumbents yield the most power (Layton, 2014; Kennedy et al., 2017). In the case of the adoption of renewable energy for the power grids of small island developing states, consumers, international agencies, and governments facing the ravages of climate change are challengers to the current system. Formal and informal institutions join with monopolistic electric utilities in some island nations to form the most powerful human-controlled parts of the system (see Figure 3.2). At the other end of the balance of power, individual consumers and isolated island governments exhibit weak to marginal ability to effect change.

Table 3.2 The Roles of the Key Stakeholders

Challengers	Incumbents	Governance Units
Foreign direct investors	Oil producers, fossil fuel	Small island developing
Formal and informal institutions	manufacturers	state governments
	Electric utilities	
Aid programmes, development banks, other NGOs		International agencies
Consumers		Trade agreements

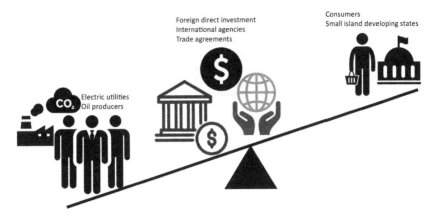

Figure 3.2 Balance of Power in Renewable Energy Adoption by Island Nations

Strategic Recommendations Drawn from Macro-Social Marketing

Strategic, macro-social marketing thinking about how to enable more uptake of renewable energies in small island developing nations stems from assessing the directives and the motivating narratives of each stakeholder. A consideration of the critical action fields and relative roles next leads to ideation of examples of social marketing initiatives that consider the system in which the larger problem is embedded. The goal of this consideration is to drive discussion and change. This is a dynamic process, however, meaning that each stage of implementation of any social marketing initiative should inspire a new, refreshed analysis of the systems and the changing structures involved (as in Figure 3.1). How have social marketing initiatives shuffled the deck of competing needs and the power balance between incumbents, challengers, and governance units?

Table 3.3 proposes how such an initial examination might yield social marketing initiatives. This examination is based on the preceding analysis of the marketing system involved in both maintaining and challenging the current petroleum-based economies of small island developing nations. Such initiatives are grounded in the macro system surrounding the problem. The needed behaviour change of greater uptake of renewable energy resources is thus viewed as a push and pull between micro-, meso-, and macro-level forces and competing and/or complimentary narratives. Importantly, the impact of any initiative necessitates a re-evaluation of the system, via the steps in Table 3.1 and Figure 3.1.

What is critical for penetration of renewables in these small developing economies is not merely technological capabilities. Renewable energy capability must emerge in lockstep with support from governmental

Table 3.3 Increasing Share of Renewable Resources in Small Island Developing States: Key Insights for Macro-Social Marketing Initiatives and Future Research

Directive	Motivating Narratives	Critical Action Fields and Relative Roles	Insights for Social Marketing Initiatives
Goal: Increase social acceptance of renewable resources.	Problem/narrative: Wind turbines aren't beautiful (Vecchiato, 2014), yet visible elements increase consumer connection to renewable energy (Wiser, 1998).	Co-creation between government, investors, and publics.	Aesthetics of landscape with turbines (i.e., with windmills as pastoral, romanticised). Return to a perception of a clean agrarian past with a clean, services-based economy of today. Sell visibility of local renewable energy resources as a status symbol with social approval. Future-focused as opposed to punitive mitigation of past missteps (i.e., Menegaki, 2012).
Goal: Harness the growth and incoming dollars of tourism to build a larger share of renewable energy in the power grids of the biggest tourist-drawing islands.	Narratives: – Clean, green destination that matches the sparkling island backdrop of many of these microstates. – Persistent, pervasive support for a clean environment.	Consumers have little power, but the rising strength of tourism operators and the hospitality industry on many islands can help agitate for more informal and formal support for uptake of renewables. For instance, the Caribbean island of Bonaire, which relies on dive tourism, derives the majority of its energy from renewable wind power. Reframing this island as an eco-paradise destination could draw more tourists to the country, to in turn fuel more investment in the renewable infrastructure.	Create a 'green' culture or a clean, green brand image that drives further hospitality and tourism. Create visible hallmarks of the country's renewable energy that intermingles with the island nation's natural beauty. If images of pastoral, bucolic agrarian past can include windmills, why can't images of a clean, green, service oriented future include wind turbines and fields of solar panels? Think: White sands, palm trees, and wind turbines as part of the preservation of pristine nature.

Goal: Procure more micro-lending and risk-sharing funds to promote uptake of renewable energy among island homeowners and businesses.	Narratives: – Banks are reluctant to provide loans for renewable energy installation for homes and small businesses (The World Bank, 2016). – Lending is also sparse to further educate, maintain, and repair renewable technologies once installed.	Small energy companies work with banks to install renewable technologies. But manpower and funding are limited for both install and later maintenance. Consumers seek to expand their use of renewables, but have little access to future funding to grow and maintain their current installations.	Invite altruism via developed world consumers to co-sponsor microloans, or encourage communities or families to adopt a community or family in small island developing nations working to get on the renewable power grid. Investment must be enough to fund start-up, maintenance, and expansion within a community (vs. one-time lock and leave loans).
Goal: Facilitate more investment in localised, boutique renewable technologies in island nations.	Narratives: – Are conditions right on my island for this renewable technology? No one wants a corroded wind turbine. And other technology-questions from dominant electric providers (Ince, 2013). – Knowledge must be transferred and renewable technology must be adopted to local climates, needs, and geographies on the islands.	Facilitate introductions of investors with moderate power with informal institutions that exert greater power in the balance of renewable energy adoption in the islands.	Creation of international incubation centres targeting investors in renewables, and connecting them with engineering firms that can localise a renewable tech solution for a specific island's needs.

(Continued)

Table 3.3 (Continued)

Directive	Motivating Narratives	Critical Action Fields and Relative Roles	Insights for Social Marketing Initiatives
Goal: Stabilise funding support to small island developing states' governments via international agencies.	Narrative: Funding is driven in large part by the changing winds of policy from international agencies and coalitions of funders. Changes in policy make small island developing states vulnerable to losing access to much-needed financial support to build renewable infrastructure in projects that are long-term and deeply costly to set up.	Funding agreement meeting between AoSIS and the U.N. to secure untouchable grants for governments in small island developing states that issue clear renewable energy goals (such as Tonga, Fiji).	Create a clear commitment for funding via such bodies as the U.N., AOSIS, Pacific Centre for Renewable Energy and Energy Efficiency, and the Caribbean Center for Renewable Energy and Energy Efficiency.
Goal: Attract more foreign direct investment to smaller scale renewable energy projects.	Narrative: There is a will to increase uptake of renewables. But financial backing and international support are highly necessary for governments to make up more of their energy balance with renewable resources.	Governance units can seek to woo foreign direct investment through creating clear renewable energy plans and marketing their countries and commodities. For instance, Fiji has the capacity to support biomass with its pine trees, and now with Korean backing, has a wood pellet plant to export this biomass fuel as a renewable energy resource to other island nations.	Social marketing aimed at investors around the returns that they can see from coalitions to fund renewable energy. See the case of Fiji with Korean investment in the Nabou Green Energy Plant. Fiji had to be willing to give regulatory support and incentives to achieve their investment.

agencies and international bodies along with investors (local and foreign), and the willingness of consumers to accept such renewable energies to power their households. The first clear directive, then, is to enable increased acceptance for and demand of renewable energy resources among residents of the small island developing states.

Directive: Increase Social Acceptance of Renewable Resources

Dimensions of social acceptance for renewable energies include sociopolitical, community, and market acceptance (Wustenhagen et al., 2007). Market acceptance in particular includes consumer motivations unique to the islands.

Foreign oil dependence, political and social misgivings about spending on foreign (vs. domestic) product, and environmental impact are key motivators unique to most island residents' potential willingness to adopt renewable resources. Barbados provides an illustrative case with almost complete dependence on fossil fuels. Just over 95% of the petroleum products in Barbados are imported (Ince et al., 2016; REEEP, 2014). The resultant risks for an island nation for energy security, the country's budget, and negative environmental impact are immense. In short, *"any strategy that seeks to address petroleum product consumption will, by default, contribute to the sustainability of Barbados and its mitigation efforts against harmful emissions and climate change"* (REEEP, 2014, np).

Social marketing during the introduction and growth stage of the renewable energy life cycle has been key to reaching full commercialisation in developed economies (Menegaki, 2012). This suggests that the core positioning of renewable energy services as bringing *"sustainability and a cleaner environment"*, and expressing a *"forward looking"* stance for development of renewables, can be effective motivating narratives for consumers (Menegaki, 2012, p. 38). Many consumers in small island developing nations actively seek to protect their land and livelihood, and look forward to building more opportunity for their families (i.e., Connell & Conway, 2000).

Among the best predictors of consumer investment and attraction to green energy projects are the marketing of more tangible, visible, and local sourcing. This includes rooftop solar panels, or community-based neighbourhood solar energy systems and local wind projects (Wiser, 1998). Visibility helps consumers identify with being supporters of renewable energy. The marketing of local and domestic sourcing of renewables has emerged as a clear consumer preference (Kaenzig et al., 2013). Providing visible proof of a customer's commitment, via rooftop solar panels or even bumper stickers, helps facilitate social approval as well as a consumer's own altruistic interest in paying more for renewable, sustainable energies (Wiser, 1998). Yet some consumers disapprove of the high visibility of renewable energy projects, worrying it will ruin the beauty of a landscape (Vecchiato, 2014). One social marketing opportunity is therefore turning visibility of turbines, solar panels, and biomass plants into a symbol of pride, environmental protections, and future-proofing.

Important in particular for small island developing states is further strategising that allows the visibility of renewable energy technologies to attract more tourism dollars vital to the economies and livelihoods of these islands.

Directive: Harness the Growth and Incoming Dollars of Tourism to Build a Larger Share of Renewable Energy in the Power Grids of the Biggest Tourist-Drawing Islands

Opportunity may exist for social marketers at the meso level of the system, working midstream or downstream on social capital support programmes and tactical interventions (i.e., Kennedy, 2016; Hasting & Domegan, 2017) to drive demand for renewable procurement on small developing island states. This is especially the case as tourism dollars begin to exert a greater impact on some island economies. For instance, the Caribbean's St. Lucia saw record numbers of tourists arriving, up 11% in 2017 (CTO, 2018). The country relies on solar panels to heat water that services hotels and homes alike. Yet such usage is far less visible to many tourists and contributes negligible productivity to the island's power grid (REEEP, 2014). Solar panels are tucked away behind hotels, and renewable energy adoption has stalled. St. Lucia's sole monopoly electricity provider has an exclusive license to provide power until 2045, giving it a dominant stake in maintaining fossil fuel dependence for the island and its 174,000 residents and 1.1 million tourists per year (Ince, 2013; CTO, 2018). Yet strategic initiatives to reposition the island's brand as a green-power paradise presents an opportunity for macro-social marketers.

Beyond natural capital and economics, social capital and social acceptance play a determining role in wind farm projects in developing economies in Costa Rica and Ecuador and are thus core areas for social marketers to consider (Espinoza & Vredenburg, 2010). Such social capital factors as the 'green' reputation of the country's brand, motivation and risk taking for environmental entrepreneurship, and sharing learning helped determine the success of these wind projects (Espinoza & Vredenburg, 2010). Pioneers, the 'green' culture, and the collaborative climate are significant informal institutions in Latin America's renewable energy efforts. Importantly, Costa Rica has emerged as an 'eco-paradise' fuelled in part by its high rate of adoption of renewable energies. Tourism is the third-largest source of income for Costa Rica, rising from 329,000 tourists in 1988 to 2.9 million tourists in 2016 (ICT, 2017). Tourism is both driven by and driving the ability of Costa Rica to invest in more renewable energy resources. The green, eco-paradise brand of the country has made it a clear destination. In addition, the investment possible from tourist dollars has helped reaffirm that brand for the country by driving increased adoption of renewable energy infrastructures. Costa Rica is a benchmark developing nation for uptake of renewables, as it sets and then breaks green power records for the world. In 2017, the entire country's grid was powered by renewable resources for 300 days straight (Embury-Dennis, 2017).

Yet even the prospect of establishing a clean, green tourism brand may not survive the stranglehold of dominant petroleum-based electric utility interests in the battle for more renewable resources. More funding alongside fewer funding interruptions to achieve project goals will be key to allowing isolated governments to build out their renewable infrastructure, as will direct social marketing to facilitate acceptance and adoption.

Directive: Procure More Micro-Lending and Risk-Sharing Funds to Promote Uptake of Renewable Energy Among Island Homeowners and Businesses

Upstream social marketing work in renewables has traditionally taken the shape of macro-level lending that shapes entire government policy, such as intergovernmental cooperation and NGO support. Yet small island developing states have found help from small energy companies, micro-lending opportunities from banks, and the altruism of developed-economy consumers and businesses to fund start-up renewable projects. The resulting midstream social marketing strategy has taken the form of practical financial assistance for right-sized projects in the smaller island jurisdictions. Renewable technology in particular can be modular and small-scale, such as individual households powered by solar panels or villages and neighbourhoods that adopt a community wind farm or burn biomass fuels.

Such small-scale developments are friendlier for micro-lending opportunities. For instance, The World Bank (2016) spearheaded 60 micro-loans to install solar panels and educate homeowners in Fiji. This project start-up is step one in ensuring 60 households have access to renewable energy, which helps power their own homes as well as generate excess electricity for the power grid in their communities. Yet little to no follow-up education and funds were made available for maintenance, expansion, and repair of the solar panel systems. There is a clear social marketing opportunity for such projects to be adopted, funded, and supported by micro-lenders looking to help homeowners and businesses in small island developing states reach renewable energy goals. Importantly, such micro-lending should cultivate localised expertise alongside small-scale funding opportunities within the islands.

Local knowledge and adaptation emerge as clear directives for macro-social marketing efforts to ensure that green power initiatives thrive. One clear social marketing outcome for small island states is thus to encourage the adaptation and development of renewable technologies for specific island conditions.

Directive: Facilitate More Investment in Localised, Boutique Renewable Technologies in Island Nations

The United Nations Development Programme identified four barriers to uptake of renewable energy in information, policy, finance, and capacity (Ince, 2013). The UNDP has goals to reduce these barriers in the Caribbean and Pacific, which are to promote the adoption of such energies by lessening barriers and costs. The Pacific Centre for Renewable Energy and Energy Efficiency, and the Caribbean Centre for Renewable Energy and Energy Efficiency, are both aimed at mitigating barriers to renewable energy adoption and increasing sustainability efforts among the small island developing states. Their goals are to function as knowledge disseminators. They promote renewable energy and energy efficiency investments, markets, and industries, in part helping share the lessons learned (i.e., Kay & Cherry, 2018). These international lobbying groups also see their chief function to help improve the islands' ability to withstand the effects of climate change.

Upstream social marketing initiatives aimed at policy formation and budget allocation can help motivate the further incubation of centres of knowledge transfer and engineering and technology specialisation to meet UNDP's goals. Investors, engineers, technology specialists, and policy makers should be targeted to help localise renewable technology among the small island developing states. This results in midstream social marketing efforts as well as subsidies and training in skills development, which take centre stage for the smaller jurisdictions in the islands. Individual governments are also key to this support and specialisation.

Directive: Stabilise Funding Support to Small Island Developing States' Governments Via International Agencies

Governments operating alone in small island jurisdictions tend to have less influence and power, especially in relation to policy that can drive adoption of renewable energy. They are remote and mostly less moneyed island states, with sometimes fraught political histories.

However, governments are trying to legislate their way into energy efficiency and energy independence, working closely with international partners. The Kingdom of Tonga seeks to have 50% renewables by 2020, and 70% by 2030 (Kay & Cherry, 2018). The Tonga Energy Road Map

(2010) sought to create *"a ten year road map to reduce Tonga's vulnerability to oil price shocks and to achieve an increase in quality access to modern energy services in an environmentally sustainable manner"* (2010, p. iii). Development assistance has been key to Tonga's renewable energy push. Organisations including New Zealand Aid Programme, Asian Development Bank, and the International Union for Conservation of Nature have supported Tongan projects such as solar farms, solar water pumps, network upgrades, and solar mini grids (Kay & Cherry, 2018). Clear and uninterrupted funding and support can mean the difference for a small island developing state's increasing uptake of renewables. This represents a clear space for strategic social marketing initiatives, both upstream and midstream, to seek commitment of funds and further build expertise among policy makers.

Directive: Attract More Foreign Direct Investment to Smaller Scale Renewable Energy Projects

Corporations are increasingly sourcing renewable energy to power their activities, as part of their own reputation management and adherence to sustainability standards. Renewable energy procurement is thus an emerging business strategy. By some estimates corporate sourcing of renewables by companies in 75 countries in 2017 was *"close to the overall electricity demand of France"* (IREA, 2018, np). Opportunity thus exists for businesses to drive demand for renewable procurement on small, developing island states. Businesses that seek to grow their green-power, sustainable brand, and reputation would be the most viable partners for small island developing states. Here is where macro-social marketing processes can offer strategic insight for social marketing tactics.

The Korean-owned Nabou Green Energy plant opened in Fiji in 2017. Nabou now powers 6% of Fijian energy from local Fiji pine and wood fibre, which is burned to produce steam as biomass energy. This makes it the first biomass renewable energy plant of its kind in the South Pacific (Nasokia, 2017). This level of foreign direct investment grew from Nabou's desire to both add capital to its holdings and further establish itself as a green-power provider worldwide. Fiji provided regulatory support and other incentives for the Koreans to enter their island marketplace. In this way, island policy makers should also be the target of social marketing efforts to help islands secure partners in foreign direct investment.

Summary

If people know it's hurting the planet to use fossil fuels, why do we still use oil and gas? The answer is a complex web of interrelated needs, demands, motivations, and narratives—in short, it's a wicked problem (Rittel &

Weber, 1973). And it's a wicked problem that requires a series of strategic, coordinated, and creative responses to drive behaviour change.

Macro-social marketing (Kennedy et al., 2017; Kennedy, 2016) proposes one tool for marketing researchers, social marketers, and policy makers. This tool asks researchers and practitioners to first analyse the system in which a wicked problem is embedded. As in Table 3.1, a macro-social marketer must next understand the key players and their relative power before designing behaviour change initiatives to alter the current course. Yet any introduced initiative must be studied carefully, in its systems and institutional context (Layton, 2014). As Figure 3.1 shows, each of those initiatives, once implemented, can alter the current trajectory of a wicked problem.

This chapter presents a static snapshot of the wicked problem of increasing uptake of renewable energy resources among small island developing states in the Pacific and Caribbean from a market needs orientation (i.e., Martinot et al., 2002). Macro-social marketing is proposed as a framework and backdrop against which to analyse the problem and its most impacted stakeholders. This chapter undertakes steps to pinpoint key motivating power struggles, opportunities, and ultimately behaviour change initiatives. To make it dynamic, however, any researcher who implements the proposed social marketing interventions (i.e., Table 3.3) must re-filter results through the macro-social marketing framework (Figure 3.1). This allows them to continuously assess impacts on the targeted populations in the marketplace, and on the interconnected system.

Ample sun, wind, hydro, and biomass resources exist in the small island developing nations of the world. What does not yet fully exist is the infrastructure, political will, knowledge transfer, and funding to make the changes needed to harness these renewable resources and end the cycle of fossil fuel use and harmful emissions. In the face of such a wicked problem, implementation of the macro-social marketing process can nudge key players into action.

References

Agterbosch, S., Glasbergen, P., & Vermuelen, W. J. V. (2007). Social barriers in wind power implementation in the Netherlands: Perceptions of wind power entrepreneurs and local civil servants of institutional and social conditions in realizing wind power projects. *Renewable and Sustainable Energy Reviews*, *11*, 1025–1055.

Brown, R. P. C., & Ahlburg, D. A. (1999). Remittances in the South pacific. *International Journal of Social Economics*, *26*(1–3), 325–344.

Bull, S. R. (2001). Renewable energy today. *Proceedings of the IEEE*, *89*(8), 1216–1226.

Camillus, J. C. (2008). Strategy as a wicked problem. *Harvard Business Review*, *86*(5), 98–106.

CompareMySolar. (2012). *Electricity price per kwh – Comparison of big six energy companies and tomorrow*. Retrieved May 28, 2018, from http://blog.comparemysolar.co.uk/electricity-price-per-kwh-comparison-of-big-six-energy-companies/

Conklin, J. (2006). Wicked problems and social complexity. In J. Conklin (Ed.), *Dialogue mapping: Building shared understanding of wicked problems* (pp. 3–40). Chichester, UK: John Wiley.

Connell, J., & Dennis, C. (2000). Migration and remittances in island micro-states: A comparative perspective on the south pacific and the Caribbean. *International Journal of Urban and Regional Research, 24*(1), 52–78.

CTO, Caribbean Tourism Organization. (2018). *Saint Lucia tourism arrivals register record breaking increase for 2017*. Retrieved May 30, 2018, from www.onecaribbean.org/saint-lucia-tourism-arrivals-register-record-breaking-increase-2017/

Embury-Dennis, T. (2017, November 22). Costa Rica's electricity generated by renewable energy for 300 days in 2017. *The Independent*. Retrieved August 31, 2018, from www.independent.co.uk/news/world/americas/costa-rica-electricity-renewable-energy-300-days-2017-record-wind-hydro-solar-water-a8069111.html.

Espinoza, J. L., & Vredenburg, H. (2010). The development of renewable energy industries in emerging economies: The role of economic, institutional, and socio-cultural contexts in Latin America. *International Journal of Economics and Business Research, 2*(3–4), 245–270.

French, J. & Gordon, R. (2015). *Stretegic Social Marketing*. London, Sage, 2015.

Hastings, G., & Domegan, C. (2017). *Social marketing, rebels with a cause* (3rd ed.). London, UK: Routledge.

Head, B. W., & Alford, J. (2015). Wicked problems implications for public policy and management. *Administration and Society, 47*(6), 711–739.

ICT. (2017, February 8). *Costa Rica supero los 2 milliones 900 mil llegadas internacionales*. Retrieved August 31, 2018, from www.centralamericadata.com/docs/Cifras_llegadas_internacionales_CR_2016.pdf

Ince, P. D. M. (2013). *Drivers and barriers to the development of renewable energy industries in the Caribbean* (Doctoral thesis), University of Calgary. Calgary, Alberta, Canada.

Ince, P. D. M., Vredenburg, H., & Liu, X. (2016). Drivers and inhibitors of renewable energy: A qualitative and quantitative study of the Caribbean. *Energy Policy, 98*, 700–712.

International Renewable Energy Agency IREA. (2018, May 24). *Corporate sourcing of renewables growing, taking place in 75 countries*. Retrieved May 30, 2018, from www.irena.org/newsroom/pressreleases/2018/May/Corporate-Sourcing-of-Renewables-Growing-Taking-Place-in-75-Countries

Jobert, A., Laborgne, P., & Mimler, S. (2007). Local acceptance of wind energy: Factors of success identified in French and German case studies. *Energy Policy, 35*, 2751–2760.

Kaenzig, J., Heinzle, S. L., & Wustenhagen, R. (2013). Whatever the customer wants, the customer gets? Exploring the gap between consumer preferences and default electricity products in Germany. *Energy Policy, 53*, 311–322.

Kay, R., & Cherry, C. (2018). *Empowering renewable energy development in Pacific Island countries*. Retrieved May 30, 2018, from www.climatelinks.org/blog/empowering-renewable-energy-development-pacific-island-countries

Kennedy, A-M. (2016). Macro-social marketing. *Journal of Macromarketing, 36*(3), 354–365.

Kennedy, A-M., Kapitan, S., Bejaj, N., Bakonyi, A., & Sands, S. (2017). Uncovering wicked problems' system structure: Seeing the forest for the trees. *Journal of Social Marketing, 7*(1), 51–73.

Kreuter, M. W., De Rosa, C., Howze, E. H., & Baldwin, G. T. (2004). Understanding wicked problems: A key to advancing environmental health promotion. *Health Education and Behavior, 31*(4), 441–454.

Layton, R. (2014). Formation, growth, and adaptive change in marketing systems. *Journal of Macromarketing, 35*(3), 302–319.

Martinot, E., Chauery, A., Lew, D., Moreira, J. R., & Wamukonya, N. (2002). Renewable energy markets in developing countries. *Annual Review of Energy Environment, 27*, 309–348.

Menegaki, A.N. & Tsagarakis, K.P. (2015). Rich enough to go renewable, but too early to leave fossil energy? *Renewable and Sustainable Energy Reviews, 41*, 1465–1477.

McAuley, A. (2014). Reflections on a decade in social marketing. *Journal of Social Marketing, 4*(1), 77–86.

Menegaki, A. N. (2012). A social marketing mix for renewable energy in Europe based on consumer preference surveys. *Renewable Energy, 39*, 30–39.

Nasokia, W. (2017, July 26). Nabou biomass plant to open. *The Fiji Sun*. Retrieved May 31, 2018, from http://fijisun.com.fj/2017/07/26/nabou-biomass-plant-to-open/

Normann, R. (2001). *Reframing business: When the map changes the landscape*. Chichester, UK: John Wiley & Sons.

North, D. C. (1990). *Institutions, institutional change and economic performance*. Cambridge: University of Cambridge Press.

NPR National Public Radio. (2011). *The price of electricity in your state*. Retrieved May 27, 2018, from www.npr.org/sections/money/2011/10/27/141766341/the-price-of-electricity-in-your-state

Prism. (2018). *22 million in South pacific*. Custom data recalled May 26, 2018 from https://prism.spc.int/regional-data-and-tools/population-statistics/169-pacific-island-populations

REEEP. (2012). *Saint Lucia (2012)*. Retrieved May 30, 2018, from www.reeep.org/saint-lucia-2012

REEEP. (2014). *Barbados (2014)*. Retrieved May 27, 2018, from www.reeep.org/barbados-2014

Rittel, H. W., & Weber, M. M. (1973). Dilemmas in a general theory of planning. *Policy Sciences, 4*(2), 155–169.

Russo, M. V. (2003). The emergence of sustainable industries: Building on natural capital. *Strategic Management Journal, 24*(4), 317–331.

Rytz, M. (dir.). (2018). *Anote's ark* [Motion Picture]. Canada.

Siddle, J. (2014, February 3). Kiribati: Tiny island's struggle with overpopulation. *BBC Science Radio Unit*. Retrieved May 30, 2018 from www.bbc.com/news/science-environment-26017336

Thogerson, J., & Gronhoj, A. (2010). Electricity savings in households- a social cognitive approach. *Energy Policy, 38*, 7732–7743.

Toka, A., Iakovou, E., Vlachos, D., Tsolakis, N., & Grigoriadou, A-L. (2014). Managing the diffusion of biomass in the residential energy sector: An illustrative real-world case study. *Applied Energy, 129*, 54–69.

UN DESA. (2017). United nations department of economic and social affairs, population division. *World population prospects: The 2017 revision.* Custom data recalled May 26, 2018 from www.un.org/development/desa/en/

Vecchiato, D. (2014). How do you like wind farms? Understanding people's preferences about new energy landscapes with choice experiments. *AESTIMUM, 64*, 15–37.

Wasserman, S., Reeg, M., & Nienhaus, K. (2015). Current challenges of Germany's energy transition project and competing strategies of challengers and incumbents: The case of direct marketing of electricity from renewable energy sources. *Energy Policy, 76*, 66–75.

Wiser, R. H. (1998). Green power marketing: Increasing customer demand for renewable energy. *Utilities Policy*, 107–119.

World Bank. (2016). *Fiji: Growing a renewable energy industry while expanding electricity access.* Retrieved July 30, 2018, from www.worldbank.org/en/news/feature/2016/05/24/fiji-growing-a-renewable-energy-industry-while-expanding-electricity-access

Wustenhagen, R., Wolsink, M., & Burer, M. J. (2007). Social acceptance of renewable energy innovation: An introduction to the concept. *Energy Policy, 35*, 2683–2691.

4 Using the Socio-Ecological Model as an Holistic Approach to Behavioural Change

Ekant Veer, Maja Golf-Papez, and Kseniia Zahrai

This chapter examines the use of the socio-ecological model (SEM) as a basis for promoting macro-social marketing behavioural change. By taking a broader perspective of macro-social marketing change the SEM can be an influential driver of pro-social behavioural change, as it focuses on a multi-layered approach to behavioural change rather than solely relying upon individual responsibility for change. The SEM has been used numerous times in academic health promotion literature as a means of encouraging positive behavioural change by taking a systemic approach to understanding and influencing behaviour. The SEM encourages health practitioners to take an holistic approach to a person's condition and then look at multi-layered means of affecting that behaviour in a positive manner. That is, rather than focus on individual responsibility alone, there needs to be a greater level of change occurring in the target population's environment and society that would allow change to become naturalistic. It is reasoned that an environment that provides the correct determinants for positive health will naturalistically lead to more positive health outcomes. However, very few studies have looked at the use of the SEM outside of specific health goals. This is not to say that the same theoretical rationale could not (and is not) used to drive positive behavioural change, but rather that the framework provided from SEM is not often explicitly employed when dealing with non-health behaviour determinants and outcomes. To this end, we suggest that the SEM and other multi-layered approaches to positive behavioural change could be employed by social-and macro-social marketers, as well as policy makers as a means of understanding the complexities associated with both health and non-health related behavioural change but also the various determinants of success at various levels that can influence this change.

In this chapter we explore the role that SEM plays in extant research and practice to drive positive behavioural change; we then compare SEM to other common holistic models of healthy behaviour change before providing an integrative model of behavioural change that looks beyond health as the unit of analysis, but rather focuses on 'behaviour' as the determinant outcome. This chapter begins by providing a brief history of the development of the socio-ecological model and its application before comparing it with similar models. We offer examples that have been used globally as well as examine the role that indigenous cultural values play in the development of holistic models of behavioural change in New Zealand (a glossary of key New Zealand Māori terms has been included at the end of this chapter). We conclude by illustrating how multi-level ecological models of behavioural change may guide the application of social marketing initiatives. This chapter offers social marketers and policy makers tools and practices that create an opportunity to examine social problems from a holistic perspective by applying the broad principles of the SEM and other similar multi-layered models to understanding and actioning both health and non-health related behavioural change.

What is the Socio-Ecological Model of Health Promotion?

The socio-ecological model is an approach to behaviour change, primarily used in health promotion, which incorporates a systemic approach to behaviour change that draws on multiple levels of influence. The SEM emerged from work by Bronfenbrenner (1979), who represented humans and human development as being subject to multiple layers of confounding influence. That is, one is not isolated in themselves or their immediate family, but the wider ecosystem that a person lives within affects their lives and behaviour. In the same way, the SEM looks not just at the final patient or target population but at the wider influential factors leading that behaviour to exist in the first instance and what levers can be used to encourage naturalistic behavioural change.

These levels of influence allow the health promoter to not just focus on the individual and intrapersonal factors affecting health but also the wider community, organisational, and macro effects that affect behaviour. In this way, the SEM does not only seek to affect the health outcomes of the final target population but also influence the wider 'determinants of health' that may have an indirect impact on final healthfulness. Table 4.1 outlines these levels of influence and how they apply to the SEM in particular.

The term 'socio-ecological' attempts to encapsulate how this holistic approach to behaviour change is based on social aspects of behaviour change but also on the notion that in ecological systems there is a fundamental appreciation for the relationship between an organism of interest and its natural surroundings (Stokols, 1996). In this way, an understanding of the social elements associated with human behaviour and the role that one's naturalistic environment plays in one's ability to thrive is necessary for promoting positive health or any other positive social marketing behaviour change. Without such a perspective we are faced with a situation where an individual may feel a powerful personal drive to seek

Table 4.1 Levels of Influence in the Socio-Ecological Model

Levels of Influence	Description of Behaviours	Entity Examples
Intrapersonal	Individual characteristics that influence behaviour, such as knowledge, attitudes, beliefs, and personality traits	Individuals
Interpersonal	Interpersonal processes and primary groups that provide social identity, support, and role definition	Close peer relationships, whanau (family), friends
Organisational	Rules, regulation, policies, and informal structures, which may constrain or promote recommended behaviours	Work, wider family, local community, and religious group norms and regulations
Community	Social networks and norms, or standards, which exist as formal or informal among individuals, groups, and organisations	Informal groupings associated with a wider community or participation groups, such as regional identity, cultural norms, and social grouping practices
Public policy	Local, state, federal policies and laws that regulate or support healthy actions and practices for disease prevention, early detection, control, and management	Any governing body that has a macro-policy focus, such as local, state, and national (federal) government bodies/ministries of health.

Micro Meso Macro

Source: (Adapted from Robinson, 2008)

a healthy behavioural change, but if they are part of a social system that does not value the chosen behaviour and in an environment that dissuades the behavioural change, the likelihood of the behaviour changing is lessened, irrespective of personal drive and success factors. The nature of the SEM is that the individual difference and behavioural change may be the final outcome measure for many health professionals. However, the influence of those in the meso and macro level cannot be ignored. Indeed, a process that allows for more macro-social marketing interventions that enable the alteration of the macro environment encourages positive health outcomes to be organically realised. The following section outlines some of the applications of the SEM to show its broad-based approach to not only take a macro-social marketing lens but also a meso and micro approach to encouraging behavioural change for the greater social good.

Applications of the Socio-Ecological Model

As mentioned previously, the predominant use of the SEM has been in the health promotion arena. The focus of its application has been not only as a lens to analyse the epidemiology of a health outcome but also as a basis for theoretical and practical interventions that can impact behavioural changes. For example, Robinson (2008) applied the lens of the SEM to understand the various drivers associated with fruit and vegetable consumption amongst low-income African Americans. The findings from the study show that the intersectionality of effects associated with culture, poverty, macro-level social norms, and more micro-level tastes all impact consumption patterns. The confluence of factors affecting the families that participated in the study meant that a personal responsibility perspective was unlikely to have a lasting effect on fruit and vegetable consumption. Townsend and Foster (2013) showed that interpersonal and wider community influences were stronger determinants on healthy eating practices amongst secondary school students than intrapersonal influences or personal choices. Bae et al.'s (2008) study of over 985 Korean patients showed that the strongest influencers of seeking a gastric cancer screening were interpersonal relationships and recommendations rather than intrapersonal factors. Only one intrapersonal factor, the participant's age, showed any significant impact on likelihood of having a gastric cancer screen test. They concluded that a multi-level approach is necessary in order to drive positive behavioural change. Similarly, DiClemente, Salazar, Crosby, and Rosenthal (2005) showed that social interactions and macro-level policy shifts were necessary in order to drive effective change in preventing and controlling sexually transmitted infections amongst U.S. based adolescents. Interestingly, Salm Ward and Doering (2014) were able to conceptualise their study on infant mortality as having the infant as the unit of analysis in their socio-ecological model and then the maternal relationship as being one level greater than this, before incorporating wider family, community, and other intrapersonal factors into the health risks that drive infant mortality rates. Their study not only showed the adaptability of socio-ecological style models but also further conceptualised the importance that non-physical factors play in driving behaviour, with maternal depression being seen as a key aspect that may lead to infant bed-sharing rates, increasing infant mortality risk.

Beyond the health context, the most common application of socio-ecological models are found in fields where studies of systemic interaction are prevalent, such as ecology and conservation. This chapter does not seek to fully explain these applications, but it is important to note that in these fields the examination of complex systems over a long period of time is an accepted norm and a necessary part of the research process (Singh, Haberl, Chertow, Mirtl, & Schmid, 2012). For example, Haberl et al.'s (2009) examination of biodiversity in European bird populations required the use of multi-level analysis to not only understand what may be driving practices that hinder biodiversity at the micro level but also the social practices and evolutionary choices that lead to bird biodiversity at a meso and macro level.

In short, social marketing interventions that forgo the impact that interpersonal influencing factors, such as community and social groups, have on individual behaviour may be missing a key driver of positive behavioural change. Equally, macro-level policy work that does not seek to understand the impact that these policies have on the lives of individual members of a population may not see the true efficacy intended from a policy change. The SEM and related models argue that it is only through taking an holistic view of behaviour and drivers of behaviour that a richer and more effective understanding of behavioural change is reached. The following section looks to examine a few examples of these alternative holistic models that are popular in health promotion and social marketing.

Alternative Holistic Models of Behavioural Change

The use of holistic models of behavioural change, especially in the health promotion field, is not uncommon. Many health promoters continue to utilise multi-level influencer approaches to understand the intersectionality of health issues and how determinants of health can be useful in creating structures and systems that support positive health outcomes. In this section we outline two popular multi-level models of health in the Ottawa Charter and Barton and Grant (2006) Health Map. We also present two multi-level models of health that are based on indigenous knowledge in New Zealand or *Kaupapa Māori*: the *Te Pae Māhutonga* and the *Te Whare Tapa Whā* approaches to wellbeing.

The Ottawa Charter

Possibly the best known multi-level model in health promotion is the Ottawa Charter. The Ottawa Charter was signed in 1986 at the World Health Organisation's first International Conference on Health Promotion (World Health Organization, 1986). The Charter was designed to explicitly recognise the impact that wider determinants of health have on individual wellbeing and health. To that end, concepts such as peace, shelter, justice, equity, income, and a stable ecosystem were seen as being fundamental to a healthy population and not just medical interventions, such as vaccinations, access to affordable healthcare, and the like. That is, there needs to be a focus on Salutogensis (factors affecting health and wellbeing) and not just pathogenesis (factors that cause disease—Antonovsky, 1979; Becker, Glascoff, & Felts, 2010; Lindström & Eriksson, 2005). The outcome from the conference was a signed agreement that a multi-level approach to health promotion needs to be adopted to provide both preventative care in health and aid in combatting existing health problems. The Charter identified five key elements to tackle, as shown in Table 4.2.

There have been many criticisms associated with the effectiveness of the Ottawa Charter as a means of creating efficacious change in societies, most notably the complexity of collecting and validating evidence of change in health as a result of adopting the stated practices (Dooris, 2006; Evans, Hall, Jones, & Neiman, 2007). However, what is well accepted is that the adoption of a wider lens to promote the healthfulness of an individual or population does aid in driving policy, the intersectionality of health issues and, in particular, the impact that societal inequities play in affecting health (Potvin & Jones, 2011).

The Barton and Grant (2006) Health Map

The Barton and Grant (2006) health map was presented as a means of understanding the intersection of human wellbeing and healthy human habitats. The health map again shows the importance of a multi-level approach to understanding health issues and the impact that a wider ecological approach has on individuals' wellbeing, a summary of which can be found in Table 4.3. In this case the health map grows from the centre, where individuals are situated, beyond the influence of federal government policy to a global influential perspective on health. This allows social marketers and policy makers to understand the impact that global issues, such as climate change, have on health needs in individuals. As a result, it can be argued that a protectionist approach to national healthcare directions at the expense of global issues does not necessarily benefit the individual nation state, and a connected global lens is necessary

Table 4.2 The Ottawa Charter's Five Action Areas (World Health Organization, 1986)

Action Area	Explanation	Example of Action
Developing Personal Skills	A focus on building education and action at the individual level to support and promote one's own healthfulness.	Arranging appointments with one's primary healthcare provider when there is a change in one's health. Ensuring that medical advice is adopted and actioned appropriately.
Strengthening Community Action	Ensuring that the wider community are engaged in actions and interventions that drive healthy living.	Community led initiatives that support healthy foods in schools or promote physical activity by organising and supporting community sports.
Creating Supportive Environments	A multi-level approach to the micro, meso, and macro environments a person operates within. Ensuring that messaging is supportive and social norms promote wellbeing interventions.	Diminishing the stigmatisation associated with health seeking behaviour. Providing adequate support networks for those suffering from illness.
Reorienting Health Services	Redistribution of resourcing to preventative care and health promotion rather than curing illnesses after they arise.	A greater level of health spending being given to health promotion advocates and a greater use of social marketing to aid in preventing diseases.
Building Healthy Public Policy	A drive to de-politicise policy regarding health and take a bipartisan approach to creating policies that benefit a healthy environment.	Agreements on accessible healthcare funding that are entrenched beyond elected governments.

Table 4.3 Characteristics of the Barton and Grant (2006) Health Map

Factor	Example	
People	Personal characteristics, such as age, sex, hereditary factors.	Micro
Lifestyle	Personal behaviours and practices, such as exercise regimes.	
Community	The impact that social networks and social capital play in health outcomes.	
Local Economy	The role that opportunities for wealth creation and local markets play in driving behaviour.	
Activities	The wider social norms around behaviour, such as expectations of work, shopping, activity, learning.	Meso
Built Environment	The way the infrastructure around a person impacts their behaviour, such as street/pavement quality, availability of open spaces etc.	
Natural Environment	The impact that the natural environment plays on one's health outcomes, such as the quality of air, water, land, and local ecosystems.	
Global Ecosystem	The role the wider global ecosystem plays on individual behaviour, such as the impact of climate change, biodiversity change, etc.	Macro

in order to ensure the health and wellbeing of all persons. The health map, like the other models described here, takes the intersection of social interaction and an ecological perspective as a means of understanding the various influencers and levers that drive healthfulness in individuals to ensure that social marketers and policy makers can design preventative measures at all levels, rather than focus on disease control and pathogenesis.

However, despite the broad reaching nature of the health map, its application has been primarily in the area of urban planning and meso-level interventions. For example, Barton (2005) utilised the health map approach to show the wider impact that the built environment has on healthy populations in European cities. Whilst Carmichael, Barton, Gray, and Lease (2013) show the impact that infrastructure and public support networks in built environments play in creating proactive and effective health intervention plans. Townsend and Foster (2013) combine both the socio-ecological model and the Barton and Grant (2006) health map approach to create and test the efficacy of an intervention that promotes healthy eating in schools, but ultimately both tools were used as a means of understanding the influencing factors on healthy choices and not necessarily able to manipulate and measure the effectiveness of a specific intervention in a population. This complexity of measurement and gathering of evidence does appear to be endemic to complex multi-level models, such as the SEM, as the various factors of influence are so difficult to control for and measure that true statistical effectiveness may be impossible to determine. This is not to say that multi-level models are completely irrelevant to health promotion, indeed, the ability to incorporate nuanced perspectives of culture and values into a multi-level model makes them extremely powerful for encouraging alternative perspectives of health, such as when indigenous health models are used.

Te Pae Māhutonga: Southern Cross Constellation

The Te Pae Māhutonga model was proposed by Professor Mason Durie (1999) as a means of executing a model of health and wellbeing from an indigenous New Zealand Māori perspective. The Te Pae Māhutonga was not an adaptation of 'western' health models to a Te Ao Māori (Māori world view) but rather an explanation of how Māori understand and practice health in a way that supports them, their family (whanau), and wider society. The model is made up of six key elements and is often visually represented in the form of the Crux star constellation, an important astronomical feature in the skies of New Zealand, which is important to Māori both in their folklore and as a navigational guide (Leather & Hall, 2004). Table 4.4 replicates the Te Pae Māhutonga model in a text format. The original model, however, presents the different aspects in the form of the Southern Cross and Pointers constellation.

In line with the other multi-level models, the Te Pae Māhutonga model recognises the importance of both the individual (Toiora) and community (Te Oranga) in healthy outcomes, but also goes further to offer key associations with a Māori world view by including cultural identity (Mauriora) and the importance of autonomy and self-determination around one's own health outcomes (Te Mana Whakahaere). In this way, the Te Pae Māhutonga model was able to draw on perspectives and cultural groundings that are central to the identity of the Māori population of New Zealand, but still incorporate elements of a socio-ecological approach, where societal/community connectivity and engagement in the wider environment (Waiora) are determinants of health outcomes.

Te Whare Tapa Whā: A House of Four Walls

More recently there has been acceptance and adoption of a new model of health and wellbeing that draws on the notion that wellness is related to four key elements central to Tikanaga Māori (Māori customs). The Te Whare Tapa Whā model seeks to represent an holistic approach to

Table 4.4 Adaptation of Te Pae Māhutonga Model of Health (Durie, 1999)

Factor	Translation	Impact	
Te Oranga	Healthy Lifestyles	The active practices that an individual undertakes to engage in health behaviour.	Micro
Te Mana Whakahaere	Autonomy	The importance of self-determination and individual responsibility to change.	
Waiora	Participation in Society	The responsibility that individuals have to engage and participate in the wider community.	
Ngā Manukura	Community Leadership	The role Rangatira (leaders) in the community play to lead change at the meso level.	Meso
Toiora	Physical Environment	The physical surroundings that may influence behavioural change practices.	
Mauriora	Cultural Identity	One's connection to a wider cultural base and its importance to you as an individual.	Macro

understanding health from four different factors of health: *Te Taha Hinengaro* (psychological health), *Te Taha Wairua* (spiritual health), *Te Taha Tinana* (physical health), and *Te Taha Whanau* (family health) (Durie, 2004; Rochford, 2004). The tool is used as part of a person's clinical assessment as a means of understanding how both individual factors related to the patient and extraneous factors may be affecting the person's health (McNeill, 2009). Interestingly, the importance of spirituality appears in the Te Whare Tapa Wha model that has been absent in other multi-level models of health promotion, which fits closely in line with the customs and practices of many Māori people, but also shows the grounding of the theory from a Māori world view, as opposed to having a solution placed upon Māori from a Te Ao Pākehā (western/non-Māori world view). There is evidence that a strong spiritual connection is connected to overall health outcomes (Seybold & Hill, 2001), but it also often incorporates the physical link to a wider community group and support network that may benefit an individual suffering from poor health (Eliade, 1958; Hill & Pargament, 2008).

The notion of physical health is also not simply related to one's physical self but also the wider physicality that one occupies and how that may have a naturalistic effect on one's health, again, in line with the principles of the SEM.

The Te Whare Tapa Whā model has most commonly been adopted within New Zealand, but has shown that it offers a valuable lens that impacts not only Māori but also non-Māori health outcomes. It provides the holistic lens that does not focus solely upon the individual as the unit of analysis (Glover, 2005; Pistacchi, 2008) and holds promise for understanding and influencing not only health behaviour change but also other social marketing related behaviour changes.

Beyond Health Outcomes: Implications for Social Marketers, Macro-Social Marketers, and Policy Makers

All the multi-level ecological models presented focus on understanding the systems and intersectionality of multiple layers of influence to primarily affect health outcomes. However, it is reasoned that the same principles that underpin the socio-ecological model of health can be applied to any behavioural change programme. By taking an integrative approach to understanding the commonalities behind these models, a programme of study and investigation can be developed regardless of the final end state desired. These commonalities include:

1. A multi-layered, **holistic** approach to understanding the influencing factors on behavioural outcomes. What role do micro-, meso-, and macro-level influencers have on behaviour and how can all be utilised to create an environment that supports positive behavioural change? How can a redistribution of resources be purposefully utilised to ensure that all levels are attended to in a manner that equitably influences final change?
2. A focus on wellbeing **beyond the physical.** How can mental, spiritual, and emotional levels of influence be utilised in a manner that will drive positive behavioural outcomes? How can equitable weighting be assigned to the impact that poor non-physical outcomes play in influencing or hindering positive behavioural change?
3. A **systemic** approach to understanding the agency associated with behavioural change and that higher order effects do create environments that hinder or encourage positive behaviour. What are the competing or compounding factors that affect positive behavioural change and the equity of accessing the resources necessary to enact these behavioural change processes? How can an understanding of the systemic intersection of multiple influencers help macro-social marketers and policy makers understand the complexity of behaviour change?

4. The importance that **welfare** plays in ensuring that behavioural outcomes are valenced in a positive manner. Although the same principles can be used to cause harm and hinder positive social change, how can all models be used in a manner that encourages positive welfare and wellbeing for the individual and the society of which they are a part, a key element in social marketing (Andreasen, 1994)?

These four common influencing factors offer an insight into the way that the socio-ecological model has crossover associations with other ecological models. By maintaining these core principles it is possible to show the effect of applying this socio-ecological lens to create, install, and maintain social marketing interventions that have a wider reaching impact beyond the focus on individual ability and singular behavioural change. By not only focusing on the individual but also on the determinants of behavioural change, such as the wider environment that a person lives and operates within, it is possible to create an integrated and holistic approach to social marketing and behavioural change that could drive more positive behavioural outcomes. The ideal may be for a singular, well-organised and managed entity influencing all levels of the environment to drive behavioural change; however, in reality it may be more viable to establish effective partnerships between entities that have access and influence at specific levels of the environment. As long as the strategic vision and values are aligned and trust established between these entities, there is the possibility for partnerships to be created that drive systemic behavioural change in a similar way to how strategic alliances exist in business (Das & Teng, 2001; Mowery, Oxley, & Silverman, 1996).

Table 4.5 attempts to show how these influencing factors can be applied in both health and non-health initiatives. These examples provide some practical tools for social marketing interventions but are not limited to the examples provided.

One of the key criticisms associated with the socio-ecological model is that the systemic nature of the interventions required means that individual level interventions become very attractive to install. A social marketer would be able to easily create an intervention that encourages positive individual level change at the consumer level. However, influencing policies and meso-level structural changes to affect systemic change can be seen as daunting and expensive. It is at this point where social marketers' roles grow beyond the traditional marketing technologies that encourage adoption and perhaps consider more wide ranging forms of impact, such as social activism to engender behaviour changes (den Hond & de Bakker, 2007; Tymoczko, 2000). For example, Aguilera, Rupp, Williams, and Ganapathi (2007) show how multi-level theories of social change were able to harness social activism as a mechanism for driving corporate social responsibility. Similarly, the role academia can play can stretch beyond journal publications and provide expert support

Table 4.5 Overarching Principles Applied to Macro-Social Marketing Interventions

Influencing Factor	Tobacco Cessation Example (Health)	Sustainable Consumption Example	Charitable Donation Example
Holistic	Creating policies at the macro level that ban smoking for persons underage. Disallowing smoking in local spaces, such as public parks, to restrict its use and acceptance at a meso level. Having a strong commitment to quitting smoking in conjunction with appropriate support and medical intervention from a doctor at the micro/individual level.	At the macro level, creating a national identity and public image that supports a clean/green environment and the importance of maintaining that brand image for the entire population, such as New Zealand's "100% Pure" tourism campaigns. At the meso level, making rubbish bins easily accessible across a city and providing adequate instructions as to how recycling can be accomplished for your suburb. For individuals, creating a sense of ownership and pride for one's own recycling efforts and encouraging personal reminders to recycle.	Create macro level policies that reward donations to registered charities with tax rebates as well as have strict accreditation practices to ensure charities are genuinely fulfilling their mandate. Support charities at the meso level with community led activities that raise awareness and funds for local charities. Provide individual level interventions that encourage people to donate easily to a chosen charity directly from their wages.
Non-Physical	Providing emotional and spiritual support to a person recovering from a physical ailment related to smoking, such as having pastoral and religious support in hospitals. Providing counselling support for persons quitting smoking as well as medical interventions.	Creating a sense of pride and positive attitudes towards recycling that overcomes the inherent physical discomfort of separating one's rubbish.	Create interventions that recognise donors who wish to be named. Make public statements of appreciation to encourage pride and attachment to a charity being supported.
Systemic	Understanding that quitting smoking may be seen as counter-cultural and that a sense of identity separation when quitting smoking may impact one's success as it could lead to separation from social groups and community.	Ensuring that national level policies are done in conjunction with consumer support and practice, such as the removal of single-use plastic bags leading to consumer frustration.	Show the flow-on effects from the work carried out by a chosen strategy and the ongoing effect a small donation can have on the wider community.
Welfare Focused	Ensuring that smoking cessation practices and policies are truly in place to encourage a healthier population and do not lead to compensatory behaviour that is also harmful.	Put in place interventions that encourage consumption practices that lead to an active improvement in the environment and society and not simply used as a 'green-washing' marketing tool.	Create interventions that not only ensure that donations are used appropriately but that donors feel a sense of wellbeing by being connected into their community.

and examination into causes that can have an effect at multiple levels of influence (Ozanne et al., 2016).

This systemic nature of effect that the SEM takes also makes evaluation of campaigns extremely complex. As such, many of the socio-ecological style models offer a broad lens of enquiry as opposed to a roadmap that allows a single social marketing body to create a systemic intervention. Many organisations lack the resources or scope to affect change at all levels effectively, but many still appreciate the importance of lobbying policy at the macro level, supporting communities at the meso level, and working with individuals seeking to create positive behavioural change in their lives. As a result, the most influential bodies that are able to affect such wide-sweeping changes are often governments, and the influence of political agendas on health and other social marketing problems is evident in many parts of the world. For instance, Evans and Van Lerberghe (2008) describe government controlled ministries of health as often suffering from myopia and that the focus is on the short-term placation of voting blocs rather than long-term sustainability of a wider health population. One famous example of government intervention on a mass scale was China's implementation of their 'one-child family policy' that not only put in place macro-level legislation regarding multiple births (Hesketh, Lu, & Xing, 2005) but also influenced meso-level cultural change with education curriculum being changed to support the one child policy (Nie & Wyman, 2005). At an individual level, the state supported the use of orphanages for families to leave their second child or a disabled child they cannot support (Johnson, 2016) to be cared for, which were later described as 'dying rooms' in the 1995 documentary on the subject (Blewett & Woods, 1995). The implementation of multi-levelled approaches to behavioural change does show that they can be effective in driving positive behavioural change, but are also extremely susceptible to government will and influence, making the need for a non-politicised approach to health and population wellbeing vital. How realistic this strategy is, is yet to be determined. In an ideal system there would be opportunities to lobby the government to create bi-partisan approval for health and wellbeing in a population. In reality it is well established that healthcare is often politicised (Jackson, 2018; Rushton, Ingram, & Kett, 2011).

Conclusion

In summary, the purpose of the SEM and similar multi-level models is to provide a way of exploring a phenomena from multiple perspectives and appreciating the varying levels of impact that determinants of behavioural change have on individual level change. The SEM offers further evidence that micro-level social marketing interventions alone are not sufficient to enable behavioural change. Equally, however, the adoption of a macro-social marketing approach without appreciation for the meso- and micro-level influences is also insufficient. An holistic approach is proposed in this chapter to show how multiple drivers of behaviour exist at multiple levels of influence. Beyond this, the presence of environments, culture, and community that support a positive behaviour is theorised to create an ecology that naturalistically drives positive behavioural change. In the same way that ecological theory predicts that organisms thrive in an environment that supports growth and development, so behaviour will thrive in an environment and social structure that encourages that behaviour. There is, therefore, little doubt that holistic level change is likely to provide the most efficacious pathway to positive or negative behavioural change. However, the complexity, cost, and long-term nature of many systemic multi-levelled behavioural change programs make the task of intervening at all levels almost impossible to implement. We argue that taking a broader lens provides a richer understanding of the whole system and its effects on individual behaviour. This broader perspective should be encouraged by social marketers, macromarketers, health promoters, and public policy makers alike, but the efficacy of programs that are able to be implemented at all tiers is yet to be truly implemented and tested.

The use of a multi-level systemic approach to understanding behaviour and social interactions is not unique to the SEM. We have shown here that indigenous knowledge can benefit our understanding of current market practices and consumer engagement in an environment that promotes or deters wellbeing. We call for further investigation into the role that indigenous practices and knowledge can be incorporated into social marketing examination and interventions not just as a means of reaching indigenous target populations but also for understanding the impact that indigenous knowledge may play in understanding wider populations.

Examination of socio-ecological effects over time is carried out in the ecology under the banner of 'Long-Term Socio-Ecological Research'. This practice shows that the methodologies exist and it is possible to examine and provide predictive value to an ecosystem if the studies are well-funded and the drive is there from researchers and practitioners alike (Singh et al., 2012).

For many social marketers, the task may appear too large and the complexities too great to tackle. As long as the levers of influence reward quick, low-cost research and interventions to drive behavioural change, it is likely that wide ranging change mechanisms are unlikely to become normative practice. The SEM and related models demand the use of partnerships, leadership, and engagement from experts and practitioners at all levels to ensure that long-term social marketing behavioural change is actionable and sustainable.

Glossary of Key Māori Terms

Māori   Indigenous people of Aotearoa/New Zealand.

Pākehā   Non-Māori; typically used to refer to British settlers in New Zealand.

Kaupapa Māori   A Māori approach to understanding/knowledge creation.

Tikanga   Customs and practices.

Te Ao Māori   Māori perspective on the world; a pre-colonisation Māori world view.

Te Ao Pākehā   A non-Māori perspective on the world; a post-colonisation world view.

Te Whare Tapa Whā   A House of Four Walls; a Te Ao Māori approach to health that incorporates four key aspects of wellbeing.

Te Pae Māhutonga   Southern Cross Constellation; a Te Ao Māori approach to health that looks at the wider systemic impacts on individual behaviour.

References

Aguilera, R. V., Rupp, D. E., Williams, C. A., & Ganapathi, J. (2007). Putting the S back in corporate social responsibility: A multilevel theory of social change in organizations. *Academy of Management Review, 32*(3), 836–863.

Andreasen, A. R. (1994). Social marketing: Its definition and domain. *Journal of Public Policy and Marketing, 13*(1), 108–114.

Antonovsky, A. (1979). *Health, stress, and coping*. San Francisco, CA: Jossey-Bass.

Bae, S. S., Jo, H. S., Kim, D. H., Choi, Y. J., Lee, H. J., Lee, T. J., & Lee, H. J. (2008). Factors associated with gastric cancer screening of Koreans based on a socio-ecological model. *Journal of Preventive Medicine and Public Health, 41*(2), 100–106.

Barton, H. (2005). A health map for urban planners. *Built Environment, 31*(4), 339–355.

Barton, H., & Grant, M. (2006). A health map for the local human habitat. *Journal of the Royal Society for the Promotion of Health, 126*(6), 252–253.

Becker, C. M., Glascoff, M. A., & Felts, W. M. (2010). Salutogenesis 30 years later: Where do we go from here? *International Electronic Journal of Health Education, 13*, 25–32.

Blewett, K., & Woods, B. (1995). *The dying rooms* [Film]. Lauderdale Productions.

Bronfenbrenner, U. (1979). *The ecology of human development: Experiments by nature and design*. Cambridge, MA: Harvard University Press.

Carmichael, L., Barton, H., Gray, S., & Lease, H. (2013). Health-integrated planning at the local level in England: Impediments and opportunities. *Land Use Policy, 31*, 259–266.

Das, T. K., & Teng, B-S. (2001). Trust, control, and risk in strategic alliances: An integrated framework. *Organization Studies, 22*(2), 251–283.

den Hond, F., & de Bakker, F. G. A. (2007). Ideologically motivated activism: How activist groups influence corporate social change activities. *Academy of Management Review, 32*(3), 901–924.

DiClemente, R. J., Salazar, L. F., Crosby, R. A., & Rosenthal, S. L. (2005). Prevention and control of sexually transmitted infections among adolescents: The importance of a socio-ecological perspective – A commentary. *Public Health*, *119*(9), 825–836.

Dooris, M. (2006). Healthy settings: Challenges to generating evidence of effectiveness. *Health Promotion International*, *21*(1), 55–65.

Durie, M. (1999). Te pae māhutonga: A model for Māori health promotion. *Health Promotion Forum of New Zealand*, *49*(2–5), 8.

Durie, M. (2004). An Indigenous model of health promotion. *Health Promotion Journal of Australia*, *15*(3), 181–185.

Eliade, M. (1958). *Patterns in comparative religion*. (R. Sheed. Trans.). London: Sheed and Ward.

Evans, L., Hall, M., Jones, C. M., & Neiman, A. (2007). Did the Ottawa charter play a role in the push to assess the effectiveness of health promotion? *Promotion and Education*, *14*(Suppl 2), 28–30.

Evans, T., & Van Lerberghe, W. (2008). *The world health report 2008: Primary health care, now more than ever*. Geneva, Switzerland: WHO Press.

Glover, M. (2005). Analysing smoking using Te Whare Tapa Wha. *New Zealand Journal of Psychology*, *34*(1), 13–79.

Haberl, H., Gaube, V., Díaz-Delgado, R., Krauze, K., Neuner, A., Peterseil, J., . . . Vadineanu, A. (2009). Towards an integrated model of socioeconomic biodiversity drivers, pressures and impacts: A feasibility study based on three European long-term socio-ecological research platforms. *Ecological Economics*, *68*(6), 1797–1812.

Hesketh, T., Lu, L., & Xing, Z. W. (2005). The effect of China's one-child family policy after 25 years. *New England Journal of Medicine: Boston*, *353*(11), 1171–1176.

Hill, P. C., & Pargament, K. I. (2008). Advances in the conceptualization and measurement of religion and spirituality: Implications for physical and mental health research. *Psychology of Religion and Spirituality*, *S*(1), 3–17.

Jackson, S. (2018). *Politicizing the white coat: Physician activism and Asylum Seeker healthcare in Canada, Germany and England* (thesis). Retrieved from https://macsphere.mcmaster.ca/handle/11375/23448

Johnson, K. A. (2016). *China's hidden children: Abandonment, adoption, and the human costs of the one-child policy* (1st ed.). Chicago: University of Chicago Press.

Leather, K., & Hall, R. (2004). *Work of the gods: Tātai arorangi: Māori astronomy*. Wellington, NZ: Viking Sevenseas NZ Ltd. Retrieved from https://vikingsevenseas.co.nz/products/work-of-the-gods-tatai-arorangi-maori-astronomy-book-1

Lindström, B., & Eriksson, M. (2005). Salutogenesis. *Journal of Epidemiology and Community Health*, *59*(6), 440–442.

McNeill, H. N. (2009). Maori models of mental wellness. *Te Kaharoa*, *2*(1), 96–115.

Mowery, D. C., Oxley, J. E., & Silverman, B. S. (1996). Strategic alliances and interfirm knowledge transfer. *Strategic Management Journal*, *17*(Suppl 2), 77–91.

Nie, Y., & Wyman, R. J. (2005). The one-child policy in Shanghai: Acceptance and internalization. *Population and Development Review*, *31*(2), 313–336.

Ozanne, J. L., Davis, B., Murray, J. B., Grier, S., Benmecheddal, A., Downey, H., . . . Veer, E. (2016). Assessing the societal impact of research: The relational engagement approach. *Journal of Public Policy and Marketing, 36*(1), 1–14.

Pistacchi, A. (2008). Te whare tapa wha: The four cornerstones of Maori health and Patricia Grace's dogside story. *Journal of New Zealand Literature: JNZL, 26*, 136–152.

Potvin, L., & Jones, C. M. (2011). Twenty-five years after the Ottawa charter: The critical role of health promotion for public health. *Canadian Journal of Public Health/Revue Canadienne de Sante'e Publique, 102*(4), 244–248.

Robinson, T. (2008). Applying the socio-ecological model to improving fruit and vegetable intake among low-income African Americans. *Journal of Community Health, 33*(6), 395–406.

Rochford, T. (2004). Whare tapa wha: A Māori model of a unified theory of health. *Journal of Primary Prevention, 25*(1), 41–57.

Rushton, S., Ingram, A., & Kett, M. (2011). Politicizing aid: Healthcare provision and strategic objectives. *Medicine, Conflict and Survival, 27*(1), 1–4.

Salm Ward, T. C., & Doering, J. J. (2014). Application of a socio-ecological model to mother – Infant bed-sharing. *Health Education and Behavior, 41*(6), 577–589.

Seybold, K. S., & Hill, P. C. (2001). The role of religion and spirituality in mental and physical health. *Current Directions in Psychological Science, 10*(1), 21–24.

Singh, S. J., Haberl, H., Chertow, M., Mirtl, M., & Schmid, M. (2012). *Long term socio-ecological research: Studies in society-nature interactions across spatial and temporal scales.* Netherlands: Springer Science and Business Media.

Stokols, D. (1996). Translating social ecological theory into guidelines for community health promotion. *American Journal of Health Promotion, 10*(4), 282–298.

Townsend, N., & Foster, C. (2013). Developing and applying a socio-ecological model to the promotion of healthy eating in the school. *Public Health Nutrition, 16*(6), 1101–1108.

Tymoczko, M. (2000). Translation and political engagement. *The Translator, 6*(1), 23–47.

World Health Organization. (1986). *Health promotion: Ottawa charter.* Ottawa, Canada: World Health Organisation. Retrieved from http://apps.who.int/iris/bitstream/handle/10665/59557/WHO_HPR_HEP_95.1.pdf?sequence=1andisAllowed=y

5 The Power of 'Talk'

Frames and Narratives in Macro-Social Marketing

Joya A. Kemper and Paul W. Ballantine

Introduction

Wicked problems are complex, highly politicised issues, which have competing frames and world views (Head, 2008). Obesity is one of the many wicked problems society faces (Parkinson et al., 2017), as many countries are now facing the simultaneous issues of malnutrition and obesity, requiring governments to balance scarce resources for both food security and preventable diseases (Roberto et al., 2015). However, while most high-income countries have implemented obesity policies, they have largely favoured micro-level (individual) initiatives such as social marketing and/or support services, and voluntary agreements or self-regulation, without any support from macro-level policies (i.e., taxation, subsidies—Roberto et al., 2015).

The implementation of micro-level initiatives shows a preference for limited government intervention and the framing of obesity as a personal, not social problem. So, while researchers have offered policy suggestions and frameworks that address the macro level, support from policy makers, industry, and the public for actual implementation must also be addressed. One way forward is to use the framework provided by the multi-level perspective (MLP) of socio-technical transitions to explore macro-social marketing actions (Kemper & Ballantine, 2017). Simply put, the MLP looks at how technological and social innovation enable transitions. Specifically, transitions occur due to a reduction in the power and resources of dominant regime actors (such as industry leaders), with this power moving towards niche actors (such as smaller, niche companies), because of changes in technological innovation, and the social and cultural landscape.

In this chapter, we discuss how to articulate and create landscape pressure—that is, communicate the social, cultural, political, and natural environmental changes that occur in the macro level of society to highlight the need for system change. We specify that macro-social marketers can help highlight such macro-level changes that are favourable to addressing wicked problems by expressing these changes in a way which induces individual and system change. Specifically, we utilise the creation and management of framing and narratives to affect systematic change. The case study of obesity interventions and its discourse is used to showcase and expand our understanding.

Macro-Social Marketing and the Multi-Level Perspective of Socio-Technical Transitions

In systemic change, institutional norms need to be shifted for both the marketing system that preserves normative behaviours and the assumptions of governmental (formal institutional) support. Specifically, social marketers need to address the larger 'master frame' of the assumptions of personal responsibility (i.e., individualism) and limited government (i.e., the free market). This is related to Peattie and Peattie's (2003) phenomenon of the competing idea of 'social discouragement', where social marketing competes with existing social values or myths. While the competing ideas of personal responsibility and limited government run contrary to all macro-social marketing initiatives, as governments and organisations encourage and may limit individuals to act in certain ways, other myths and frames distort causes and viable solutions to specific wicked problems. In the case of obesity, a myth that is commonly perpetuated is that of the 'lazy' individual.

The MLP organises socio-technical systems into niches, regimes, and landscapes (Geels, 2010). Socio-technical regimes are those that benefit the most from the status quo; they are the current dominant players in an industry. Regimes are strong because they *"are structures constituted from a co-evolutionary accumulation and alignment of knowledge, investments, objects, infrastructures, values and norms that span the production-consumption divide"* (Smith, Voß, & Grin, 2010, p. 441). These incumbent regimes (e.g., transportation providers, current energy and food systems), are heavily dependent on interlinked actors, such as employees, key suppliers, competitors, and institutions (Geels, 2004).

Socio-technical niches (e.g., organic, fair trade, free-range, or local food) compete with incumbent regimes (Smith, Stirling, & Berkhout, 2005). However, niches are not prone to the same pressures and changes prevailing in regimes (i.e., existing funding, infrastructure, routines, and practices) as their norms are different and less established than regimes, which makes them inherently unstable but more open to innovation, change, and new thinking (Smith, 2006; Smith et al., 2010). Moreover, niches have the ability, when supported through funding, institutions, and infrastructure, to replace existing regimes.

Lastly, the socio-technical landscape is the larger macro sphere which involves social, cultural (i.e., social movements), economic, political (i.e., ideology, political party strength, regulatory), or natural (i.e., draught, natural resource depletion) changes that prompt responses from the regime and niches. Theoretically, these landscape changes are more favourable to niches, as they are able to adapt and respond to changes more quickly and easily than regimes (Geels, 2010).

'Lock-in' mechanisms occur in regimes and affect the capacity to adapt to landscape pressures. These mechanisms include scale economies, sunk investments, infrastructures, and core competencies. Beyond material costs, 'lock-in' mechanisms also involve informal institutions such as the deeply ingrained culture, norms, shared beliefs, and discourses of regime stakeholders. These informal institutions stabilise existing systems (Unruh, 2000) and are unstable in niches (Geels & Schot, 2007; Smith et al., 2005). Specifically, informal institutions can be divided into normative (role relationships, values, behavioural norms) and cognitive rules (belief systems) (Geels, 2004). Normative and cognitive rules allow individuals, organisations, industries, and even new ideas to gain legitimacy (Scott, 1995). Specifically, Suchman (1995) contends that *"legitimacy is a generalized perception or assumption that the actions of an entity are desirable, proper, or appropriate within some socially constructed system of norms, values, beliefs and definitions"* (p. 574). Indeed, the changes in these 'rules' alongside regulatory (formal) change help to explain how innovations and markets lose their legitimacy and go through processes of (de)institutionalisation, and thus a socio-technical transition (Fuenfschilling & Truffer, 2014).

Macro-social marketing intervenes to frame and leverage landscape pressure(s) (Smith et al., 2005). Traditionally, in social marketing, the articulation of pressures can be achieved through increasing public, government, and business knowledge of the wicked issue. In macro-social marketing we can extend this further by communicating the pressure in a coherent and persuasive way, through framing or narrative tools, to gain support for initiatives (i.e., new regulations, increased funding) and encourage behaviour change. Beyond articulation, macro-social marketing at the meso level can leverage landscape pressures and mobilise and support social movement(s). This can be on various scales, from local community groups to national grassroots movements, consumer associations, or niche industry groups.

Joining the Policy Debate and Public Sphere: The Creation and Management of Framing and Narrative

Macro-social marketing's implementation of formal interventions, such as regulation, legislation, and other education/programme funding (e.g., hotlines, nutrition classes), is embroiled within public policy debates. Policy viability is not just about effectiveness but also about acceptance from individuals, governments, and industry (Lang & Rayner, 2007). Consequently, support for policies must be garnered. Widespread taken for granted assumptions and norms present serious challenges to the implementation of policies towards public health (Roberto et al., 2015); these assumptions revolve around the responsibility of the individual and the government, particularly prevalent in issues of unhealthy food, tobacco, and alcohol consumption (Beauchamp, 1976; Weishaar et al., 2016). Thus, macro-social marketing needs to understand dominant regime frames and narratives to ascertain their hold on power, and understand how to construct counter-frames and narratives.

Narrative and discursive struggles initiate change in both formal and informal institutions through reciprocal relationships (North, 1990). Informal institutional (cultural, social) change supports individual behaviour change (i.e., see the need for, willingness, and self-efficacy to change, shifting personal and social norms), as well as social change through the support of initiatives (i.e., policy). Similarly, formal regulations reinforce the informal norms present in society. Therefore, macro-social marketing must *"engage in cultural framing actions"* (Geels, 2010, p. 506) to legitimise new ways of thinking, social practices, and innovations, and thus break away from dominant regime power and discourse (Kemper & Ballantine, 2017). To do so, we expand on framing and narratives to help transform current informal institutions (i.e., individual responsibility norms), which in turn provide public and political support for formal institutional change.

A new and emerging body of socio-technical transitions research examines the social representations, discursive struggles, storylines, and narratives appearing in transitions, such as in energy (Hermwille, 2016; Malone, Hultman, Anderson, & Romeiro, 2017). Moreover, social movement theorists have now long since recognised the importance of framing alongside resource mobilisation and political opportunity processes in social change (Benford & Snow, 2000). Considering this social and political turn in socio-technical research, we discuss the potential for macro-social marketing to contribute to this emerging literature.

Blending the functionalist and structuralist view of culture, we use the interpretative approach to culture which focuses on agency and the creation of meaning and discourse theory to focus on the collective meanings and sense making around particular issues (Geels & Verhees, 2011). This borrows heavily from institutional theory and logics, particularly institutional work (Fuenfschilling & Truffer, 2014). We use the term 'cultural legitimacy', coined by Geels and Verhees (2011), to combine normative and cognitive rules. Both normative and cognitive rules refer to 'wider society', both of which are two forms of informal institutions. Thus, the causal mechanisms which help produce cultural legitimacy are through discourse and framing struggles (Geels & Verhees, 2011; Phillips, Lawrence, & Hardy, 2004; Van Dijk, 1989). In line with Geels and Verhees (2011, p. 913), we build on the discursive view:

> suggest[ing] that the cultural legitimacy of technologies derives from the content and meaning of discourses, which depend on the way

that deep-structural elements, concepts, ideas, metaphors, arguments and images are ordered and related. For innovation journeys, actors aim to produce legitimacy by articulating positive discourses around new technologies.

Therefore, cultural actions are performed to influence and convince (i.e., through sense making but also influencing attitudes and beliefs) particular audiences that something (new ideas, products, regulations) is right, appropriate, or desirable (Geels & Verhees, 2011). This institutional work, the *"purposive actions of individuals and organisations aimed at creating, maintaining and disrupting institutions"* (Lawrence & Suddaby, 2006, p. 215), sets to disrupt the institutional logics (material practices, beliefs, assumptions) present in socio-technical regimes. As such, sense making and discursive struggles take place on public stages (e.g., news media, social media, public debates) and are performed by social marketers, organisations, industry associations, policy makers, special interest groups, and non-governmental organisations (Geels & Verhees, 2011). These different frames compete on the public stage for dominance and influence on general discourse (Geels & Verhees, 2011; Van Dijk, 1989).

Therefore, a stakeholder analysis must be undertaken to understand the key players, their voices (opinions), and dominance in the landscape. For example, Morone, Lopolito, Anguilano, Sica, and Tartiu (2016) explored the sources of landscape pressure through interviews with stakeholders in the waste management domain. Key stakeholders in most discursive struggles include a variety of incumbents, challengers, and governance units (Layton, 2015), such as governments, regime or niche organisations, industry or consumer associations, public interest groups, and the media. The relative power held in these discursive struggles is directly related to the actors' ability to mobilise resources, including financial, political, and cultural.

The distinction between frames, discourse, narratives, and storylines is not always clear in the literature. We adhere to Geels and Verhees's (2011) distinction between discourses and frames. Thus, discourses are considered to be shared, general ways of knowing and talking about particular innovations (e.g., sugar-sweetened beverages), while frames focus on the interpretation of a specific innovation and related issue (e.g., health risks associated with sugar-sweetened beverages, responsibility of government to regulate sugar-sweetened beverages). A frame is an *"active, processual phenomenon that implies agency and contention at the level of reality construction"* (2000, p. 614). Narratives are associated with frames, but differ as narratives are stories which are personal and emotional in nature (Olsen, 2014). Discourse and frames are mostly associated with contested, discursive struggles and issues of power (Van Dijk, 1989), while traditionally, narratives are employed to outline emotional stories with a plot, characters (hero, villain), and a moral ('right' behaviour). Therefore, a narrative is a story with a temporal sequence of events, a plot with moments, symbols, and archetypal characters, which culminates in a moral to the story (Jones & McBeth, 2010) and which *"connect events in a meaningful way for a definite audience and thus offer insights about the world and/or people's experiences of it"* (Hinchman & Hinchman, 1997, p. xvi). We now expand on how frames and narrative in wicked issues, specifically obesity, can help shift informal institutions and provide discursive, social, and political support for specific formal institutional initiatives (i.e., taxation).

Frames

Framing is both a micro- and macro-level construct. This relates to how individuals use information (and how it's presented) to develop beliefs (micro) and the mode of presentation used by the media, industry, and other actors (macro) (Scheufele & Tewksbury, 2006). Previous research has examined message framing from the micro perspective in health and prosocial communications (Loroz, 2007; McGregor, Ferguson, & O'Carroll, 2012; Rothman & Salovey, 1997). Additionally, while research has addressed the use of framing in communications, it has only done so within the downstream and midstream social marketing perspective and on frame creation (Daellenbach & Parkinson, 2017), which leaves out a crucial element of the contested process of counter-framing and interaction with opponent actions on the macro level. We aim to address this gap.

The resultant outcome of framing activities is termed collective action frames (CAF), which inspire and legitimise campaigns (Benford & Snow, 2000). The objective of CAF is to *"mobilize potential adherents and constituents, to garner bystander support, and to demobilize antagonists"* (Snow & Benford, 1988, p. 198). To understand the macro-social marketing potential of frames, we discuss two important ways to frame issues; these include the need to address three core framing activities and the development of a frame(s).

According to Benford and Snow (Benford & Snow, 2000; Snow & Benford, 1988), core framing tasks of diagnostic, prognostic, and motivational framing facilitate agreement and action within a social movement. These can be seen in Table 5.1. Diagnostic framing involves the articulation of the issue needed to be solved (i.e., caloric overconsumption, lack of exercise) and who is to blame (causality; i.e., food companies and marketing). As such, 'injustice frames' are commonly used, especially when advocating for political or economic reform by identifying the victims (Benford & Snow, 2000). Here, the power of large multi-nationals in politics and marketing can be highlighted. 'Adversarial' framing, for example, can be used as a *"normative reference point for the attribution of responsibility and blame . . . [and] by making the character and*

Table 5.1 Diagnostic, Prognostic, and Motivational Framing

Frame	Processes	Obesity case	Related to . . .
Diagnostic framing	Identification of problem	Caloric overconsumption, lack of exercise	Education and credibility of source(s). Also includes stigmatisation issues
	Identification of culpable agent	Food companies	Related to 'boundary' or 'adversarial' framing. Connected to heroes and villains in narrative storytelling (see below)
Prognostic framing	Articulation of solution	Government responsibility	Storytelling of 'appropriate' behaviour (see below)
	Strategies for 'attack'	Counter-frame the individual responsibility and hands-off approach government	Contested processes (see later)
Motivational framing	Rationale for taking action and extends to changing individual behaviour	Slow food movement, which promotes greater work-life balance	Value exchange discussed in social marketing literature (Domegan, 2008; Hastings & Haywood, 1991)

practices of their opponents part of the problem" (Knight & Greenberg, 2011, p. 325). The use of narrative storytelling can be used to highlight the 'heroes' and 'villains'. However, due to identifying the problem, placing blame, and victimising, there are issues surrounding stigmatisation which need to be taken into account (e.g., Gurrieri, Previte, & Brace-Govan, 2013). For example, other frames in the obesity debate need to examined, such as the social justice frame, which investigates discrimination issues in obesity (Kwan, 2009). Here, participatory methods can be used to account for the voices of all actors in a social issue (discussed more later).

Next, prognostic framing involves the articulation of a solution and the strategies for achieving those solutions. The focus here is as much on the proposed solution by proponents, such as government intervention, as it is on discounting the opponent's proposed solutions (counter-framing), such as their stances on individual responsibility and as an anti-tax proponent (Van Gorp & Vercruysse, 2012). Here, macro-social marketing must articulate frames which emphasise the need for intervention by changing formal institutions (i.e., regulation and legislation), as well as promoting the regimes' shortcomings (i.e., unhealthy/unsustainable products, manipulative tactics, lobbying which occurs behind closed doors). This is related to counter-framing. For example, 'boundary' framing may be utilised, communicating how the frame differs from others (Silver, 1997). The process ultimately results in competitive frame contests between actors (Benford & Snow, 2000; Scheufele & Tewksbury, 2006). Here, proponents will need to counter-frame the individual responsibility and hands-off approach to government from its opponents.

Lastly, motivational framing is the agency component of frames, providing the rationale for taking action against the status quo. The motivational frame applies when trying to mobilise or further support existing social movements (e.g., veganism), local community groups, online communities (e.g., The Healthy Mummy), consumer associations (e.g., The Canadian Health Food Association), niche industry associations (e.g., The Soil and Health Association), and academic research groups (e.g., Oxford Food Research Network). In another manner, motivational framing can be used in relation to individual and community behaviour change, specifically utilising value exchange theory discussed in social marketing literature to provide reasons *for* behaviour change (Domegan, 2008; Hastings & Haywood, 1991). For example, the slow food movement can be emphasised for its health and sustainability focus and its work-life balance for increased family time.

While the core tasks of framing aim to articulate and create buy-in of social issues (i.e., their seriousness, need for action, specific interventions), we now turn to frame development and generation. The development of frames is suggested to include the three processes of discursive, strategic, and contested actions (Benford & Snow, 2000), but most relevant to macro-social marketing are strategic and contested processes. Strategic processes are those which are deployed to achieve a specific purpose (i.e., convince, mobilise, acquire resources) and may be aligned with either actors' existing frames (particularly those of other movements to combine resources and leverage combined power), beliefs, or values, or other actor or opponent interests (e.g., Khayatzadeh-Mahani, Ruckert, & Labonté, 2018). Lastly, all CAF are involved in contested processes with opponents, bystanders, the media, and actors, and include counter-framing (Atanasova & Koteyko, 2017; Kwan, 2009) and frame disputes within proponent movements. We provide descriptions and examples in Table 5.2.

In the case of obesity, strategic and contested processes can be used to shift institutional norms in both individual behaviour change and policy acceptance. The strategic process includes frame bridging, amplification, and extension (Benford & Snow, 2000; Snow, Rochford, Worden, & Benford, 1986). Macro-social marketing can focus on bridging frames with sustainability (Tilman & Clark, 2014), as many healthy foods are also sustainable (Swinburn et al., 2019) and align with existing family values, such as family dinner meals (e.g., Bacon, 2018), the seriousness of the health risks (e.g., through narratives), the role of industry (e.g., marketing practices), increasing self-efficacy (e.g., nutrition education), and communicating the effectiveness of government intervention. The frame articulated by macro-social marketers can also align with interest in the non-health sectors, such as agriculture, transportation, education, finance, and urban planning (Atanasova & Koteyko, 2017). Particularly, there is a potential for the healthy food movement and macro-social marketing to *"progress action when it facilitates joint efforts with stakeholders across and between, micro, meso, exo and macro levels"* (Parkinson et al., 2017, p. 397).

Counter-framing is possibly the most important element of macro-social marketing. The effectiveness of counter-frames may depend on the timing and repetition of the frame (Chong & Druckman, 2012) and the relative power (which may be social, political, and/or economic) of actors. Counter-frames in the obesity debate may include the responsibility of industry frame countering the free market frame (Beauchamp, 1976) and the overconsumption of high caloric food frame countering the need to exercise frame (Jenkin, Signal, & Thomson, 2011). There is also a need to take into account the internal frame disputes within the public health arena. This may include discussion within the proponent group about the solutions advocated, such as taxation on sugar-sweetened beverages, advertising regulation, acceptance about working with industry/opponents like campaigns or associations with the food industry (i.e., The American Council for Fitness and Nutrition) (Ludwig & Nestle, 2008), and connection with larger cultural frames/issues.

Table 5.2 Core Tasks of Framing

Process	Sub-processes	Definition	Obesity Case
Strategic	Frame bridging	Alignment with existing frames	Alignment with sustainable frames, particularly in the food context (Tilman & Clark, 2014)
	Frame amplification	Alignment with existing values	Alignment with family values (i.e., family meals, leisure activities) (e.g., Bacon, 2018)
		Alignment with existing beliefs—seriousness	Discussion of serious health risks associated with obesity
		Alignment with existing beliefs—blame	Attribution (the environment), organisations (food industry)
		Alignment with existing beliefs—antagonistic	The food industry, its marketing in particular
		Alignment with existing beliefs—probability for change	Increase self-efficacy in social marketing messages and education. Also communication of the effectiveness (and thus needs) of government intervention
	Frame extension	Alignment with other actors or opponent interests	Alignment (policy actions/recommendations) with the goals and interests of non-health sectors (Atanasova & Koteyko, 2017)
Contested	Counter-framing	Countering opponents' arguments and frames	Countering individual responsibility framing prominent with opponents
	Internal frame disputes	Arguments within the proponent group about framing	Discussion within the proponent group about solutions advocated, acceptance about working with industry/opponents, and connection with larger cultural frames/issues

More specifically, the framing of obesity, and divergent beliefs about what drives and sustains social issues, contributes to many of the barriers preventing intervention on obesity (Roberto et al., 2015). Personal responsibility has been used by the food industry to defend itself from criticism, legislation, and litigation (Brownell & Warner, 2009). Research has shown that the media also helps perpetuate the personal responsibility idea by covering stories and using language which places the blame on individuals (Saguy & Almeling, 2008). Through research, macro-social marketers can carefully frame and target messages to the public regarding social issues (Kemper & Ballantine, 2017, p.386).

Moreover, we can learn from 'fights' or cases which demonstrate framing issues in the obesity context, as well as others, such as tobacco and alcohol. For example, successful campaigns framing the issue of sugar taxation in California demonstrate that highlighting the harmful behaviour of corporations is particularly effective (Somji et al., 2016). However, the commercial interests in public health are rarely discussed in relation to processed food and beverage companies (Weishaar et al., 2016). This is where we can learn from the relative success of the anti-tobacco movement. For example, the movement gained momentum when it was able to speak out against the negative impact of commercial interests, a case-in-point being California's successful anti-smoking campaign highlighting that the *"tobacco industry is not your friend"* (Reid, 2005; Weishaar, Amos, & Collin, 2015). In addition, shifting the frame from 'right to smoke' (industry lead) to the 'right to breathe clean air' (public health lead) helped garner public and policy support to reduce exposure to second-hand smoke (Wolfson, 2017). However, the challenge is to understand how ideas and imagery mobilise citizens and engage the public (Huang et al., 2015).

Frames can go beyond the written and can be visualised through images (Rodriguez & Dimitrova, 2011; Schwalbe, Silcock, & Keith, 2008). Thus, we could transmit the 'new normal' family meal, which may not include a main meat product, for example. Initiatives in primary schools already show the creation of a new food culture, firstly through encouragement to eat healthy and then the banning of non-water beverages and the requirement of one piece of fruit (in some New Zealand schools), which over time creates a healthy food culture at school, which may in turn translate to the child's home. Specifically, macro-social marketers can spread, through various mediums (e.g., social media, television, news), ideas and imagery (e.g., children's lunchbox, family meal) that support the new institutional norm(s). Considering downstream social marketing campaigns often use imagery in media, TV, and print appeals, research on visual framing can broaden our understanding of the use of imagery in highlighting particular frames.

Various avenues exist to undertake research to understand frames being used by the media, communities, and individuals. For example, much research surrounds the frames used in the media around obesity (e.g., Barry, Jarlenski, Grob, Schlesinger, & Gollust, 2011; Jeong, Gilmore, Bleakley, & Jordan, 2014; Kim & Anne Willis, 2007; Lawrence, 2004; Sun, Krakow, John, Liu, & Weaver, 2016), and such analysis (and future research conducted by social marketers) can aid macro-social marketing to understand how to counteract frames used in the media. The creation of counter-frames or narratives can be aided through a participatory approach (McHugh, Domegan, & Duane, 2018), using methodologies such as Narrative Workshops (Shaw & Corner, 2017). For example, recent research has even examined, through in-depth interviews, the diagnostic, prognostic, and motivational framing used by parents to talk about the family meal and compared this to advertising campaigns (Bacon, 2018).

Extending the participatory process to social marketing, macro-social marketers can also work with community groups to help wield their power and apply pressure on policy makers (Wallack & Dorfman, 1996). Active public pressure can impact both business and political actions (Huang et al., 2015; Moodie et al., 2013). Further, the institutionalisation process is cemented through the help of community groups and projects advocating for an institutional norm (Kuhn, 2005). Citizen protest and activism brought together by a common cause can affect social and political change.

Consequently, macro-social marketing also needs to bring together and mobilise groups and individuals who wish to have their voices heard. Petitions, marches, protests, and active debate online or on TV can be some of the ways the public can have a voice and participate in the political process. A similar principle can be applied to partnerships and coalitions between organisations, NGOs, and government agencies to coordinate research, funding, and political powers, among others. Indeed, recent calls from socio-technical transition researchers actively question the role of coalitions (Roberts et al., 2018). Thus, macro-social marketing can act as *"the 'glue' that holds multi-stream initiatives together"* (Parkinson et al., 2017, p. 397). There is much room to improve our knowledge about social change and citizen mobilisation with social movement theory and research.

Narratives

The use, role, and study of narratives and storylines in marketing is not new (Shankar, Elliott, & Goulding, 2001; Van Laer, De Ruyter, Visconti, & Wetzels, 2013). However, marketing research usually focuses on the individual act of consumption and has rarely examined this from a systematic and macro perspective. Narratives can be utilised through communication, social marketing, and other interventions (Gordon, Waitt, Cooper, & Butler, 2018). Indeed, narratives, rather than statistical data, have been advocated to be used in health behaviour change (Hinyard & Kreuter, 2007).

While narratives and storytelling are often used interchangeably (e.g., Olsen, 2014; Polkinghorne, 1988), frames and narratives are more distinct. Olsen (2014, p. 250) elaborates that *"while frames specify a diagnosis and prognosis of a problem, narrative draws the audience in with the features of emplotment and temporality . . . they are engaged in an unfolding sequence of events that contains moral or practical consequences"*. Thus, narratives differ from frames as they include a temporal dimension, which Bushell, Buisson, Workman, and Colley (2017) argue makes narratives better at communication. Narratives can explain why and when events occur and how people should behave to achieve a desirable outcome (Bushell et al., 2017; Gordon et al., 2018). For example, Gordon et al. (2018) created 'collective video storytelling', which combined scientific and lay knowledge about domestic energy use, and featured real people and stories, to provide guidance to Australian households about effective energy efficiency management. The study utilised social practice theory and payed particular attention to transformation-narrative theory (Van Laer et al., 2013). Transporting the listener or reader into the story is unique to narratives, allowing a personal connection and a focus on the emotional (Olsen, 2014; Van Laer et al., 2013).

Narratives are useful to make sense of 'chaotic' events such as personal, social, or environmental problems (Becker, 1997), and the conversion of these issues into stories provides reorder to the chaos (White, 2014). In this sense, plot structure is important. These plot structures have been categorised as tragedy, romance, comedy, and satire (White, 2014). For example, plotlines are common in energy transitions, and Janda and Topouzi (2015) demonstrate this through the uses of 'learning stories' (overcome challenge), 'hero stories' (technology), or 'horror stories' (preparation for social and environmental issues). The former of which Janda and Topouzi (2015) recommend researchers utilise to motivate the public and policy makers to enact change. However, Polletta (2009) argues that narratives do little to change the status quo as they are less authoritative than framing. Nevertheless, new research on strategic narratives might shine a light on the possibilities for the use of stories to incite and inspire change (Bushell et al., 2017).

Analysing the narratives and storylines used by government and businesses can shed light on how institutions have already been successful in social, economic, and political change. Malone et al. (2017) show the various storylines used in the U.S. (nuclear power), Brazil (sugar cane ethanol), and Sweden (biomass energy) to develop their energy pathways directly related to their existing political-cultural national narratives. Similarly, the U.K., Germany, and Japan all utilised different narratives in their response to the Fukushima disaster and subsequently affected policy and energy transformation (Hermwille, 2016). While these studies use historical analyses, they demonstrate the potential for descriptive and analytical tools to inform strategic opportunities to create specific narratives or reframe issues to induce desirable systemic change.

As an example, narrative forms of communication are often used in health behaviour change campaigns. Communication researchers have demonstrated that the use of entertainment education, journalism, literature, testimonials, and storytelling can impact behaviour change (Kreuter et al., 2007). Specifically, narrative communication can have powerful effects on increasing motivation and overcoming resistance, facilitating information processing, providing social and supportive connections, and addressing emotional issues and coping mechanisms (Kreuter et al., 2007). Thus, there is room for macro-social marketing to utilise narrative communication research for downstream and upstream social marketing. Next, we focus on providing a spotlight on effecting frames and narratives used in the media.

The Media: A Case in Point for the Use of Frames and Narrative

The media plays a large role in the construction of social reality (Scheufele, 1999). There are a number of ways social marketing can involve and account for media influence. At a macro level, macro-social marketing campaigns can have an implicit impact on media portrayals and subsequently affect the discourse surrounding an issue. Specifically, research demonstrates that the Philadelphia sugar-sweetened beverage reduction media campaign (radio and TV), in coordination with other initiatives, may have helped media to shift from the focus on the individual to other social and contextual factors such as food and beverage companies (Jeong et al., 2014).

Another way is to directly influence media stories through the provision of information and expertise. The media often relies on external sources to inform news articles; at the very least about half of journalists utilise press releases and corporate public relations materials (30% can be traced verbatim—Lewis, Williams, & Franklin, 2008). Consequently, there is a role to play in supplying media with stories, research findings, and debates to advance the resolution of wicked issues.

Storylines featured in television shows and on social media also have the potential to influence the framing and narratives surrounding social issues. Morgan, Movius, and Cody (2009) examine the impact of organ donation storylines of the U.S. television dramas *CSI: NY*, *Numb3rs*, *House*, and *Grey's Anatomy* on attitudes, knowledge, and behaviours. They found that if narratives helped viewers become emotionally involved, they were more likely to become an organ donor, particularly if the show explicitly encouraged donation, portrayed characters as becoming donors (including how), and discussed the merits of donating.

Whether social marketers can influence storylines on television shows remains to be seen, however, there is an ability to strive to attach more explicit messages to the end of an episode (such as those relating to mental illness or bullying). These more explicit calls to action can also occur, and research has examined the effectiveness of explicit persuasive appeal in entertainment-education interventions (Shen & Han, 2014). While social marketers might aim to join issue coalitions with television studios or shows, merely analysing the storylines present in shows, social media, and public discourse can also help to understand the broader environmental context in which social marketing messages are received.

Overall, research in media and communications, particularly media advocacy, holds valuable information for social and macro-social marketing which has largely been neglected (Wallack, 2002).

Concluding Thoughts

Wicked problems add complexity to policy design and implementation. There are differences in the understanding of a problem and therefore the frames generating the possible solutions (Head, 2008). Landscape events, shocks, and changes impact upon regimes and niches, but they will only generate enduring pressure "*if discursively prominent narratives become available that allow to translate the landscape shock into the socio-political environment*" (Hermwille, 2016, p. 243). While the ability for change has been highlighted historically in transitions research through the use of discourses, frames, and narratives by regimes and niches (Bosman, Loorbach, Frantzeskaki, & Pistorius, 2014; Hermwille, 2016; Kim & Kim, 2014; Roberts, 2017), it is now time for macro-social marketing to change formal and informal institutions through designing communications which articulate and leverage landscape pressures. It is only through the use of discourse, framing, and narrative understanding, analysis, and deployment that macro-social marketing can be a part of "*creating desirable images of change*" (Kennedy & Parsons, 2012, p. 37). Therefore, there is much room for future research.

While strategic frames and narratives offer a way to provide support for formal and informal institutional change, more insight and targeted approaches to initiate change in social practices are needed. However, the socio-technical approach may still provide insight into the need to take into account all aspects of social practices. The MLP of socio-technical transitions provides a mid-range theory (Geels, 2010) to help theorise change at the micro, meso, and macro levels. At the micro level, individuals are embedded in social practices and 'scripts' that shape action; at the meso level, structural regime rules and technological trajectories limit (in)action; and at the macro level, infrastructures, social/cultural norms, values, and broad consumption patterns provide material and immaterial constraints to actions (Geels, 2018). There is an opportunity for future research in macro-social marketing to examine closely the social practices related to (un)sustainable and (un)healthy consumption through the lens of the MLP.

While our examples apply to obesity, many other wicked issues should be examined and helped with macro-social marketing analysis and implementation, including issues of climate change, sustainability, and alcohol and drug control. Interdisciplinary research, whether conceptual or empirical, is needed to examine the full potential of framing effects. Specifically, research is needed which crosses communications and media effects with public relations research, and should include topics such as agenda setting and lobbying.

References

Atanasova, D., & Koteyko, N. (2017). Obesity frames and counter-frames in British and German online newspapers. *Health*, *21*(6), 650–669.

Bacon, T. (2018). Framing the family meal: A comparison of social marketing campaigns and parents' views. *Journal of Family Issues*, *39*(1), 78–103.

Barry, C. L., Jarlenski, M., Grob, R., Schlesinger, M., & Gollust, S. E. (2011). News media framing of childhood obesity in the United States from 2000 to 2009. *Pediatrics*, *128*(1), 132–145.

Beauchamp, D. E. (1976). Public health as social justice. *Inquiry*, *13*(1), 3–14.

Becker, G. (1997). *Disrupted lives: How people create meaning in a chaotic world*. Berkeley, CA: University of California Press.

Benford, R. D., & Snow, D. A. (2000). Framing processes and social movements: An overview and assessment. *Annual Review of Sociology*, *26*(1), 611–639.

Bosman, R., Loorbach, D., Frantzeskaki, N., & Pistorius, T. (2014). Discursive regime dynamics in the Dutch energy transition. *Environmental Innovation and Societal Transitions*, *13*, 45–59.

Brownell, K. D., & Warner, K. E. (2009). The perils of ignoring history: Big Tobacco played dirty and millions died. How similar is Big Food?. *The Milbank Quarterly*, *87*(1), 259–294.

Bushell, S., Buisson, G. S., Workman, M., & Colley, T. (2017). Strategic narratives in climate change: Towards a unifying narrative to address the action gap on climate change. *Energy Research and Social Science*, *28*, 39–49.

Chong, D., & Druckman, J. N. (2012). Counterframing effects. *Journal of Politics*, *75*(1), 1–16.

Daellenbach, K., & Parkinson, J. (2017). A useful shift in our perspective: Integrating social movement framing into social marketing. *Journal of Social Marketing*, *7*(2), 188–204.

Domegan, C. T. (2008). Social marketing: Implications for contemporary marketing practices classification scheme. *Journal of Business and Industrial Marketing*, *23*(2), 135–141.

Fuenfschilling, L., & Truffer, B. (2014). The structuration of socio-technical regimes – Conceptual foundations from institutional theory. *Research Policy*, *43*, 772–791.

Geels, F. W. (2004). From sectoral systems of innovation to socio-technical systems. *Research Policy*, *33*(6–7), 897–920.

Geels, F. W. (2010). Ontologies, socio-technical transitions (to sustainability), and the multi-level perspective. *Research Policy, 39*(4), 495–510.

Geels, F. W. (2018). Disruption and low-carbon system transformation: Progress and new challenges in socio-technical transitions research and the multi-level perspective. *Energy Research and Social Science, 37,* 224–231.

Geels, F. W., & Schot, J. (2007). Typology of sociotechnical transition pathways. *Research Policy, 36,* 399–417.

Geels, F. W., & Verhees, B. (2011). Cultural legitimacy and framing struggles in innovation journeys: A cultural-performative perspective and a case study of Dutch nuclear energy (1945–1986). *Technological Forecasting and Social Change, 78*(6), 910–930.

Gordon, R., Waitt, G., Cooper, P., & Butler, K. (2018). Storying energy consumption: Collective video storytelling in energy efficiency social marketing. *Journal of Environmental Management, 213,* 1–10.

Gurrieri, L., Previte, J., & Brace-Govan, J. (2013). Women's bodies as sites of control: Inadvertent stigma and exclusion in social marketing. *Journal of Macromarketing, 33*(2), 128–143.

Hastings, G., & Haywood, A. (1991). Social marketing and communication in health promotion. *Health Promotion International, 6*(2), 135–145.

Head, B. W. (2008). Wicked problems in public policy. *Public Policy, 3*(2), 101–118.

Hermwille, L. (2016). The role of narratives in socio-technical transitions – Fukushima and the energy regimes of Japan, Germany, and the United Kingdom. *Energy Research and Social Science, 11,* 237–246.

Hinchman, L. P., & Hinchman, S. (1997). *Memory, identity, community: The idea of narrative in the human sciences.* New York: Suny Press.

Hinyard, L. J., & Kreuter, M. W. (2007). Using narrative communication as a tool for health behavior change: A conceptual, theoretical, and empirical overview. *Health Education and Behavior, 34*(5), 777–792.

Huang, T. T., Cawley, J. H., Ashe, M., Costa, S. A., Frerichs, L. M., Zwicker, L., . . . Kumanyika, S. K. (2015). Mobilisation of public support for policy actions to prevent obesity. *The Lancet, 385,* 2422–2431.

Janda, K. B., & Topouzi, M. (2015). Telling tales: Using stories to remake energy policy. *Building Research and Information, 43*(4), 516–533.

Jenkin, G. L., Signal, L., & Thomson, G. (2011). Framing obesity: The framing contest between industry and public health at the New Zealand inquiry into obesity. *Obesity Reviews, 12*(12), 1022–1030.

Jeong, M., Gilmore, J. S., Bleakley, A., & Jordan, A. (2014). Local news media framing of obesity in the context of a sugar-sweetened beverage reduction media campaign. *Journal of Nutrition Education and Behavior, 46*(6), 583–588.

Jones, M. D., & McBeth, M. K. (2010). A narrative policy framework: Clear enough to be wrong? *Policy Studies Journal, 38*(2), 329–353.

Kemper, J. A., & Ballantine, P. W. (2017). Socio-technical transitions and institutional change: Addressing obesity through macro-social marketing. *Journal of Macromarketing, 37*(4), 381–392.

Kennedy, A-M., & Parsons, A. (2012). Macro-social marketing and social engineering: A systems approach. *Journal of Social Marketing, 2*(1), 37–51.

Khayatzadeh-Mahani, A., Ruckert, A., & Labonté, R. (2018). Obesity prevention: Co-framing for intersectoral 'buy-in.' *Critical Public Health, 28*(1), 4–11.

Kim, S-B., & Kim, D-Y. (2014). The effects of message framing and source credibility on green messages in hotels. *Cornell Hospitality Quarterly, 55*(1), 64–75.

Kim, S-H., & Anne Willis, L. (2007). Talking about obesity: News framing of who is responsible for causing and fixing the problem. *Journal of Health Communication, 12*(4), 359–376.

Knight, G., & Greenberg, J. (2011). Talk of the enemy: Adversarial framing and climate change discourse. *Social Movement Studies, 10*(4), 323–340.

Kreuter, M. W., Green, M. C., Cappella, J. N., Slater, M. D., Wise, M. E., Storey, D., . . . Hinyard, L. J., (2007). Narrative communication in cancer prevention and control: A framework to guide research and application. *Annals of Behavioral Medicine, 33*(3), 221–235.

Kuhn, T. (2005). The institutionalization of alta in organizational communication studies. *Management Communication Quarterly, 18*(4), 618–627.

Kwan, S. (2009). Framing the fat body: Contested meanings between government, activists, and industry. *Sociological Inquiry, 79*(1), 25–50.

Lang, T., & Rayner, G. (2007). Overcoming policy cacophony on obesity: an ecological public health framework for policymakers. *Obesity reviews, 8,* 165–181.

Lawrence, R. G. (2004). Framing obesity: The evolution of news discourse on a public health issue. *Harvard International Journal of Press/Politics, 9*(3), 56–75.

Lawrence, T., & Suddaby, R. (2006). Institutions and institutional work. In S. R. Clegg, C. Hardy, & W. R. Nord (Eds.), *Sage handbook of organization studies* (2nd ed., pp. 215–254). Cambridge: Sage Publications, Ltd.

Layton, R. A. (2015). Formation, growth, and adaptive change in marketing systems. *Journal of Macromarketing, 35*(3), 302–319.

Lewis, J., Williams, A., & Franklin, B. (2008). A compromised fourth estate? UK news journalism, public relations and news sources. *Journalism Studies, 9*(1), 1–20.

Loroz, P. S. (2007). The interaction of message frames and reference points in prosocial persuasive appeals. *Psychology and Marketing, 24*(11), 1001–1023.

Ludwig, D. S., & Nestle, M. (2008). Can the food industry play a constructive role in the obesity epidemic? *Journal of the American Medical Association, 300*(15), 1808–1811.

Malone, E., Hultman, N. E., Anderson, K. L., & Romeiro, V. (2017). Stories about ourselves: How national narratives influence the diffusion of large-scale energy technologies. *Energy Research and Social Science, 31,* 70–76.

McGregor, L. M., Ferguson, E., & O'Carroll, R. E. (2012). Living organ donation: The effect of message frame on an altruistic behaviour. *Journal of Health Psychology, 17*(6), 821–832.

McHugh, P., Domegan, C., & Duane, S. (2018). Protocols for stakeholder participation in social marketing systems. *Social Marketing Quarterly, 24*(3), 164–193.

Moodie, R., Stuckler, D., Monteiro, C., Sheron, N., Neal, B., Thamarangsi, T., . . . Casswell, S. (2013). Profits and pandemics: Prevention of harmful effects of tobacco, alcohol, and ultra-processed food and drink industries. *The Lancet, 381*(9867), 670–679.

Morgan, S. E., Movius, L., & Cody, M. J. (2009). The power of narratives: The effect of entertainment television organ donation storylines on the attitudes, knowledge, and behaviors of donors and nondonors. *Journal of Communication*, 59(1), 135–151.

Morone, P., Lopolito, A., Anguilano, D., Sica, E., & Tartiu, V. E. (2016). Unpacking landscape pressures on socio-technical regimes: Insights on the urban waste management system. *Environmental Innovation and Societal Transitions, 20*, 62–74.

North, D. (1990). *Institutions, institutional change and economic performance*. Cambridge: Cambridge University Press.

Olsen, K. A. (2014). Telling our stories: Narrative and framing in the movement for same-sex marriage. *Social Movement Studies, 13*(2), 248–266.

Parkinson, J., Dubelaar, C., Carins, J., Holden, S., Newton, F., & Pescud, M. (2017). Approaching the wicked problem of obesity: An introduction to the food system compass. *Journal of Social Marketing, 7*(4), 387–404.

Peattie, S., & Peattie, K. (2003). Ready to fly solo? Reducing social marketing's dependence on commercial marketing theory. *Marketing theory, 3*(3), 365–385.

Phillips, N., Lawrence, T. B., & Hardy, C. (2004). Discourse and institutions. *Academy of Management Review, 29*(4), 635–652.

Polkinghorne, D. E. (1988). *Narrative knowing and the human sciences*. Albany: State University of New York Press.

Polletta, F. (2009). *It was like a fever: Storytelling in protest and politics*. Chicago: University of Chicago Press.

Reid, R. (2005). *Globalizing tobacco control: Anti-smoking campaigns in California, France, and Japan*. Bloomington: Indiana University Press.

Roberto, C. A., Swinburn, B., Hawkes, C., Huang, T. T., Costa, S. A., Ashe, M., . . . Brownell, K. D. (2015). Patchy progress on obesity prevention: Emerging examples, entrenched barriers, and new thinking. *The Lancet, 385*, 2400–2409.

Roberts, C., Geels, F. W., Lockwood, M., Newell, P., Schmitz, H., Turnheim, B., & Jordan, A. (2018). The politics of accelerating low-carbon transitions: Towards a new research agenda. *Energy Research and Social Science, 44*, 304–311.

Roberts, J. C. D. (2017). Discursive destabilisation of socio-technical regimes: Negative storylines and the discursive vulnerability of historical American railroads. *Energy Research and Social Science, 31*, 86–99.

Rodriguez, L., & Dimitrova, D. V. (2011). The levels of visual framing. *Journal of Visual Literacy, 30*(1), 48–65.

Rothman, A. J., & Salovey, P. (1997). Shaping perceptions to motivate healthy behavior: The role of message framing. *Psychological Bulletin, 121*(1), 3.

Saguy, A. C., & Almeling, R. (2008, March). Fat in the Fire? Science, the News Media, and the "Obesity Epidemic" 2. In Sociological Forum (Vol. 23, No. 1, pp. 53-83). Oxford, UK: Blackwell Publishing Ltd.

Scheufele, D. A. (1999). Framing as a theory of media effects. *Journal of Communication, 49*(1), 103–122.

Scheufele, D. A., & Tewksbury, D. (2006). Framing, agenda setting, and priming: The evolution of three media effects models. *Journal of Communication, 57*(1), 9–20.

Schwalbe, C. B., Silcock, B. W., & Keith, S. (2008). Visual framing of the early weeks of the US-led invasion of Iraq: Applying the master war narrative to electronic and print images. *Journal of Broadcasting and Electronic Media*, *52*(3), 448–465.

Scott, W. R. (1995). *Institutions and organizations*. Thousand Oaks, CA: Sage Publications, Ltd.

Shankar, A., Elliott, R., & Goulding, C. (2001). Understanding consumption: Contributions from a narrative perspective. *Journal of Marketing Management*, *17*(3–4), 429–453.

Shaw, C., & Corner, A. (2017). Using narrative workshops to socialise the climate debate: Lessons from two case studies – Centre-right audiences and the Scottish public. *Energy Research and Social Science*, *31*, 273–283.

Shen, F., & Han, J. (2014). Effectiveness of entertainment education in communicating health information: A systematic review. *Asian Journal of Communication*, *24*(6), 605–616.

Silver, I. (1997). Constructing "social change" through philanthropy: Boundary framing and the articulation of vocabularies of motives for social movement participation. *Sociological Inquiry*, *67*(4), 488–503.

Smith, A. (2006). Green niches in sustainable development: The case of organic food in the United Kingdom. *Environment and Planning C: Government and Policy*, *24*, 439–458.

Smith, A., Stirling, A., & Berkhout, F. (2005). The governance of sustainable socio-technical transitions. *Research Policy*, *34*(10), 1491–1510.

Smith, A., Voß, J-P., & Grin, J. (2010). Innovation studies and sustainability transitions: The allure of the multi-level perspective and its challenges. *Research Policy*, *39*(4), 435–448.

Snow, D. A., & Benford, R. D. (1988). Ideology, frame resonance, and participant mobilization. *International Social Movement Research*, *1*(1), 197–217.

Snow, D. A., Rochford, E. B. Jr., Worden, S. K., & Benford, R. D. (1986). Frame alignment processes, micromobilization, and movement participation. *American Sociological Review*, 464–481.

Somji, A., Nixon, L., Mejia, P., Aziz, A., Arbatman, L., & Dorfman, L. (2016). *Soda tax debates in Berkeley and San Francisco: An analysis of social media, campaign materials and news coverage*. Berkeley: Berkeley Media Studies Group.

Suchman, M. C. (1995). Managing legitimacy: Strategic and institutional approaches. *The Academy of Management Review*, *20*(3), 571.

Sun, Y., Krakow, M., John, K. K., Liu, M., & Weaver, J. (2016). Framing obesity: How news frames shape attributions and behavioral responses. *Journal of Health Communication*, *21*(2), 139–147.

Swinburn, B. A., Kraak, V. I., Allender, S., Atkins, V. J., Baker, P. I., Bogard, J. R., . . . Ezzati, M., (2019). The global syndemic of obesity, undernutrition, and climate change: The lancet commission report. *Lancet*, *393*(10173), 741.

Tilman, D., & Clark, M. (2014). Global diets link environmental sustainability and human health. *Nature*, *515*(7528), 518–522.

Unruh, G. C. (2000). Understanding carbon lock-in. *Energy Policy*, *28*, 817–830.

Van Dijk, T. A. (1989). Structures of discourse and structures of power. *Communication Yearbook*, *12*, 18–59.

Van Gorp, B., & Vercruysse, T. (2012). Frames and counter-frames giving meaning to dementia: A framing analysis of media content. *Social Science and Medicine, 74*(8), 1274–1281.

Van Laer, T., De Ruyter, K., Visconti, L. M., & Wetzels, M. (2013). The extended transportation-imagery model: A meta-analysis of the antecedents and consequences of consumers' narrative transportation. *Journal of Consumer Research, 40*(5), 797–817.

Wallack, L. (2002). Public health, social change, and media advocacy. *Social Marketing Quarterly, 8*(2), 25–31.

Wallack, L., & Dorfman, L. (1996). Media advocacy: A strategy for advancing policy and promoting health. *Health Education and Behavior, 23*(3), 293–317.

Weishaar, H., Amos, A., & Collin, J. (2015). Best of enemies: Using social network analysis to explore a policy network in European smoke-free policy. *Social Science and Medicine, 133*, 85–92.

Weishaar, H., Dorfman, L., Freudenberg, N., Hawkins, B., Smith, K., Razum, O., & Hilton, S. (2016). Why media representations of corporations matter for public health policy: A scoping review. *BMC Public Health, 16*(1), 899.

White, H. (2014). *Metahistory: The historical imagination in nineteenth-century Europe*. Baltimore: The Johns Hopkins University Press.

Wolfson, M. (2017). *The fight against big tobacco: The movement, the state and the public's health*. Piscataway: Routledge.

6 Macro-Level Interventions in Systems of Wicked Consumption

Davide C. Orazi, Matthias Koch, and Srishti Varma

Introduction

The consumption of products containing addictive substances such as sugar, nicotine, and alcohol represent a major risk for non-communicable diseases including diabetes and cancer. Despite this threat, eradicating these 'wicked consumptions' (Koch & Orazi, 2017) is challenging for at least two reasons. First, wicked consumptions are habitual and addictive, leading to the automatisation and repetition of the consumption behaviour with minimal effort and ignoring information challenging the consumption. Habituality and addictiveness thus make wicked consumption behaviours resistant to individual-level interventions aimed at behavioural change. Second, wicked consumptions are embedded in complex and interconnected market systems we term 'systems of wicked consumption'. These systems facilitate the proliferation of wicked consumptions through enticing promotion, placement, and pricing strategies. This chapter begins by introducing the etiology of wicked consumptions, focusing on their habituality and addictiveness. Next, we bring forth the notion of systems of wicked consumption, and explain the tensions arising between the conflicting stakeholders embedded therein. We conclude by presenting a range of macro-level interventions that, by targeting the very structure of wicked systems, may prove to be far more effective than individual-level interventions in curbing the diffusion of wicked consumptions.

Etiology of Wicked Consumptions

Habituality and Addictiveness of Wicked Consumptions

Wicked consumption behaviours define the *"inflated consumption of unhealthy commodities such as soft drinks, foods high in fat and sugar, tobacco, and alcohol"* (Koch & Orazi, 2017, p. 356). The consumption of such commodities is referred to as 'wicked' not only because mounting medical research links it to negative health outcomes (Schulze et al., 2004), but also because the inherent habituality and addictiveness of these consumption behaviours trigger wicked, self-reinforcing behavioural cycles that increase resistance to individual-level interventions (Verplanken & Wood, 2006). Behaviours are considered habitual when actions are developed as repetitive responses to specific contextual stimuli (Verplanken & Wood, 2006). Opening a beer before turning on the TV, or lighting up a cigarette after a coffee, are examples of the behavioural link established between a contextual stimulus (e.g., turning on the TV) and an unrelated action (e.g., opening a beer) which, if repeated over time, leads to the formation of a habit. Engaging in a habit occurs with minimal awareness and effort (Verplanken & Wood, 2006). Opening a can of soda, chain-eating chips, lighting up a cigarette are all actions that can be performed without allocating substantial cognitive or conative resources to the task. The minimal awareness and effort required by habitual consumption is termed behavioural automatisation. Habitual behaviours, however, are not only automatic, but also resistant to information challenging the habit. Warning labels on beer bottles and cigarette packs, for instance, tend to be ignored by habitual consumers (Andrews, Netemeyer, Kees, & Burton, 2014), a process termed informational irresponsiveness.

Behavioural automatisation and informational irresponsiveness are intrinsic to habits and are further aggravated by the fact that most of the substances at the core of wicked consumptions are addictive, but not illegal (Koch & Orazi, 2017). Traditionally, addiction has been defined as a repetitive, hard to control habitual behaviour that leads to short-term rewards (e.g., hedonic gratification) but long-term losses (e.g., increased risk of non-communicable diseases—Marlatt, Baer, Donovan, & Kivlahan, 1988). Historically, emphasis was placed on the (a) illegality, and (b) level of intoxication produced by the addictive substance (Gearhardt, Roberts, & Ashe, 2013). This definition led governments and policy makers to focus predominantly on drugs and, during the 1920–1933 period of U.S. Prohibition, alcohol. Following the groundbreaking discovery that nicotine was addictive and not just habit-forming (Stolerman & Jarvis, 1995), the definition of 'addictive' has progressively shifted to encompass substances whose consumption is hard to control and stop despite the negative health consequences they produce (Gearhardt et al., 2013). Nicotine, sugar, and alcohol all fall under this definition: these neuroactive compounds produce immediate gratification and lead to the formation of habits, but have long-term detrimental effects on individual health and societal wellbeing. Nicotine has proven effects in contributing to cancer development (Stolerman & Jarvis, 1995). Sugar leads to obesity and the formation of Type-II diabetes (Pomeranz, 2012). While the consumption of alcohol, as little as one standard drink per day, was recently linked to an increase in the relative risk of developing breast and oral cavity cancer (Burton & Sheron, 2018).

The Epidemic Life Cycle of Wicked Consumptions

Despite the proliferation of wicked consumptions, individual consumers cannot be held fully accountable for their outbreak. During the times of Prohibition, moral models of addiction placed the burden entirely on the individual, blaming people's weak character and lack of willpower if they failed to self-regulate (Strug, Priyadarsini, & Hyman, 1986). Needless to say, these models have received little empirical support over the decades (Marlatt et al., 1988), partly because individual wicked consumptions cannot be considered in isolation from the systems they are embedded into. Contrary to this view, compensatory models of addiction (Marlatt et al., 1988) posit that, while individuals may be personally accountable for putting effort in controlling or ceasing wicked consumptions, they are not fully responsible for their etiology. We echo these models and explain why, at least in part, we are victims of not only our own devices but, in many cases, of our own neurocortical system.

A combination of evolutionary and systemic factors has facilitated the epidemic outbreak of wicked consumptions (Koch & Orazi, 2017). Think about sugar. Our cells need sugar to survive. At the same time, sugar is addictive and activates brain regions related to craving, facilitating over-consumption and increasing the risk of negative health consequences (Volkow, Wang, Fowler, & Telang, 2008). This apparent paradox only manifests in modern society with the advent of added sugar in processed foods (Pomeranz, 2012). Throughout our evolutionary history, sugar was a substance scarce in nature, and the human taste evolved to crave it to offset the risk of starvation (Drewnowski, 1997). Finding a ripe fruit after hours of search also led to calorie-rich rewards compensating the caloric effort invested in their achievement. Even then, sugar found in fruits (i.e., fructose) is also accompanied by high amounts of water and fiber, which help slow its absorption (Gearhardt et al., 2013). The rapid economic development of the past century, however, has resulted in faster production and easier accessibility to processed foods high in added sugar and often stripped of water and fibers. As Gearhardt and colleagues (2013) state, "*naturally rewarding foods have been altered in such a way that significantly increases reward potency* [. . .] *and may increase risk for the development of a potentially addictive substance*" (p. 47). Coupled with the advent of global retail systems, this economic development has created an over-supply of unhealthy commodities high in added sugar that propagate following a life cycle akin to an epidemic outbreak (Koch & Orazi, 2017).

The four stages of the epidemic life cycle of wicked consumption behaviours are documented by Koch and Orazi (2017). The first stage is *epidemic outbreak*. During this phase, manufacturers and commercial marketing forces support product diffusion with product and promotional strategies. The aim is to introduce in the market a product that offers short-term rewards and facilitates the formation of habitual and addictive consumption patterns, leveraging the lack of research on the long-term negative effects.

The second stage is *epidemic multiplication*. Reinforcing wicked consumptions through strong distribution networks and global marketing campaigns (Koch & Orazi, 2017), global manufacturers are able to expand in different markets while capitalising on revenues. At this stage, however, medical and policy research is typically initiated with the aim of establishing a causal link between wicked consumptions and negative health outcomes. Examples of how medical research starts curbing the diffusion of wicked consumptions include the Surgeon General's report in 1964 on the link between smoking and lung cancer, and Stolerman and Jarvis's groundbreaking discovery in 1995 that nicotine is addictive.

Research typically culminates in the third stage, defined as *epidemic intervention and host reaction*. Based on mounting research, governmental institutions start trialing policy interventions and preventive campaigns to assist consumers in becoming informed decision makers. In response, marketers react, 'evolving' their products as viruses do: Low-nicotine cigarettes and low-sugar sodas are two examples of 'healthier' alternatives to current wicked offerings. These products, however, often turn out to be even unhealthier. Smokers of low-tar cigarettes pull harder and develop lung cancer in deeper areas in the lungs (Brooks et al., 2005). Low-sugar products often compensate by adding fat, which at parity of volume has more caloric content and can lead to obesity much faster, or reduce the amount of sugar with natural sweetener but position the new product as healthy when in fact it is not. The recent case of Coke Life shows how a product that still contains almost 30 grams of sugar per 100 ml is positioned as a green-packaged, healthy product with 35% less sugar than the original (Mayer, 2013).

The fourth stage of the epidemic life cycle defines the decline in wicked consumption supported by mounting research, policy interventions, and social marketing initiatives. Different scenarios are possible at this stage, and we refer to Koch and Orazi (2017) for a detailed account. What warrants reflection here is that the general epidemic life cycle of wicked consumptions is not likely to stop in the short term based on a systematic rewiring of our cortical system. Evolution, albeit inexorable, is an extremely slow process, and we cannot expect individuals to stop craving sugar if this response evolved as an adaptive strategy against starvation. Rather than targeting individuals at the micro level, we need to understand that greater change can be achieved by acting at the macro level, targeting wicked systems of consumption. But if the system is partially to blame for the proliferation of wicked consumption, then it falls on researchers, policy makers, and social marketers to monitor the outbreak of wicked consumptions and the development of wicked consumption systems.

Wicked Consumption Systems

The discourse around the etiology of wicked consumptions suggests a systemic nature for the issue at hand. According to systems theory, wicked problems are multi-causal, involve multiple stakeholders with different goals, and display an inherent interconnectedness between processes and structures within the system (Head & Alford, 2015). Due to these factors, wicked problems, of which wicked consumptions are a sub-type, are extremely hard to tackle. Wicked consumptions indeed proliferate because they are embedded in wicked systems where different stakeholder groups interact, including marketers of unhealthy commodities, consumers, and counter-marketing forces (e.g., public health officials, policy makers, and social marketers). The actions of these stakeholder groups are guided by different objectives and differentially affect the proliferation of wicked consumptions. In the next section, we use the case of added sugar as an illustration of how the stakeholders involved in wicked consumption systems act and react based on their priorities and objectives.

Stakeholder Dynamics in Wicked Consumption Systems: The Case of Added Sugar in U.S. Nutritional Labels

While sugar is naturally found in fruit and vegetables, it can also be extracted from cane and beetroot, refined, and added to food and beverages. The U.S. Food and Drug Administration (FDA), in particular, defines added sugars as *"sugars that are either added during the processing of foods, or are packaged as such, and include sugars (free, mono- and disaccharides), sugars from syrups and honey, and sugars from concentrated fruit or vegetable juices that are in excess of what would be expected from the same volume of 100 percent fruit or vegetable juice of the same type"* (US Food and Drug Administration, 2016, np). U.S. citizens aged 6 to 54 consume a daily average of 87 grams of *added* sugar (Pomeranz, 2012), which is significantly in excess to the recommended maximum dose of 50 grams per day determined by the FDA in 1993. Sweetened soft drinks, in particular, are the major contributor to added sugar consumption (Pomeranz, 2012). The original U.S. Nutrition Labeling and Education Act (NLEA) in 1990, however, led to the enforcement of nutrition labels that only disclose the amount of total sugar contained. Added sugar amounts were not displayed due to, at the time, a lack of scientific consensus on the link between added sugar consumption and adverse health consequences such as obesity. In the decades following, the mounting research evidence on the link between sugary drinks and obesity prompted public health officials to call for additional regulations, including the disclosure of added sugar amounts (Gearhardt et al., 2013).

Three different non-consumer stakeholders have been interacting in this scenario to support their interests. Following the creation of uniform front-of-package labelling (Pomeranz, 2012), in 2011 the FDA announced their resolution to introduce revised regulations disciplining the information disclosed on food and beverages labels. Answering the call, the Institute of Medicine (IOM), a professional, research-driven organisation, recommended to display the amount of added sugar in the front-of-package labels. In response, the Grocery Manufacturers Association (GMA), a lobby of food and beverage producers, reacted by criticising the IOM proposition and countering with their own labelling system disclosing only the total amount of sugar, with no further distinction between natural and added sugar (Pomeranz, 2012). Supporting this counter-move was the narrative that obesity is a wicked problem caused by several interlinked factors, including lack of physical activity and social environment. Following this rhetoric, marketers of sugary drinks pointed out that singling out one ingredient as the key responsible for the obesity epidemic is unfair and more efforts should be invested in socio-environmental interventions.

Marketers of sugary drinks tapped onto this debate using promotional efforts as well. Coca-Cola's involvement in the Global Energy Balance Network, for instance, was aimed at incentivising a healthier and more active lifestyle to shift the focus of the conversation from nutrition to exercise (O'Connor, 2015). Accordingly, funded scientists started advocating that the U.S. population was overly fixated with calorie consumption instead of healthy weight and exercise. The campaign caused strong reactions from several public health experts and scientists, who felt it reminiscent of the 'Big Tobacco Playbook' times when scientific experts were recruited to cast doubts about the health risks of smoking (O'Connor, 2015). After mounting research demonstrating a link between sugar intake and chronic diseases, in May 2016 the FDA finally announced that nutrition labels will now display the amount of added sugar to reflect the increased health risk stemming from sugar consumption (US Food and Drug Administration, 2016). We will return to the specific design elements of this intervention when discussing *macro-level interventions in wicked consumption systems*.

The previous example captures the interwoven and often conflicting agendas of institutional stakeholders, but does not include consumer desires and behaviours. Consumers value freedom of choice and yet also wish to be informed decision makers when it comes to their health (Gearhardt et al., 2013; Orazi & Newton, 2018). The conflicting agendas of marketing and counter-marketing forces, however, can lead to confusion on the best course of action to take. For sugar consumption, some consumers may still believe that exercising is an effective compensatory strategy to counter an unhealthy diet, when in fact the effect is minimal (Thomas et al., 2012; Wilks et al., 2011). As pointed out by Pomeranz (2012), "*specific standards can be developed to increase information on the nutrition facts panel, create daily reference values, develop a disqualifying level for manufacturers to make health claims, and develop a front-of-package system that includes sugar in its nutritional criteria*" (p. e14). However, even if policy makers and social marketers treat consumers as rational cognitive beings when delivering interventions, the fact that consumers are subject to cognitive biases, habits, and addictions (Orazi & Newton, 2018; Verplanken & Wood, 2006) further reduces the likelihood of them adopting healthy behaviours.

Representing Wicked Consumption Systems

The previous scenario clarifies that the complexity and interconnectedness of wicked systems eludes linear representations and makes it less-than-optimal to consider their constitutive elements in isolation. Stock-and-flow diagrams are more effective to visualise wicked systems (Cohen, 2017). Consider our simplified wicked consumption system for sugar and assume we are focusing on the consumption of sugary beverages, which result in the ingestion of high amounts of sugar (i.e., up to 44 grams per 330 ml). Stocks define the number of consumers that are either in a state of potential consumption or have turned into consumers of sugary drinks. Stocks are typically represented as rectangles (Meadows, 2008). The stock of potential consumers thus 'flows' into the stock of actual consumers, from which it can return to a state of potentiality through corrective actions.

In our simplified wicked consumption system, the rate at which potential consumers flow into the stock of actual consumers (i.e., conversion rate) depends on the competing actions of marketers and counter-marketing forces. Advertising campaigns, price promotions, and new product releases are but a few of the marketing tactics employed by manufacturers of unhealthy commodities to entice consumers to eat and drink unhealthy but profitable products (Koch & Orazi, 2017). At the opposite end of the fight, counter-marketing forces seek to reduce the conversion rate by adopting counter-marketing efforts that range from macro-level interventions affecting the system at its roots, such as sin taxes and product bans, to micro-level interventions putting the emphasis on individual responsibility, such as preventative campaigns. We will return to the different types of intervention available to counter-marketing forces, specifically macro-social marketing interventions, when discussing *macro-level interventions in wicked consumption systems*. For the time being, it is important to consider the multiplicity of stakeholders involved in wicked consumption systems.

Beyond marketers and counter-marketers, consumers also influence the conversion rate by initiating reinforcing or balancing loops through word of mouth and other social influence mechanisms. These loops can be either virtuous or wicked depending on whether they increase or decrease the conversion rate. For instance, being embedded in a social circle in which everyone consumes soda drinks has a wicked, reinforcing effect on the conversion rate from potential to actual consumers due to peer pressure and potential unavailability of drink alternatives. A health-conscious peer with a keen interest in research papers, however, may be considered as a virtuous force or 'balancing loop' that opposes the wicked direction of the system (Meadows, 2008). Of course actual consumers of unhealthy commodities can then be persuaded to behavioural change by persuasive campaigns and other individual-level interventions, flowing back to a state of potentiality. In our system, however, adopters never flow away from the system; rather, they flow back to a state of potentiality where the risk of relapse is always present. Figure 6.1 illustrates a simplified wicked consumption system.

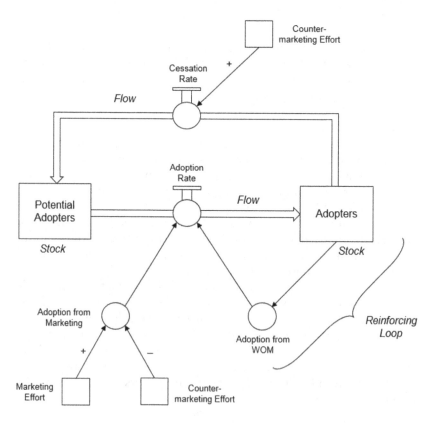

Figure 6.1 Structure of a Wicked Consumption System

Macro-Level Interventions in Wicked Consumption Systems

We now turn to the types of interventions available to social marketers and policy makers to counter-act marketing efforts. First, we review common downstream or micro-level interventions aimed at empowering consumers in making healthier choices. After discussing the inherent limits of individual self-regulation, we then turn to upstream or macro-level interventions in general and the need to balance restriction and enablement interventions when intervening on wicked systems of consumption. From a systemic perspective, these macro-level interventions can affect either the stock of the system, by limiting the amount of potential adopters (e.g., banning sales to certain age categories), or the flow of the system, by rendering harder the transition from potential to actual adopters (e.g., banning soft-drinks vending machines from campuses).

The Inherent Limits of Micro-Level Interventions

Empowering consumers to become informed decision makers remains a critical strategy to ensure consumers build resilience against marketing attempts aimed at promoting wicked consumptions (Koch & Orazi, 2017; Orazi & Newton, 2018). Downstream or micro-level interventions target the individual and require individual effort to be effective, with the ultimate aim of facilitating the increase or maintenance of virtuous behaviours and the decrease or cessation of wicked ones (Andreasen, 2002). Educational strategies such as school programs (Stigler, Neusel, & Perry, 2011; Rundle-Thiele et al., 2015) and preventive campaigns (Orazi, Bove, & Lei, 2016) remain key to improving consumers' knowledge about the long-term negative consequences associated with wicked consumptions (Seiders & Petty, 2004; Verplanken & Wood, 2006). The provision of support services such as quit lines or Alcoholics Anonymous can also ease the conversion from adopters to potential adopters, and decrease the risk of relapse (Michie, van Stralen, & West, 2011). Similarly, disclosure remedies are mandated through regulations to increase transparency and require manufacturers to notify of health-related information on the package of the products, such as warning labels on cigarette packages. The FDA regulation to disclose nutritional information on food and beverage labels is an example of a disclosure remedy (Balasubramanian & Cole, 2002).

Following up on our example of added sugar consumption, consider the recent history of food labelling in the U.S. Four years before the implementation of the revised nutrition labels, Pomeranz (2012) advocated revised labels that could either disclose added sugars or separate the types of sugars with the total sugars sub-heading. An additional suggestion included providing a daily reference value for added sugars to support consumers in understanding how much a nutrient in a serving of food contributes to a daily diet of about 2,000 calories. In May 2016, the FDA published the rules for the revised nutrition labels for packaged food and drinks to reflect the new scientific evidence linking added sugar consumption to negative health outcomes. The revised labels incorporate much of the consensus generated in the preceding years, notably displaying (a) total calories in the top centre of the label, in a large bold type font, and (b) the amount of added sugar. Following the publication of the revised rules for packaged foods labelling, the FDA set the compliance date to the 26th of July 2018. Figure 6.2 illustrates the revised nutrition labels.

It has to be noted, however, that after listening to feedback from manufacturers and industry groups, the FDA decided to extend the compliance

Nutrition Facts

Serving Size 2/3 cup (55g)
Servings Per Container About 8

Amount Per Serving

Calories 230	Calories from Fat 72

	% Daily Value*
Total Fat 8g	**12%**
Saturated Fat 1g	**5%**
Trans Fat 0g	
Cholesterol 0mg	**0%**
Sodium 160mg	**7%**
Total Carbohydrate 37g	**12%**
Dietary Fiber 4g	**16%**
Sugars 12g	
Protein 3g	

Vitamin A	10%
Vitamin C	8%
Calcium	20%
Iron	45%

* Percent Daily Values are based on a 2,000 calorie diet. Your daily value may be higher or lower depending on your calorie needs.

	Calories:	2,000	2,500
Total Fat	Less than	65g	80g
Sat Fat	Less than	20g	25g
Cholesterol	Less than	300mg	300mg
Sodium	Less than	2,400mg	2,400mg
Total Carbohydrate		300g	375g
Dietary Fiber		25g	30g

Nutrition Facts

8 servings per container
Serving size   2/3 cup (55g)

Amount per serving

Calories   230

	% Daily Value*
Total Fat 8g	**10%**
Saturated Fat 1g	**5%**
Trans Fat 0g	
Cholesterol 0mg	**0%**
Sodium 160mg	**7%**
Total Carbohydrate 37g	**13%**
Dietary Fiber 4g	**14%**
Total Sugars 12g	
Includes 10g Added Sugars	**20%**
Protein 3g	

Vitamin D 2mcg	10%
Calcium 260mg	20%
Iron 8mg	45%
Potassium 235mg	6%

* The % Daily Value (DV) tells you how much a nutrient in a serving of food contributes to a daily diet. 2,000 calories a day is used for general nutrition advice.

Figure 6.2 Original Versus Revised Food Labels Comparison

Note: Revised nutritional label on the right. Notable changes include a larger, bolder type font for servings (on top); a substantially larger type font indicating the total calories, now moved in the top centre of the label; and the inclusion of added sugars under the "total sugars" sub-heading. Sourced from www.fda.gov, "Changes to the Nutrition Facts Label", and reproduced under by the FDA. The material on FDA website is not copyrighted. It is in the public domain and may be republished, reprinted and used freely without obtain permission from FDA. Please view the statement on FDA's website regarding the use of information on the agency's website, see the section on "https://www.fda.gov/AboutFDA/AboutThisWebsite/WebsitePolicies/default.htm" Website Policie date to the 1st of January 2020 for manufacturers with USD 10 million or more annual sales, and to the 1st of January 2021 for food manufacturers with less than USD 10 million annual sales. The FDA justified this decision by declaring that "*additional time would provide manufacturers covered by the rule with necessary guidance from FDA, and would help them be able to complete and print updated nutrition fact panels for their products before they are expected to be in compliance*" (US food and Drug Administration, 2018, np). This episode further speaks to how stakeholders' tensions cause delays in the implementation of governmental interventions. This is an inherent feature of a multi-stakeholder system where stakeholders have competing interests. The weakest link in this intervention chain, however, is still the individual. Disclosure remedies still target the individual by disclosing useful information, but imply individuals pay attention to whatever is disclosed (Verplanken & Wood, 2006; Kennedy, 2016).

Yet the habituality of wicked consumptions makes them prone to behavioural automatisation and informational irresponsiveness (Verplanken & Wood, 2006), limiting the effectiveness of interventions based on the communication of information. Further exacerbating the situation is the fact that our self-regulation resources are limited and deplete in response to external stressors (Muraven & Baumeister, 2000). According to theories of ego depletion and the active self as an expendable resource (Muraven & Baumeister, 2000; Baumeister, 2014; Vohs et al., 2018), each consecutive attempt to refrain from consumption becomes harder, progressively depleting self-regulating resources until the point the consumer gives in to wicked consumption. As wicked consumptions rests on habit, they are more frequent and thus require more frequent self-regulatory attempts, eventually depleting regulatory resources and giving into wicked consumptions. For these reasons, macrosystemic interventions seem more apt to tackle the root of the problem by restricting access to wicked consumption at the system's level.

Macro-Social Marketing: Balancing Restrictive and Enabling Interventions

When the aim is to intervene at the system level, macro-social marketing is well equipped to counterbalance marketing efforts (Kennedy, 2016). Macro-social marketing focuses on designing interventions that influence the system where marketers and consumers are embedded. In so doing, macro-social marketing aims at both restricting marketing efforts and bypassing the weaknesses inherent to individual decision making. In reviewing seminal frameworks on macro-social marketing interventions (Seiders & Petty, 2004; Verplanken & Wood, 2006; Michie et al., 2011; Kennedy & Parsons, 2012), we found several commonalities and complementarities among the types of macro-level (or upstream) interventions listed. With the exception of disclosure remedies such as enforcing regulation on nutritional labels (Seiders & Petty, 2004), most macro-level interventions adopt a form of restriction to the marketing mix. These systemic interventions can reduce both the stock of potential adopters and the flow from potential to actual adopters. An example of restrictive interventions that affect the stock of potential users is product bans, which bar access to the commodities and thus eliminate the stock of potential adopters legally sourcing the product. An example of restrictive interventions affecting the flow of the market, on the other hand, is the introduction of sin taxes on sugar, which make the product less financially attractive and thus decrease the flow from potential to actual adopters.

Restrictive interventions affect the stock and flow of wicked systems. They do so through regulations and legislations aimed at limiting or preventing access to unhealthy commodities, typically targeting elements traditionally associated with the marketing mix. Drawing on several intervention frameworks (Seiders & Petty, 2004; Verplanken & Wood, 2006; Michie et al., 2011; Kennedy & Parsons, 2012), we thus classify existing restrictive interventions based on (a) their focus on different aspects of the marketing mix of commercial manufacturers, and (b) their effect on either the stock or flow of the system.

Table 6.1 illustrates this classification.

Product. Restrictive interventions applied to products include bans and restrictions to sell. Product bans eliminate the availability of the product for the whole system, making the wicked product unavailable and thus eliminating the system itself. For example, marijuana is legally banned in several Australian states and its possession is a criminal offence in states such as Queensland. Product bans, however, often lead to the creation of parallel systems (in this case, a black market) where the banned product becomes available outside the institutionalised system of consumption. Restrictions to sell, on the other hand, refer to the protection of specific customer segments and prevent access to certain consumers. Policies preventing minors to buy cigarettes fall within the restriction to sell intervention category. Restrictive remedies at the product level affect the stock of the system, drastically reducing the amount of potential adopters.

Table 6.1 Macro-Level Restrictive Interventions in Wicked Systems

Marketing Mix	Restrictive Remedies	System Element Targeted (Effect)
Product	Product bans	Stock (strong)
	Restriction to sell	Stock (moderate)
Promotion	Advertising bans	Flow (moderate)
	Advertising restrictions	Flow (weak)
Price	Financial restrictions	Flow (moderate)
Place	Distribution bans	Flow (weak)
	Consumption restrictions	Flow (weak)

Promotion. Similar to product restrictions, restrictive interventions applied to promotion include advertising bans and restrictions. Advertising bans prohibit the promotion of wicked commodities (Koch & Orazi, 2017), such as the case of tobacco advertising bans in Australia. Advertising restrictions prohibit promotion at specific times to protect vulnerable audience or restrict the use of specific communication elements in the design of the promotion. Broadcasting ads for computer games classified as R18+ in Australia can only happen at specific times (typically in zone coded as M: 7.30pm and 6.00am, 12pm to 3.00pm; and M15+: 8.30pm to 5.00am—Free TV Australia, 2016). As restrictive remedies at the promotion level are geared towards making the availability of a certain product less salient in the mind of the consumer, they affect the flow of the system, reducing the conversion rate from potential to actual adopters.

Price. Restrictive interventions applied to price take the form of financial remedies or added taxes (Michie et al., 2011). Sin taxes impose a burden on both marketers and consumers in the form of higher prices, as happens with cigarettes in Australia, sold at an average of AUD\$25. Resources obtained through sin taxes can then be used for downstream interventions and communication campaigns. Increasing the price of a wicked product also has the effect of switching consumption choice towards more accessible alternatives (French, 2003). Restrictive remedies at the price level affect the flow of the system, reducing the conversion rate from potential to actual adopters by means of making the product financially unattractive.

Place. Restrictive remedies applied to place counter-act the distribution capillarity of market systems, limiting the points of sale and distribution. Within place restrictions, we further distinguish between distribution bans and consumption restrictions. Distribution bans limit accessibility to the product by banning, for instance, vending machines of soft-drinks in school campuses (Stead & Lancaster, 2000) or pokies in all casinos of Western Australia except in one specific location (Online Pokies, 2016). Consumption restrictions prohibit the consumption of wicked products in designated areas, for instance cigarettes in smoke-free campuses or alcohol in the streets. Restrictive remedies at the place level affect the flow of the system, physically limiting purchase and consumption opportunities. The effectiveness of place-based interventions, however, is highly dependent on the number of available sites where consumers can purchase and consume the restricted product adjacent to the restricted area.

Restrictive interventions, however, need to be accompanied by enabling interventions. The habitual and addictive nature of wicked consumptions implies that restricting access to wicked commodities may prove detrimental if no alternatives are provided. The case of U.S. Prohibition is emblematic in this regard: Banning alcohol led to the proliferation of even more wicked consumption systems, fueling bootlegging and a black market. Where restrictive interventions affect the stock and flow of wicked systems, enabling interventions alter the structure by providing access to products that enable the transition outside of the wicked system and towards less detrimental or even healthier options. For instance, nicotine gums and patches enable tobacco consumers to exit the system and adopt a substitute product that assists with overcoming nicotine addiction (Koch & Orazi, 2017). That being said, restrictive interventions are still necessary to support the transition to the substitute; in the example of tobacco gums, this equates to banning tobacco advertising campaigns, making the product financially unattractive through sin taxes, and restricting access by locking distribution channels (Stead & Lancaster, 2000; French, 2003).

Conclusion

Wicked consumption systems are widespread and well known to social marketers and policy makers. Deeply rooted in our evolutionary history, the neuroactive compounds contained in the unhealthy commodities at the core of wicked consumption systems decrease the effectiveness of many individual-level interventions, especially those based on the communication of information. Habit formation around wicked consumptions further enhances the wickedness of these systems, making it hard for consumers to transition away from wicked systems if unaided. This chapter presents a brief etiology of wicked consumptions and explains the factors responsible for their epidemic life cycle and the formation of wicked consumption systems. Our conceptualisation of multi-stakeholder wicked systems brings forth the challenges that social marketers and regulators need to face in pursuit of eradicating wicked consumptions. By explaining the dynamics of wicked consumption systems in terms of stocks and flows, we also introduce different macro-level interventions aimed at transitioning consumers to either a state of potentiality or directly away from the wicked system itself. We hope this brief review will help both the uninitiated to get a better picture of the complexities inherent to wicked consumption systems and the adept to consider future research avenues based on the empirical validation of these theoretical models. The biggest limitations to extant literature on macro-social marketing systems and wicked consumption remain the lack of empirical validation. Future research using dynamic modelling is warranted to capture the effects of macro-level interventions on the state of a wicked system over time, also taking into account marketing and counter-marketing forces, as well as balancing and reinforcing loops initiated by consumers.

References

Andreasen, A. R. (2002). Marketing social marketing in the social change marketplace. *Journal of Public Policy and Marketing*, 21(1), 3–13.

Andrews, J. C., Netemeyer, R. G., Kees, J., & Burton, S. (2014). How graphic visual health warnings affect young smokers' thoughts of quitting. *Journal of Marketing Research*, 51(2), 165–183.

Balasubramanian, S. K., & Cole, C. (2002). Consumers' search and use of nutrition information: The challenge and promise of the nutrition labeling and education act. *Journal of Marketing*, 66(3), 112–127.

Baumeister, R. F. (2014). Self-regulation, ego depletion, and inhibition. *Neuropsychologia*, 65, 313–319.

Brooks, D. R., Austin, J. H., Heelan, R. T., Ginsberg, M. S., Shin, V., Olson, S. H., . . . Stellman, S. D. (2005). Influence of type of cigarette on peripheral versus central lung cancer. *Cancer Epidemiology and Prevention Biomarkers*, 14(3), 576–581.

Burton, R., & Sheron, N. (2018). No level of alcohol consumption improves health. *Lancet*, 392(10152), 987–988.

Cohen, M. (2017). A systemic approach to understanding mental health and services. *Social Science and Medicine*, 191, 1–8.

Drewnowski, A. (1997). Taste preferences and food intake. *Annual Review of Nutrition*, 17(1), 237–253.

French, S. A. (2003). Pricing effects on food choices. *Journal of Nutrition*, 133(3), 841S–843S.

Gearhardt, A., Roberts, M., & Ashe, M. (2013). If sugar is addictive what does it mean for the law? *Journal of Law, Medicine and Ethics*, 41, 46–49.

Head, B. W., & Alford, J. (2015). Wicked problems: Implications for public policy and management. *Administration and Society*, 47(6), 711–739.

Kennedy, A-M. (2016). Macro-social marketing. *Journal of Macromarketing*, 36(3), 354–365.

Kennedy, A-M., & Parsons, A. (2012). Macro-social marketing and social engineering: A systems approach. *Journal of Social Marketing*, 2(1), 37–51.

Koch, M., & Orazi, D. C. (2017). No rest for the wicked: The epidemic life cycle of wicked consumer behavior. *Journal of Macromarketing*, 37(4), 356–368.

Marlatt, G. A., Baer, J. S., Donovan, D. M., & Kivlahan, D. R. (1988). Addictive behaviours: Etiology and treatment. *Annual Review of Psychology*, 39(1), 223–252.

Mayer, A. (2013). Soft-drink makers accused of using 'big tobacco playbook'. *CBC News*. Retrieved from www. cbc. ca/news/health/soft-drink-makers-accused-of-using-big-tobacco-playbook-1.1362598

Meadows, D. H. (2008). *Thinking in systems: A primer*. Vermont: Chelsea Green Publishing.

Michie, S., Van Stralen, M. M., & West, R. (2011). The behaviour change wheel: A new method for characterising and designing behaviour change interventions. *Implementation Science*, 6(1), 42.

Muraven, M., & Baumeister, R. F. (2000). Self-regulation and depletion of limited resources: Does self-control resemble a muscle? *Psychological Bulletin*, 126(2), 247–259.

O'Connor, A. (2015). Coca-Cola funds scientists who shift blame for obesity away from bad diets. *New York Times*. Retrieved from www.nytimes.com

Online Pokies. (2016). *Pokie regulations in Australia*. Retrieved from www.onlinepokies.com/state-regulations.htm#wa

Orazi, D. C., Bove, L. L., & Lei, J. (2016). Empowering social change through advertising co-creation: The roles of source disclosure, sympathy and personal involvement. *International Journal of Advertising, 35*(1), 149–166.

Orazi, D. C., & Newton, F. J. (2018). Collaborative authenticity: How stakeholder-based source effects influence message evaluations in integrated care. *European Journal of Marketing, 52*(11), 2215–2231.

Pomeranz, Y. (2012). *Functional properties of food components.* Academic Press.

Rundle-Thiele, S., Schuster, L., Dietrich, T., Russell-Bennett, R., Drennan, J., Leo, C., & Connor, J. P. (2015). Maintaining or changing a drinking behaviour? GOKA's short-term outcomes. *Journal of Business Research, 68*(10), 2155–2163.

Schulze, M. B., Manson, J. E., Ludwig, D. S., Colditz, G. A., Stampfer, M. J., Willett, W. C., & Hu, F. B. (2004). Sugar-sweetened beverages, weight gain, and incidence of type 2 diabetes in young and middle-aged women. *Jama, 292*(8), 927–934.

Seiders, K., & Petty, R. D. (2004). Obesity and the role of food marketing: A policy analysis of issues and remedies. *Journal of Public Policy and Marketing, 23*(2), 153–169.

Stead, L. F., & Lancaster, T. (2000). A systematic review of interventions for preventing tobacco sales to minors. *Tobacco Control, 9*(2), 169–176.

Stigler, M. H., Neusel, E., & Perry, C. L. (2011). School-based programs to prevent and reduce alcohol use among youth. *Alcohol Research and Health, 34*(2), 157–162.

Stolerman, I. P., & Jarvis, M. J. (1995). The scientific case that nicotine is addictive. *Psychopharmacology, 117*(1), 2–10.

Strug, D. L., Priyadarsini, S., & Hyman, M. M. (1986). *Alcohol interventions: Historical and sociocultural approaches* (vol. 2). Haworth Press.

Thomas, D. M., Bouchard, C., Church, T., Slentz, C., Kraus, W. E., Redman, L. M., . . . Heymsfield, S. B. (2012). Why do individuals not lose more weight from an exercise intervention at a defined dose? An energy balance analysis. *Obesity Reviews: An Official Journal of the International Association for the Study of Obesity, 13*(10), 835–847.

US Food and Drug Administration. (2016). *Changes to the nutrition facts label.* Published online at: www.fda.gov/Food/GuidanceRegulation/Guidance DocumentsRegulatoryInformation/LabelingNutrition/ucm385663.htm. FDA, Silver Spring, MD

US Food and Drug Administration. (2018). *FDA in brief: FDA issues final rule to extend compliance date on updated nutrition facts label and serving size rules to allow industry more time to make required changes.* Retrieved from www. fda.gov/NewsEvents/Newsroom/FDAInBrief/ucm606436.htm

Verplanken, B., & Wood, W. (2006). Interventions to break and create consumer habits. *Journal of Public Policy and Marketing, 25*(1), 90–103.

Vohs, K. D., Baumeister, R. F., Schmeichel, B. J., Twenge, J. M., Nelson, N. M., & Tice, D. M. (2018). Making choices impairs subsequent self-control: A limited-resource account of decision making, self-regulation, and active initiative. In *Self-regulation and self-control* (pp. 45–77). United Kingdom: Routledge.

Volkow, N. D., Wang, G. J., Fowler, J. S., & Telang, F. (2008). Overlapping neuronal circuits in addiction and obesity: Evidence of systems pathology.

Philosophical Transactions of the Royal Society of London B: Biological Sciences, 363(1507), 3191–3200.

Wilks, D. C., Sharp, S. J., Ekelund, U., Thompson, S. G., Mander, A. P., Turner, R. M., . . . Lindroos, A. K. (2011). Objectively measured physical activity and fat mass in children: A bias-adjusted meta-analysis of prospective studies. *PLoS ONE, 6*(2), e17205.

7 Macro-Social Marketing and the Complexity of Value Co-Creation

Christine Domegan and Patricia McHugh

Introduction

Macro-social marketing deals with complex problems in a complex world. Working with this complexity becomes important to macro-social marketing if the quality of lives of citizens and societies is to be improved. Complexity is defined as the "*state of having many parts and being difficult to understand or find an answer to*" and complexities as the "*features of something that make it difficult to understand or find an answer to*" (Cambridge Dictionary, 2019). Complexity does not see individual behaviours as separate or discreet from their context, environment, or surrounding relationships and structures. Rather, an individual's behaviour is dependent on their daily lives, the way they live, and their relationships. In the same way that a single water molecule cannot express the wetness and viscosity of water, complexity, says the macro-social marketer, cannot isolate or reduce the person and their behaviours to a series of non-interacting events. Instead, complexity asks the macro-social marketer to take a holistic or systems perspective of a problem or issue where the interests of the individual, their community, and society are interrelated and adaptive (Layton, 2007, 2009, 2011, 2015). Complexity within a 'system' is made up of diverse citizens and stakeholder organisations interconnected and networked to produce their own patterns of behaviour over time. It is where the sum of the whole is greater than the sum of the parts, meaning the behaviour of different citizens and stakeholders within a context cannot be easily uncovered or predicted.

Complexity acknowledges the temporal and spatial distance between people, their behaviours, value exchanges, and their outcomes. Put another way, complexity in macro-social marketing sees value co-creation within communities and networks (Barrutia & Echebarria, 2013) partly as a result of differing micro, meso, and macro reactions and responses, and partly due to feedback or cumulative causation—a chain or loop of causes and effects between the actors in a system. As a result, there is "*room for multiple interpretations of value in parallel*" with dynamic complexity (Hillebrand, Driessen, & Koll, 2015, p. 414). One such example of multiple interpretations of value in parallel with dynamic complexity is Foresight's obesity map. The obesity map visualises the multiple value interpretations surrounding healthy eating and physical activity contextualised against food production, food consumption, biology, the activity environment, individual activity, psychology, and societal influences (Butland et al., 2007). What's evident are the interfaces between subsystems—food production with food consumption; the activity environment with an individual's activity—together with interfacing adjacent systems; the food system with the physical activity system. Healthy Victoria (Venturini, 2015) and WHO (2015) summarise the complexity of these interconnections and linkages as requiring a global approach with a local touch. For example, in the RARE Pride environmental campaigns, adaptive management is utilised to re-align upstream and downstream efforts regarding fish conservation demand and supply factors operating for fishermen, their families, the local council, shops, markets and schools, and members of the community (Jenks, Vaughan, & Butler, 2010).

For the macro-social marketer, complexity on the ground translates into three critical issues. First, there is a broadened stakeholder mindset. The complexity of macro-social marketing requires an understanding of a vast range of stakeholders, at macro, meso, and micro levels including citizens, all of whom have different lives, views, experiences, expectations, and needs. Second, while understanding stakeholders from a holistic or systems perspective is necessary, it is not sufficient. The issues tackled by macro-social marketing no longer lend themselves to single level, once-off solutions. A participation philosophy that is multifaceted and multilevel is central to transformative change. Thirdly, with the resolution of issues such as homelessness, marine pollution, fast fashion, obesity, and climate action no longer residing with one citizen, one stakeholder, or one organisational group, social value is about co-creating change and value co-creation is a process of co-discovering, co-designing, and co-delivering change.

This chapter examines the complexity of value co-creation for macro-social marketing and how it manifests through our understanding of societal or system stakeholders, our participation philosophy, and how both stakeholders and participation links to what we value, what we don't value, and the value co-creation process. By the end of this chapter you should be familiar with the idea of broadened or systems stakeholders, active participation philosophy, and the value co-creation process, and their relevance for macro-social marketing. Specifically you should understand:

- An expanded and **broadened view of stakeholders—systems or societal stakeholders**
- **Participation** and its philosophy around deeply active and collaborative actions

- The difference between 'Me' Values and 'Our' Values
- The importance of co-creating 'Our' Values and
- The importance of co-discovering, co-designing, and co-delivering new shared values into your macro-social marketing work.

A Broadened Stakeholder Perspective

In marketing, *"a single-minded focus on the customer to the exclusion of other stakeholders"* has become the new marketing myopia (Smith, Drumwright, & Gentile, 2010, p. 4; Kull, Mena, & Korschun, 2016). Similar to the customer-centric thinking in commercial marketing, historically social marketing received much criticism for its myopic tendencies to target only lay individuals in its behavioural programmes and interventions (Hastings, MacFayden, & Anderson, 2000; Andreasen, 2002; Gordon, 2013; Buyucek, Kubacki, Rundle-Thiele, & Pang, 2016). Given social marketing stimulates change in the *"social issues arena, stakeholders take on an even more important role in our considerations than they do commercially"* (Niblett, 2005, p. 11). Multiple authors (Hastings et al., 2000; Andreasen, 2002; Gordon, 2013; Buyucek et al., 2016) acknowledge the need for a broadened focus beyond lay individuals. This moves social marketing, as reflected in macro-social marketing in particular, towards systemic orientations, whereby intervention efforts target and infuse other stakeholders (Smith & Fischbacher, 2005; Gordon & Gurrieri, 2014; McHugh & Domegan, 2017) across the full ecosystem of society (Kennedy et al., 2017).

Traditional marketing perspectives analyse what the customer, as an independent entity, values as well as the economic benefits derived from an exchange for a company (Bagozzi, 1975). Customers and stakeholders were seen as equally important entities capable of creating and co-creating value, as opposed to customers taking primacy, as illustrated in Table 7.1. This first seminal shift towards stakeholders also derives

Table 7.1 Shifting Stakeholder Perspectives

Traditional Marketing Perspective	*Societal Stakeholder Perspective*
• The interests of stakeholders are viewed as independent	• The interests of stakeholders are viewed as interrelated
• Value perceptions of stakeholders are viewed as differing in importance, with customers taking primacy	• Acknowledging the value perceptions of multiple stakeholders is critical for success
• Value is viewed as created by the firm	• Value is viewed as co-created with a multitude of stakeholders
• Government & civil society as regulators of value creation	• Government & civil society as facilitators of value creation
• Management of stakeholders	• Managing for stakeholder relationships

Source: Adapted from Wasieleski and Weber (2017) and Hillebrand et al. (2015)

from Freeman (1984, p. 46) and management literature describing stakeholders as: *"any group or individual who can affect or is affected by the achievement of the organization's objectives"*. While Freeman's approach to defining stakeholders has the benefit of being comprehensive, its expansiveness has incurred the criticism of being difficult to implement (Kull et al., 2016), with Miles (2012, 2017) espousing that the concept of the 'stakeholder' continues to cause conceptual confusion and contestation. However, Freeman (1984) in his all-encompassing definition wanted marketers to move beyond traditional linear thinking, to contemplate 'who counts' and 'what really counts' for the fulfilment of both economic and social means, with only those who have no power (who cannot affect), claim, or relationship (are not affected by it) being excluded (Mitchell, Agle, & Wood, 1997).

The second seminal stakeholder shift, seen in the recent marketing and social science literature, positions stakeholders as interrelated. Rather than focus attention on one particular group of stakeholders, the inclusion of diverse networks of stakeholders has the potential to create more value and may result in improved commitment to economic, social, and behavioural means (Gummesson, 2008; Domegan, Collins, Stead, McHugh, & Hughes, 2013; Buyucek et al., 2016). This interrelated multiplicity gives rise to stakeholder marketing, defined by Hult, Mena, Ferrell, and Ferrell (2011, p. 57) as *"activities within a system of social institutions and processes for facilitating and maintaining value through exchange relationships with multiple stakeholders"*.

In essence, stakeholders in a macro-social marketing context embrace a system of stakeholders. This represents a dispersed spectrum of individuals and groups with common interests across geographical, political, resource, or social boundaries, and across subsystems. It assembles top-down/bottom-up, micro, meso, and macro levels (e.g., representatives of industry, professional associations, consumer and civil associations, leadership positions, decision makers, etc.) and cross-sectoral approaches (e.g., inland sectorial groups, local industrial sectors, local authorities and agencies, and non-profit government organisations—NGOs—including citizen associations and environmental organisations), that bring together different groups of people to enact change (Kennedy & Parsons, 2012; Brennan, Previte, & Fry, 2016; French & Gordon, 2015). This type of stakeholder interrelatedness extends beyond a traditional client focus and acknowledges multiple webs of stakeholder groups simultaneously affecting and affected by marketing and macro-social marketing environments (Gordon & Gurrieri, 2014; Buyucek et al., 2016; McHugh & Domegan, 2017).

It is evident that the thinking and contributions surrounding contemporary stakeholder marketing and analysis take a very collective approach. By taking this collective approach to defining stakeholders and their interests, theoretical progressions in macro-social marketing highlight a participative stakeholder capacity. Systems and stakeholders control assets, information, communications, and networks, and influence the success, or not, of an intervention. In most cases, their support is needed to implement change and create social value, and occasionally, they are the problem or barrier to the transformation sought. Stakeholders can *"perpetuate the problem, with multiple levels of interconnecting factors involved"* (Kennedy, 2017, p. 355). It is advised in these instances that differing and sometimes conflicting stakeholders' views and interests should be balanced to ensure attention is concurrently paid to the *"legitimate interests of all appropriate stakeholders"* (Donaldson & Preston, 1995, p. 67).

The Growing Importance of a Participation Philosophy

Bryson (2004, p. 24) argues that stakeholders, their participation, and analysis have never been more important due to the increasingly interconnected nature of the world with a heightened emphasis on *"markets, participation, flexibility and deregulation"*. Many of macro-social marketing's complex problems such as obesity, alcohol consumption, antibiotic resistance, climate change, and conservation encompass collective action and encourage individuals and groups to *"learn new skills, reflect on their social and economic conditions, and act in their collective interest, improving the ability of individual actors to understand and advance their capability to exert system-level influence"* (Hamby, Pierce, & Brinberg, 2016, p. 2).

Macro-social marketing problems are growing in number, complexity, and scale, and include multiple stakeholders with varying value (Kennedy et al., 2017). This intensifies the instinctively realistic need for macro-social marketers to develop greater stakeholder awareness and engagement. As Buyucek et al. (2016) state, a greater understanding of the stakeholders that need to be involved in a macro-social marketing process, the degree to which they are involved, and the role they play can yield powerful insights into why some interventions achieve desired behavioural change states and why others do not.

Applying stakeholder participation knowledge in macro-social marketing provides an impetus to understand stakeholders' existing values and motivations and work with them to develop mutually acceptable strategies for realising these (Hastings & Domegan, 2014; Gordon & Gurrieri, 2014). Stakeholder participation ensures that all potential groups and individuals who may be affected, involved, or have a partial responsibility to act are considered (Bryson, 2004). This kind of participation is about collaboration, empowerment, and direct active engagement with priority groups and audiences through all stages of a macro-social marketing intervention. Participation is about speaking and listening to people on their terms, being respectful of their views, experiences, needs, and wants. Participation goes significantly beyond just asking stakeholders, including citizens, for their opinions. It gives priority groups and audiences a voice in relation to the barriers to change, and ownership and responsibility for solutions to influence their welfare. Research is interactive; it is 'with' and not 'on' priority groups, audiences, and stakeholders.

Direct active participation with individuals, communities, and policy decision makers is the foundation for value co-creation and positive social outcomes. Community stakeholders are important since they have the ability to mobilise opinion, support, and engagement in favour of, or in opposition to, behavioural change actions (Hult et al., 2011). Active participation by multiple stakeholders, top down and bottom up, is more empowering because it reflects blended values, important to individuals themselves as well as the group dynamic, thereby enhancing joint decision making and co-ownership. Active participation provides the necessary dialogue, interaction, and mutual learning to manage and resolve highly complex issues, such as influencing human behaviour and the choices we make concerning a focal issue.

Attempts to influence behaviour should start with an understanding of the priority individuals and groups you want to do the changing. Macro-social marketers need to chart the stakeholders involved, their interactions, and work out why they do what they do at present, their values and motivations, and use this understanding to develop an offering that is equally appealing but with positive personal and/or social outcome (Layton, 2015; Kennedy et al., 2017). Stakeholder participation is central for co-creation, and successful behaviour change is built through a well-grounded understanding of current behaviour and the people engaged in it.

Stakeholder participation encourages macro-social marketers to tackle critical questions such as those posed by Miles (2012): Who are the stakeholders? How do stakeholders impact the focal issue? How does the focal issue impact the stakeholder? Why are the stakeholders being identified? What is the form of the stake? What is the nature of the stake and what does the stake relate to? We believe that it is in tackling these pertinent questions that a series of stakeholder participation protocols, with related sets of tasks, tools, and activities, are important practical tools for macro-social marketers to appropriately identify, classify, and map stakeholders across the focal macro-social marketing domains.

There are many different ways for citizens, policy makers, community associations, and other target stakeholders to participate in macro-social marketing. These range from social movements to education, law, structural change, and citizen science. Participation can be a form of informing citizens, creating awareness, and imparting knowledge, as found in education or citizen science. Participation can occur through consultation associated with formative research and audience insight using techniques such as focus groups and/or in-depth interviews with key stakeholders. Participation can also be concerned with collaboration, empowerment, and direct active engagement with target stakeholders through ALL stages of a macro-social marketing intervention. The movement is towards collaborating and empowering with citizens and citizen groups as seen in Figure 7.1.

The term 'participation' has come to represent the many ways in which consumers and producers might collaborate to create value for mutual benefit (Schau, Muñiz, & Arnould, 2009). The move to value co-creation is not the only antecedent for the recent interest in more collaborative, participatory ways of working in social marketing (Collins, Spotswood, & Manning, 2012; Bryant et al., 2007). A rich and instructive heritage is woven through a variety of disciplines in the social and health sciences, such as education (Freire, 2000; Kemmis & McTaggart, 2005), public health (Israel, Schulz, Parker, & Becker, 1998), community development (Fals-Borda & Rahman, 1991), theology (Berryman, 1987), and international development (Chambers, 1997; Hickey & Mohan, 2005). In the UK, policy makers' attention is turning ever more to concepts such as community engagement, which assumes public services that involve their users are likely to be of higher quality and more relevant to the communities they serve (SCDC, 2010), and co-production, which posits that *"people who use services contribute to the production of services"* and is based on the insight that service users bring expertise and assets which can help improve those services (Needham & Carr, 2009, p. 4). There is also growing interest in what has been termed the assets based or community capacities approach (El-Askari et al., 1998; Kretzmann & McKnight, 1996; Assets Alliance Scotland, 2010), focusing on a community's resources, skills, talents, and ideas for generating change, rather than on their needs and deficits (Sharpe, Greaney, Lee, & Royce, 2000).

These movements where people—citizens and other stakeholders—get directly involved in making change happen for their future is supported by Lefebvre (2011), who sees people as co-producers, collaborators,

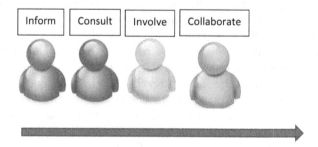

Figure 7.1 Levels of Participation Low to High participation to go with arrow flow Inform = low

Source: Adapted from McHugh, Domegan, and Santoro (2016) and Davies and Simon (2013)

facilitators, and co-learners with social marketers. Thus, value co-creation is relevant to macro-social marketing as social marketers:

- Need to understand what is of value to the target audience as well as stakeholders
- Work with the target audience and stakeholders to sense, respond, and experience new mutually acceptable value propositions while
- Jointly facilitating co-creation processes to realise these.

Furthermore, the macro-social marketer *"must also avoid this degenerating into manipulations"* (Hastings & Domegan, 2014) as value is multifaceted or reciprocal and is something that is experienced and phenomenological (Vargo & Lusch, 2008; Ballantyne, Williams, & Aitken, 2011a, 2011b).

Value Co-Creation in Macro-Social Marketing

At first glance, value co-creation seems to be highly compatible with macro-social marketing, both in theoretical terms and as an approach for designing and implementing programmes. According to Vargo and Lusch (2008, p. 6), value co-creation may be *"not only accommodative but potentially foundational"* to theory development in social marketing and is likely to have direct relevance to more general societal issues as well. The importance of value and value co-creation in macro-social marketing is captured by Lee and Kotler (2019, p. 7), who define social marketing as *"a process that applies marketing principles and techniques to create, communicate, and deliver value, in order to influence target audience behaviours that benefit society as well as the target audience"*. Thus, participants are engaged in joint analysis, development of strategy, and structured learning to achieve behavioural change. Participants in co-created projects are assumed to partake deliberately in exchange instead of being *"passive consumers of messages and programs"* (Lefebvre, 2009, p. 143). Further, value co-creation conceptually precedes and permeates every aspect of behavioural exchange (Lefebvre, 2009; Hastings & Domegan, 2014). In simple terms, the macro-social marketer is theorised as co-creating value in the form of dialogue, interaction, communication, and collaboration by facilitating target audiences into action to discover for themselves what desirable behaviours they are willing to adopt.

In addition to the fertile conceptual lens for theory building and testing offered by value co-creation, the potential benefits accruing from the active participation of the targeted stakeholders are starting to attract increasing levels of interest from macro-social marketers and from policy makers and programme designers in other fields. These benefits include 'consumer proofing' of interventions and an assumption of greater commitment to behavioural change (Holbrook, 1999; Jackson, 2005; Laczniak, 2006; Lefebvre, 2009; Hastings & Domegan, 2014). To this end it has been argued that third sector programmes *"designed and directed by community members, are far more likely to succeed than those planned and executed exclusively by outsiders"* (Bryant et al., 2007, p. 61).

Value co-creation theory in macro-social marketing rests upon people becoming direct and active participants in social change processes. Reiterating this theoretical point is fundamental: It is important for the macro-social marketer to distinguish between the target audiences' perception of the value that is created through interactions and shared value co-creation in macro-social marketing experiences (value-in-use) and the involvement of target audiences in co-creation processes (value-in-information and value-in-context). This conceptualisation of value co-creation moves macro-social marketing away from a 'power-over' managerial orientation to 'power-with', highly collaborative, and participatory processes around problem definition, programme design, and solutions (Prahalad & Venkat, 2004; Gronroos & Voima, 2013; Gummerus, 2013; Ind & Coates, 2013). It defines target audiences beyond the individual level as both clients and stakeholders. From this perspective, value co-creation in macro-social marketing can be *"a force for participation and democratisation that does create meaning for all, rather than simply an alternative research technique or a way of creating value through co-opting the skills and creativity of individuals"* (Ind & Coates, 2013, p. 92). This has the effect of opening up interactions, communications, power, and knowledge flows across and between micro, meso, and macro levels in society (Jaworski, Kohli, & Sahay, 2000; Chandler & Vargo, 2011). Target audiences for macro-social marketing value co-creation are not *"subjects of social problems or objects of social marketing projects"* (Brenkert, 2002, p. 21), that is, victims of circumstance, incapable of dealing with their own difficulties who assign responsibility for social problems to policy makers. Indeed, at the root of many unsuccessful initiatives is the failure of target audiences (clients and stakeholders) to take an active part in their own governance and a deliberative role in configuring both individual and collective value propositions. So, how might a value co-creation model in macro-social marketing integrate these concepts of value-in-use, value-in-context, and value-in-information? Authors (e.g., Vargo & Lusch, 2004; Sheth & Uslay, 2007; Chandler & Vargo, 2011; Hastings & Domegan, 2014) suggest such a value co-creation model would not be sequential but iterative in nature with value-in-use, value-in-context, and value-in-information occurring simultaneously within and across processes of co-discovery, co-design, and co-delivery.

Adopting Value Co-Creation to Close the Macro-Social Marketing Value Action Gaps

By adopting a stakeholders systems change orientation as one of three core directives for macro-social marketing, we use direct, active, meaningful participation to work on closing value-action gaps for different stakeholder groups at different levels of the system to bring about a more systemic change.

The Macro-Social Marketing Value Co-Creation Process

When talking about value, we discuss what we value and don't value. We equate value with money, price, quality, and cost. In the plural, 'values' take in high-minded principles—as in 'the values of a civilised society'. We know value is individualised and subjective, based upon experiences, actual and perceived. For example, the subjective nature of value is reflected when we talk about physical activity as fun for young children, exercise for the 30+, fitness for the 40+, and wellness for the 50+. Value cannot and does not have a single meaning. Value also presents complexity for anyone working in macro-social marketing because target groups, policy makers, stakeholders, competitors, and funders all have different values. Moreover, these diverse outlooks can seem like chalk and cheese. Think of the doctor who sees surfing as a valuable health advantage and the teenager who uses surfing to have fun, to impress, to be accepted, and to 'be cool', or as a way to rebel against the establishment and parents. This highlights one last important aspect of value—its collective generation within families, friendship groups, communities, and societies (Alderson, 1957).

Link the notion of value/values to macro-social marketing with its system thinking and societal stakeholder involvement and we are talking about people needing to get directly involved in their own futures. The values we hold and put on things are vital to this process. It will come as no surprise that macro-social marketing offerings understand existing values and then work to develop mutually acceptable new values and ways of realising sustainable change. Values are universal and explain motivations behind attitudes, actions, and behaviour. The failure to convert values into actions represents the value-action gap (Kollmuss & Agyeman, 2002). A value-action gap is a mismatch between a person's values/attitudes and behaviour or, put another way, the difference between what people say and what people do.

Value action gaps underlie most environmental and health behaviours, including the U.N.'s 17 sustainable development goals and the WHO's 'health is everyone's business'. Simply put, macro-social marketing and sustainable change are about closing different value-action gaps through active participation by individuals, communities, and policy decision makers at different levels within the system. Participation provides the necessary dialogue, interaction, and mutual learning between different macro-social marketing stakeholders to leverage and resolve complex issues. The task for the macro-social marketer is to work out why they do what they do at present, their values and motivations, and use this understanding to co-develop an offering that is equally appealing but with positive personal and/or social outcomes. Closing different value-action gaps using collaborative participation can be done through societal stakeholder value co-creation. Value co-creation is a process that can be broken down into value co-discovery, value co-design, and value co-delivery for empowered participation (Kollmuss & Agyeman, 2002; McArdle, 2015).

Value Co-Discovery

Value co-discovery is about genuine in-depth relationships with your system stakeholders. Active, versus passive, participation is more empowering because it reflects values important to active stakeholder communities for stakeholder and community participation. Value co-discovery empowers your system stakeholders in the same way, as the co-storyteller of the improved system. The system stakeholders become dynamic and equal in developing a deep understanding of experiences and the problem faced. Value co-discovery's essence lies in building relationships with the target stakeholders, who provide the necessary dialogue, interaction, and mutual learning.

Value Co-Design

Value co-design takes this full and intensely deep understanding of your system stakeholders, worked out in partnership with them, and captures it in jointly designed offerings, products, services, delivery mechanisms, solutions, and interventions. It is action orientated and about manifesting different value propositions for different stakeholders. The aim is to ensure all stakeholders have a win-win outcome—no one stakeholder group gets all of what they want, but all stakeholders get some of what is needed for progress.

Value Co-Delivery

With value co-delivery, the coordinating mechanism around shared values comes into operation, which means front-line people are important at this point. Public policy, technology, infrastructure, and media are relevant too. The macro marketing system stakeholders have to facilitate the manifestation of the new shared friendly values or they cannot come into being. In its simplest form, value co-delivery is about the systems factors beyond the control of individuals that block or facilitate the materialisation of new shared values.

For an example of value co-creation in action, see the 'Waves of Freedom' initiative (http://wavesoffreedom.org/#about-us). 'Waves of Freedom' is a non-profit organisation that utilises surfing to empower and transform women and girls into *"self-advocates and empowered change-makers in their community and beyond"*. When Easkey Britton and Marion Poizeau travelled to Iran to surf, they wanted to explore how women in Iran could get to the water and surf. They connected with pioneering Iranian sportswomen and co-created, co-designed, and co-delivered an initiative to empower women through surfing.

The value co-creation process closes value-action gaps and is all about the need to build critical capacity with policy makers, regulators, media, educators, and citizens around values and behaviours. For critical capacity to occur, macro-social marketing offerings must engage in 'value co-discovery' to understand the system stakeholders and their lived experiences, analysing their subjective values through attitudes, beliefs, knowledge, motivations, and current behaviours. Together, macro-social marketers and the system stakeholders carry out 'value co-design' to capture new meanings relevant to the problem through jointly devised product, service, price, place, partnership, policy, and promotion offerings. In 'value co-delivery', both the system stakeholders and macro-social marketing partners factor in the system's role in the new potential behaviours and associated values. The system either blocks or empowers individuals to alter their behaviours.

The 3Cs of value co-creation—Figure 7.2—are about *"critical capacity building and connecting, are mutually dependent: regulation without public support is severely weakened, whilst a politician's inclination to regulate is greatly increased by popular demand – and both are aided and abetted by effective co-created offerings"* (Hastings, 2015, p. 22)

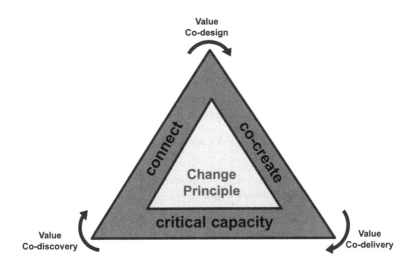

Figure 7.2 The 3 Cs Model of Value Co-Creation

Source: Adapted from Hastings and Domegan (2014) and Hastings, (2015)

Implementing a Value Co-Creation Process

Implementing a value co-creation process in macro-social marketing strategy involves a number of tasks and tools, summarised in Table 7.2. Each of these is unpacked subsequently.

Identify 'Me' Values and 'Our' Values

The first step is to identify 'Me' Values and 'Our' Values. 'Me' Values benefit an individual and are dependent upon the perceptions of others. 'Me' Values reflect self-interested only goals such as personal status, material wealth, or power. 'Me' Values are self-enhancing and importantly within the context of our work, can suppress common interests. 'Our' Values take into consideration the outcomes of our actions and can sometimes be viewed as the opposite of, or an extension of 'Me' Values. 'Our' Values integrate common interests such as a "*sense of community, affiliation to friends and family, and self-development*" (Crompton, 2010, p. 7). Figure 7.3 identifies 10 universal groups of values relevant to macro-social marketing work.

'Our' Values reflect common interests, where individuals are concerned with themselves *and* with others. These motivations and values cannot be fully expressed in economic terms. 'Me' Values, on the other hand, place less emphasis on common interests, displaying lower levels of motivation and responsibility for change that results in societal and environmental wellbeing. 'Me' Values are normally expressed in economic terms. For macro-social marketing, it's important to reflect upon 'Me' and 'Our' Values that can act in direct opposition with one another as

Table 7.2 Aims, Tasks, and Tools

I want to. . .	My tasks are to. . .	Tools I can use are. . .
Contain harmful 'Me' Values and co-create 'Our' Values for macro-social marketing change	Identify harmful 'Me' Values for containment	Tool 1.1 Identify 'Me' Values and 'Our' Values
	Identify 'Our' Values for change	Tool 1.1 Identify 'Me' Values and 'Our' Values
	Map the relative importance between harmful 'Me' Values and important 'Our' Values	Tool 1.2 Rank the Relative Importance of 'Me' Values and 'Our' Values
	Identify structural issues that encourage harmful 'Me' Values and/or block co-creating 'Our' Values	Tool 1.3 Values and Behaviours
	Build critical capacity	

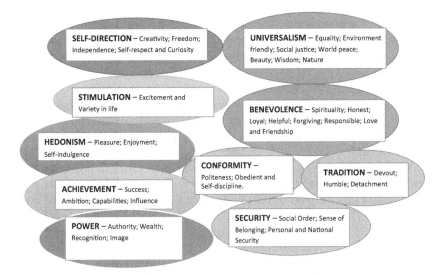

Figure 7.3 'Me' Values and 'Our' Values

Source: Adapted from Holmes, T., Blackmore, E., Hawkins, R. and Wakeford, T. (2011)

seen in Figure 7.3. For instance, if an individual stakeholder considers community feeling to be important, they are less likely to emphasise self-interested values such as wealth and authority.

Self-enhancement values such as the attainment of wealth, personal status, and success, are directly opposed to or suppress self-transcendence type values such as the wellbeing of others. Independence and readiness for change suppress conservation values such as order, honour, and the preservation of the past. The identification of 'Me' and 'Our' Values in macro-social marketing is critical in motivating collective action and responsibility. In macro-social marketing, some values will tend to occur together, e.g., hedonism, achievement, and power, while others will tend not to occur at the same time, e.g., conformity and stimulation.

Since macro-social marketing addresses bigger-than-self problems/issues, citizens and stakeholders that "*attach greater importance to self-enhancement and conservation values (particularly power and security) are found to be less concerned about environmental damage, less likely to behave in environmentally friendly ways, and less likely to engage politically*" (Crompton, 2010, p. 12). There are two take away messages here:

(1) Be a disciplined macro-social marketing thinker about values; do value inquiry work; and
(2) The strength of 'Me' Values, *relative* to 'Our' values, can speed up or slow down macro-social marketing value co-creation processes.

A Word of Caution

Watch out for complexity. We all have 'Me' and 'Our' Values at work in our daily lives, for example, a financial incentive ('Me' Value) to purchase a bike to cycle to work ('Our' Value). What's important to macro-social marketing and value co-creation is the *relative importance* and motivations behind the 'Me' Values and 'Our' Values. For example, short-term financial rewards reinforce 'Me' Values at the cost of long-term sustainable 'Our' Values. So, it is critical that macro-social marketing value co-creation offerings identify 'Me' Values whilst also co-creating strong 'Our' Values.

What we are seeing is a link between 'Me' and 'Our' Values and how we behave. However, people don't always walk the walk, that is, people have values that they hold to be important but often times, they can fail to practise what they preach (Crompton, 2010). For example, Mary may be concerned with environmental issues ('Our' Values, universalism), but she may still dump her rubbish at the beach because she doesn't like the smell of rubbish in her car ('Me' Value, conformity); John might be concerned with the depleting fish stocks ('Our' Values, universalism), but he may still eat unsustainably caught fish because it's cheaper to buy ('Me' Value, achievement). One of the reasons why stakeholders do not always act in accordance with their values is due to structural constraints. In the previous examples, Mary might also have left the rubbish at the beach because there are no immediate litter bins; while John is concerned with the depleting fish stocks, he still eats unsustainably caught fish because this is what is available in his local fishmonger's.

As a macro-social marketer, you also need to think about potential structural constraints that may restrict people from acting in accordance with their values and how these blockages may be overcome. This is all about the need to build critical capacity with the system stakeholders—our policy makers, regulators, media, educators, and target citizens around values and behaviours. For critical capacity to occur, macro-social marketing offerings must engage in 'value co-discovery' to understand stakeholders and their lived experiences, analysing their subjective values through attitudes, beliefs, knowledge, motivations, and current behaviours. Together, macro-social marketers and their stakeholders carry out 'value co-design' to capture new meanings relevant to the problem through jointly devised product, service, price, place, partnership, policy, and promotion offerings.

Summary

Achieving desired social change states sought by macro-social marketing requires a greater understanding of the complexities of our lives in our complex world. First, a broadened stakeholder mindset is needed that is an interactive and iterative method emphasising deliberations among citizens, and various micro, meso, and macro stakeholder organisations and macro-social marketers with the purpose of contributing meaningfully to the positive social outcomes (Powell & Colin, 2008). Broadened or system stakeholders ensure that the road of change is travelled together. The use and application of the protocols for stakeholder participation is an example of how processes can ensure those who are key, who count, and who have a stake are involved in the design and delivery of behavioural and social change states. It must be acknowledged that a broadened stakeholder mindset is not easy and it takes time. However, a dedication to the stakeholders in the amalgamation of a stakeholder group, who are both critics and creators of change, can bring new, creative, and innovative thinking to the focal issue or opportunities under investigation. Learning and reflecting upon the strengths and weaknesses of the stakeholders is critical. Reflexivity shapes experiences, insights, and knowledge, which in turn can improve future stakeholder participation decisions, actions, and behaviours (McHugh & Domegan, 2017).

Second, a participation philosophy moves macro-social marketing programmes and interventions beyond dyadic exchanges to system collaborations, empowering and mobilising multiple stakeholders across networks of value co-creating communities to achieve social value. Stakeholders move from passive observers to active contributors for change. To maintain and grow a participation philosophy, mutual benefit, shared values, and communication are needed (Hastings & Domegan, 2014). The establishment of trust is important, which can be limited, evolutionary, or relational, depending on an engagement strategy chosen for stakeholder participation. Deep participation associated with macro-social marketing needs does not evolve overnight. Time is needed to turn trust into commitment (Duane & Domegan, 2018) and to establish contact points, repeated interactions, and networks in order to co-create meaningful value exchanges.

Third, value co-creation allows stakeholders from different backgrounds, contexts, and expertise the opportunity to co-discover, co-design, and co-deliver change (Hastings & Domegan, 2014). An aspect worth considering is the systems dynamic of changing stakeholder relations as a result of co-creation. Working with individuals outside of a traditional silo blurs the boundaries of tacit knowledge. Stakeholders through the process of co-creation can change previously held assumptions, ideas, and values, their material interests may change, and institutional support and practices may alter (Friedman & Miles, 2002). A common issue arising from stakeholder participation is the existence of tension and conflict between individuals or groups of stakeholders. Hillebrand et al. (2015, p. 418) advocate paradoxical thinking when conflict arises. Paradoxical thinking in macro-social marketing encourages critical debate and dialogue to allow stakeholders the opportunity to voice their views and concerns, rather than *"ignore or suppress the tension"*. As a result, stakeholders get time to *"reflect on the tension to reach a joint solution that may not be perfect to all, but where all stakeholders still perceive some benefit"*. Theoretically and managerially, the world is an imperfect place and macro-social marketing, born of its complexity, operates there.

References

Alderson, W. (1957). *Marketing behaviour and executive action, a functional approach to marketing theory*. Homewood, IL: Richard D. Irwin Inc.

Andreasen, A., (2002). Marketing social marketing in the social change marketplace. *Journal of Public Policy and Marketing, 21*(1), 3–13.

Assets Alliance Scotland. (2010). *Assets alliance Scotland*. Scotland: Scottish Government/Scottish Community Development Centre (SCDC)/Long-Term Conditions Alliance Scotland (LTCAS). Retrieved from www.scdc.org.uk/news/article/Assets-alliance-scotland-report/

Bagozzi, R. P. (1975, October). Marketing as exchange. *Journal of Marketing, 39*, 32–29.

Ballantyne, D., Frow, P., Varey, R. J., & Payne, A. (2011b). Value propositions as communications practice: Taking a wider view. *Industrial Marketing Management, 40*(2), 202–210.

Ballantyne, D., Willams, J., & Aitken, R. (2011a). Introduction to service dominant logic: From proposition to practice. *Industrial Marketing Management, 40*(2), 179–180.

Barrutia, J., & Echebarria, C. (2013). Networks: A social marketing tool. *European Journal of Marketing, 47*(1–2), 324–343.

Berryman, P. (1987). *Liberation theology: Essential facts about the revolutionary movement in Latin America and beyond*. Philadelphia, PA: Temple University Press.

Brenkert, G. (2002, Spring). Ethical challenges of social marketing. *Journal of Public Policy and Marketing, 21*, 14–25.

Brennan, L., Previte, J., & Fry, M-L. (2016). Social marketing's consumer myopia. *Journal of Social Marketing, 6*(3), 219–239.

Bryant, C. A., McCormack Brown, K. R., McDermott, R. J., Forthofer, M. S., Bumpus, E. C., Calkins, S. A., et al. (2007). Community-based prevention marketing: Organizing a community for health behaviour intervention. *Health Promotion Practice, 8*, 154–163.

Bryson, J. M. (2004). What to do when stakeholders matter? *Public Management Review, 6*(1), 21–53.

Butland, B., Jebb, S., Kopelman, P., McPherson, K., Thomas, S., Mardell, F., & Parry, V. (2007). *Tackling obesities: Future choices – Project report*. London, UK: Foresight – Government Office for Science.

Buyucek, N., Kubacki, K., Rundle-Thiele, S., & Pang, B. (2016). A systemic review of stakeholder involvement in social marketing interventions. *Australasian Marketing Journal, 24*(1), 8–19.

Cambridge Dictionary. Retrieved March 24, 2019, from https://dictionary.cambridge.org/dictionary/english/complexity?q=Complexity

Chambers, R. (1997). *Whose reality counts? Putting the first last*. London: Intermediate Technology Publications.

Chandler, J. D., & Vargo, S. L. (2011). Contextualisation and value-in-context: How context frames exchange. *Marketing Theory*, *11*(1), 35–49.

Collins, K., Spotswood, F., & Manning, L. (2012). *Poverty, power and politics: Considerations for engaging citizens in social marketing programmes: Using social marketing to deliver effective and efficient citizen focused social programmes*. European Social Marketing Conference, Lisbon, Portugal.

Crompton, T. (2010). *Common cause the case for working with our cultural values*. Retrieved from http://valuesandframes.org/

Davies, A. & Simon, J. (2013). Engaging Citizens in Social Innovation: A short guide to the research for policy makers and practitioners. A deliverable of the project: "The theoretical, empirical and policy foundations for building social innovation in Europe" (TEPSIE), European Commission – 7th Framework Programme, Brussels: European Commission, DG Research.

Domegan, C., Collins, K., Stead, M., McHugh, P., & Hughes, T. (2013). Value co-creation in social marketing: Functional or fanciful? *Journal of Social Marketing*, *3*(3), 239–256.

Donaldson, T., & Preston, L. E. (1995). The stakeholder theory of the corporation: Concepts, evidence, and implications. *Academy of Management Review*, *20*, 65–91.

Duane, S., & Domegan, C. (2019). Social marketing partnerships: Substance and scope. *Marketing Theory*. Vol. 19, no. 2, pp. 169–194.

El-Askari, G., Freestone, J., Irizarry, C., Kraut, K. L., Mashiyama, S. T., Morgan, M. A., & Walton, S. (1998). The healthy neighbourhoods project: A local health department's role in catalyzing community development. *Health Education and Behaviour*, *25*(2), 146–159.

Fals-Borda, O., & Rahman, M. A. (1991). *Action and knowledge: Breaking the monopoly with participatory action research*. London: Intermediate Technology Publications.

Freeman, R. E. (1984). *Strategic management: A stakeholder approach*. Boston, MA: Pitman.

Freire, P. (2000). *Pedagogy of the oppressed*. London: Continuum International Publishing Group.

French, J., & Gordon, R. (2015). *Strategic social marketing*. Thousand Oaks, CA: Sage Publications Ltd.

Friedman, A. L., & Miles, S. (2002). Developing stakeholder theory. *Journal of Management Studies*, *39*(1), 1–21.

Gordon, R., (2013). Unlocking the potential of upstream social marketing. *European Journal of Marketing*, *47*(9), 1525–1547.

Gordon, R., & Gurrieri, L. (2014). Towards a reflexive turn: Social marketing assemblages. *Journal of Social Marketing*, *4*(3), 261–278.

Gronroos, C., & Voima, P. (2013). Critical service logic: Making sense of value creation and co-creation. *Academy of Marketing Science*, *41*(2), 133–150.

Gummerus, J. (2013). Value creation processes and value outcomes in marketing theory: Strangers or siblings? *Marketing Theory*, *13*(1), 19–46.

Gummesson, E. (2008). Extending the service-dominant logic: From customer centricity to balanced centricity. *Journal of the Academy of Marketing Science*, *36*, 15–17.

Hamby, A., Pierce, M., Daniloski, K., & Brinberg, D. (2016). The use of participatory action research to create a positive youth development program. *Social Marketing Quarterly*, *17*(3), 2–17.

Hastings, G. (2015). Public health and the value if disobedience. *Public Health*, *129*(8), 1046–1054.

Hastings, G., & Domegan, C. (2014). *Social marketing from tunes to symphonies* (2nd ed.). London: Routledge.

Hastings, G., MacFadyen, L., & Anderson, S. (2000). Whose behavior is it anyway? The broader potential of social marketing. *Social Marketing Quarterly*, *6*(2), 46–58.

Hickey, S., & Mohan, G. (2005). Relocating participation within a radical politics of development. *Development and Change*, *36*(2), 237–262.

Hillebrand, B., Driessen, P., & Koll, O. (2015). Stakeholder marketing: Theoretical foundations and required capabilities. *Journal of the Academy of Marketing Science*, *43*, 411–428.

Holbrook, M. (1999). Introduction to consumer value. In M. Holbrook (Ed.), *Consumer value: A framework for analysis and research* (pp. 1–28). London: Routledge.

Holmes, T., Blackmore, E., Hawkins, R., & Wakeford, T. (2011). *The common cause handbook*. UK: Public Interest Research Centre. Retrieved from http://valuesandframes.org/

Hult, G. T., Mena, J. A., Ferrell, O. C., & Ferrell, L. (2011). Stakeholder marketing: A definition and conceptual framework. *Academy of Marketing Science Review*, *1*, 44–65.

Ind, N., & Coates, N. (2013). The meanings of co-creation. *European Business Review*, *25*(1), 86–95.

Israel, B. A., Schulz, A. J., Parker, E. A., & Becker, A. B. (1998). Review of community-based research: Assessing partnership approaches to improve public health. *Annual Review of Public Health*, *19*, 173–202.

Jackson, T. (2005). *Motivating sustainable consumption: A review of evidence on consumer behaviour and behavioural change*. A Report to the Sustainable Development Research Network. UK: DEFRA.

Jaworski, B., Kohli, A. K., & Sahay, A. (2000). Market-driven versus driving markets. *Journal of the Academy of Marketing Science*, *28*(1), 45–54.

Jenks, B., Vaughan, P. W., & Butler, P. J. (2010). The evolution of rare pride: Using evaluation to drive adaptive management in a biodiversity conservation organization. *Evaluation and Program Planning*, *33*, 186–190.

Kemmis, S., & McTaggart, R. (2005). Participatory action research. In N. K. Denzin & Y. S. Lincoln (Eds.), *The Sage handbook of qualitative research* (3rd ed., pp. 559–605). London: Sage Publications Inc.

Kennedy, A-M. (2017). Macro-social marketing research: Philosophy, methodology and methods. *Journal of Macromarketing*, *37*(4), 347–355.

Kennedy, A-M., & Parsons, A. (2012). Macro-social marketing and social engineering: A systems approach. *Journal of Social Marketing*, *2*(1), 37–51.

Kennedy, Ann-Marie, Sommer Kapitan, Neha Bajaj, Angelina Bakonyi and Sean Sands (2017). "Uncovering wicked problem's system structure: seeing the forest for the trees", *Journal of Social Marketing*, *7*(1), 51–73.

Kollmuss, A., & Agyeman, J. (2002). Mind the gap: Why do people act environmentally and what are the barriers to pro-environmental behavior? *Environmental Education Research*, *8*(3), 239–260.

Kretzmann, J., & McKnight, J. P. (1996). Assets-based community development. *National Civic Review*, *85*(4), 23–29.

Kull, A. J., Mena, J. A., & Korschun, D. (2016). A resource-based view of stake-holder marketing. *Journal of Business Research*, 69, 5553–5560.

Laczniak, G. R. (2006). Some societal and ethical dimensions of the service-dominant logic perspective of marketing. In R. F. Lusch & S. L. Vargo (Eds.), *The service dominant logic of marketing: Dialog, debate and directions* (pp. 279–285). New York, NY: M. E. Sharpe, Inc.

Layton, R. A. (2007). Marketing systems: A core macromarketing concept. *Journal of Macromarketing*, 27(3), 227–242.

Layton, R. A. (2009). On economic growth, marketing systems, and the quality of life. *Journal of Macromarketing*, 29(4), 349–362.

Layton, R. A. (2011). Towards a theory of marketing systems. *European Journal of Marketing*, 45(1–2), 259–276.

Layton, R. A. (2015). Formation, growth and adaptive change in marketing systems. *Journal of Macromarketing*, 35(3), 302–319.

Lee, N., & Kotler, P. (2019). *Social marketing: Changing behaviors for good* (6th ed.). Los Angeles, CA: Sage Publications.

Lefebvre, C. R. (2009). Notes from the field: The change we need: New ways of thinking about social issues. *Social Marketing Quarterly*, 15, 142–144.

Lefebvre, C. R. (2011). An integrative model for social marketing. *Journal of Social Marketing*, 1, 54–72.

McArdle, M. (2015). *Closing the recycling loop – Values and reasons in the value-action gap for recycled products*. 18th Annual Irish Academy of Management Conference, National University of Ireland, Galway.

McHugh, P., & Domegan, C. (2017). Evaluate development! Develop evaluation! Answering the call for a reflexive turn in social marketing. *Journal of Social Marketing*, 7(2), 135–155.

McHugh, P., Domegan, C. & Santoro, F. (2016). Sea Change Co-Creation Participation Protocol for Work Package 5 – Governance, EU Sea Change Project, Whitaker Institute, NUI Galway, Ireland.

Miles, S. (2012). Stakeholder: Essentially contested or just confused? *Journal of Business Ethics*, 108, 285–298.

Miles, S. (2017). Stakeholder theory classification: A theoretical and empirical evaluation of definitions. *Journal of Business Ethics*, 142, 437–459.

Mitchell, R. K., Agle, B. R., & Wood, D. J. (1997). Toward a theory of stakeholder identification and salience: Defining the principle of who and what really counts. *Academy of Management Review*, 22(4), 853–886.

Needham, C., & Carr, S. (2009). Retrieved from www.developbromley.com/public/SelfDirectedSupport/Tools/SCIE.Research.Briefing.31.pdf

Niblett, G. R. (2005). Stretching the limits of social marketing partnerships, upstream and downstream: Setting the context for the 10th innovations in social marketing conference. *Social Marketing Quarterly*, 11, 9–15.

Powell, M., & Colin, M. (2008). Meaningful citizen engagement in science and technology: What would it really take? *Science Communication*, 30(1), 126–136.

Prahalad, C., & Venkat, R. (2004). Co-creating unique value with customers. *Strategy and Leadership*, 32(3), 4–9.

SCDC – Scottish Community Development Centre. (2010). *Community engagement . . . encouraging productive relationships between communities and public bodies*. Retrieved March 19, 2013, from www.scdc.org.uk/community-engagement/

Schau, H. J., Muñiz, A. M., & Arnould, E. J. (2009). How brand community practices create value. *Journal of Marketing, 73*(5), 30–51.

Sharpe, P. A., Greaney, M. L., Lee, P. R., & Royce, S. W. (2000). Assets-oriented community assessment. *Public Health Reports, 115*(2–3), 205–211.

Sheth, J. N., & Uslay, C. (2007). Implications of the revised definition of marketing: From exchange to value creation. *Journal of Public Policy and Marketing, 26*(2), 302–307.

Smith, A. M., & Fischbacher, M. (2005). New service development: A stakeholder perspective. *European Journal of Marketing, 39*(9–10), 1025–1048.

Smith, N. C., Drumwright, M. E., & Gentile, M. C. (2010). The new marketing myopia. *Journal of Public Policy and Marketing, 29*(1), 4–11.

Vargo, S. L., & Lusch, R. F. (2004). "Evolving to a New Dominant Logic for Marketing," *Journal of Marketing, 68*(1), 1–17.

Vargo, S. L., & Lusch, R. L. (2008). Service-dominant logic: Continuing the evolution. *Journal of the Academy of Marketing Science, 36*, 1–10.

Venturini, R. (2015). *Social marketing in a systems intervention: Healthy together Victoria* (pp. 148–152). World Social Marketing Conference, Sydney Australia. Retrieved April 19–21, 2015, from http://wsmconference.com/wp-content/uploads/2015/04/WSM-2015-Proceedings-book.pdf

Wasieleski, D., & Weber, J. (Ed.). (2017). *Stakeholder management (Business and society 360, Volume 1)*. Bingley, UK: Emerald Publishing Limited.

World Health Organisation. (2015). *Tailoring immunization programmes for seasonal influenza (TIP FLU), a guide for increasing health care workers' uptake of seasonal influenza vaccination*. Denmark: WHO Regional Office of Europe.

8 Social Marketing's Contribution to Macro-Social Policy and Economics, Beyond Upstream, Midstream, and Downstream Analysis

Jeff French

Introduction

The chapter starts with a discussion about the nature of the contribution that social marketing can make to social policy selection, development implementation, and evaluation. The complementary nature of social marketing, social sciences, and other forms of understanding about how to construct and deliver programmes designed to increase personal and social wellbeing is also considered.

Moving beyond these operational considerations, the chapter next focuses on the limitations of the 'stream' metaphor in social marketing and makes an argument about the need to develop social marketing theory to encompass how fundamental ideological and macroeconomic assumptions shape policy selection and their implementation, along with social marketing's contribution to this. The chapter explores some of the fundamental economic, philosophical, and ideological drivers of social policy and its implementation and how social marketing can, and is, contributing to these debates and to both social progress and wealth creation.

The chapter concludes with the setting out and discussion of a social marketing systems map that illustrates key factors and issues that need to be addressed when considering or assessing the contribution that social marketing can make to informing macro, meso, or micro economic policy and how the concepts of up, mid, and downstream social marketing can be understood in this context.

Social Marketing's Contribution to Social Policy Selection and Delivery

As Biroscak (2018) states:

> Awareness seems to be at an all-time high regarding the potential use of social marketing to stimulate behaviour change through improving policies, systems and macro- environmental factors.

(p. 27)

Social marketing theory and practice has expanded over recent years to encompass the added value, in terms of both effectiveness and efficiency, of applying social marketing principles beyond the design of better intervention projects. Social marketing contributions at policy selection, policy development, and strategy building stages of social policy (French & Gordon, 2015, Hastings & Domegan, 2018) are now well documented. A key aspect of adopting such an expanded conception of social marketing's contribution, or what has been termed 'Strategic Social Marketing' (French & Gordon, 2015), is the belief based on evidence that social marketing can make valuable contributions to social policy selection, policy development, and strategy development as well as more traditional contributions towards implementation development, management, and evaluation. Examples of such interventions are now being increasingly reported (Borden, Cohn, & Gooderham, 2018; Rubenstein et al., 2018). Strategic social marketing is concerned with contributing to all social policy development regardless of any direct marketing activity that may be associated within it. Conceived in this way 'strategic social marketing' has been defined as:

> The systemic, critical and reflexive application of social marketing principals to enhance social policy selection, objective setting, planning and operational delivery.
>
> (French & Gordon, 2015, p. 134)

As can be inferred from the preceding definition, 'strategic social marketing' is concerned with informing policy selection based on what we know about developing successful interventions, strategic goal setting, assisting with the process of determining how success will be measured, and ensuring that the right mix of interventions is selected and managed. Social marketing also has a critical role to play in ensuring that understanding and insights about the beliefs, values, and needs of citizens, community leaders, stakeholders, politicians, and professionals are captured, analysed, and fed into the policy selection and development process. The input of citizens' views about what policy imperatives exist and how to prioritise among these is a process that most politicians and policy makers understand and seek to address. Social marketing can assist with the collection and analysis of citizen understanding, views, needs, and behaviour. Through this process, social marketing can help to inform the development of achievable and acceptable behavioural objectives. Social marketing can also help policy makers with the development of targeted intervention strategies consisting of the optimum mix of intervention and by assisting with policy and strategy, impact evaluation, and assessment of the return on social investment.

All social marketing is centred on an approach to problem definition and solution generation that is built around understanding and creating social good that is valued by citizens. Adopting a strategic social marketing approach also recognises that there are multiple 'Types' and 'Forms' of intervention (French, 2011b) that can be applied. Taking a strategic social marketing approach recognises that action will be required to be directed at the causal conditions of social problems as well as the provision of direct support for individuals and families to assist them to adopt or sustain positive social behaviours. Table 8.1 summarises some of the main contributions social marketing can make to the policy making process.

At its core, strategic social marketing seeks to influence social policy selection, development, and programme delivery to reflect citizens' wants, needs, and values. Social marketing can be used in this way to ensure that understanding about participants' behaviour and preferences directly informs the identification and selection of appropriate social issues, policy, and interventions. Any social policy seeking to influence citizen behaviour that does not have the broad support of the public and does not meet the needs of the target audiences is unlikely to be successful. There is a need then, if successful social programmes are to be developed, to engender a sense of ownership among intended recipients and stakeholders. Delivering any social policy also needs the involvement of the widest possible coalition of interests if a sense of ownership is to be created and if all available expertise and resources are to be used to

Table 8.1 How Social Marketing Assists Social Issue Selection, Policy, and Strategy Development

1. Setting clear, measurable policy objectives and targets.
2. Collection and analysis of citizen behaviour, and causes of behaviour, understanding views and needs about potential social behavioural challenges.
3. Situational and environmental analysis, including PESTLE (Political, Environmental, Social, Technological, Legal, Economic) and SWOT (Strengths, Weaknesses, Opportunities, Threats) and competition analysis.
4. Gathering citizens' views on the evidence regarding the acceptability, costs, and value of possible policy and potential tactics to influence behaviour.
5. Stakeholder, partnership, and assets analysis and management.
6. Informing programme design and highlighting potential intervention approaches based on theory and evidence reviews, user experience, and feedback.
7. Development, prototyping, and pre-testing of services, products, campaigns, and other interventions.
8. Audience and stakeholder insight and segmentation development.
9. Understanding and formulating the most cost effective and acceptable mix of behavioural influence strategies and tactics.
10. Modelling and measuring impact, outcome costs, and gains, including ROI, VFM, and cost-benefit analysis.

Source: French and Gordon (2015)

inform the development and delivery of the policy. Social marketing has a role to play in creating this sense of ownership and buy-in to social policies. Social marketing can also help politicians and public officials to test potential policies and refine them through a process of target audience engagement and consultation as well as through a process of market research, prototype testing, and piloting.

The Complementary Nature of Social Marketing, Social Science, Behavioural Economics, and Other Forms of Social Influence

In recent times the application of a broad range of social science theory has been used by a growing number of policy makers to augment and inform the development of social policy implementation. An example of this application is what has been called 'behavioural economics'. Behavioural economics draws on understanding from a mixture of social-psychology, sociology, evolutionary psychology, economics biology, brain science, and related fields of study. It uses this insight to develop interventions that seek to influence evolved and learnt human preferences and biases rather than just appeals directed at rational consideration of social choices. This approach is often characterised as Nudging. Nudging is seen by some as a new and helpful approach to influencing citizens based on a philosophy labelled 'liberal paternalism', popularised by Thaler and Sunstein (2008) in their best-selling book *Nudge*. A central tenet of their position is that many behavioural challenges faced by society stem from a combination of personal preference or choice and a mix of environmental, cultural, and economic factors. They further argue that there is now a growing body of evidence from many disciplines that people do not always act in an economically logical/rational way; e.g., people do not always act in a way designed to maximise their own advantage or take full account of all the information at their disposal when making decisions. The work of Kahneman (2011) and other behavioural scientists and social policy specialists (Oliver, 2013; Shafir, 2013) has helped policy makers appreciate how this new understanding about how decisions are made can be applied to designing social policy.

Those who support 'Nudging' as a concept maintain that most people, most of the time, do not dispassionately analyse their behavioural decisions; rather many decisions are processed by what Thaler and Sunstein (2008) call the 'automatic' mental system, in a process that they term 'mindless choosing'. Influencing this mindless choosing is the focus of Nudging. In addition to designing 'choice environments' that influence 'mindless choosing', Thaler and Sunstein (2008) review a number of findings from a broad scope of scientific and economic literature to set out a set of concepts that they say can guide people with the responsibility for designing such choice situations. These 'Choice Architects' can use concepts such as social proof, discounting, overconfidence, the power of loss, representation, framing, the power of temptation, anchoring, etc. to craft successful 'Nudges'. Clearly many of these concepts are not new and many of them are the basis of every-day commercial sector marketing and social marketing and have been for many years. Some policy makers see 'Nudging' as a form of social intervention that is more in keeping with a relationship of influence with citizens that places less emphasis on laws, regulations, and information. However, Nudging is still a paternalistic approach at its core in that the people who are designing interventions are still expert choice architects rather than citizens, and potentially manipulative in that it seeks to influence unconscious preferences and biases (House of Lords, 2011). A further problem is that often this kind of liberal paternalism is focused not on tackling the determinants of issues such as obesity or crime. Behavioural science informed approaches instead often locate responsibility for actions with individuals, but also with providers of public services (Sunstein & Thaler, 2003).

There is clearly a great deal of overlap and common ground between social marketing and the application of social sciences theory and evidence. As stated by Dessart and van Bavel (2017, p. 355):

> Both disciplines share the end-goal of contributing to greater social good, and they both build on a deep behavioural analysis based on multidisciplinary approaches focused on citizens.

Social marketing itself draws on theory and evidence from all social science disciplines and augments this with understanding, theory, and know-how from fields that include management and implementation sciences, communication, education and persuasions sciences, as well as design and economics. Social marketing is also a systemic planning process and set of organising concepts that is deeply influenced by a natural science paradigm, as are the social sciences. The use of systemic planning, intervention testing, prototyping, and systematic evaluation are all common to the two fields. Conceptually from a social marketing perspective, social marketing can be seen as a super ordinate concept within which social sciences are a key set of feeder disciplines. From the perspective of social scientists, social marketing can be conceived as a helpful set of tested organising principles that can be used to guide the development, implementation, and evaluation of strategies and programmes of action that are informed by social science theory and research, and deep insights about citizens' motivations and circumstances.

A key factor influencing the connectivity or lack of it between behavioural sciences and social marketing are three fundamental questions. First, what are appropriate social goals? Second, who decides what social goals are appropriate? Third, what level should social action be directed at along the spectrum of individual choice through to macroeconomic and environmental context? A discussion of these fundamental questions is presented in the following sections of this chapter. However, before we address these questions it is worth spending a little time considering the utility of the 'stream' metaphor as it has shaped and, in many respects, restricted a discussion of these fundamental questions over recent years in the field of social marketing.

The Diminishing Utility of the 'Stream' Metaphor

As Newton and Rep (2016) have stated, the upstream and downstream metaphor:

> Has reached the end of its usefulness . . . . What is needed instead are new frameworks that can explicitly explicate the multidirectional relationships that have given rise to the ill-defined problems facing society and provide guidance as to how these problems could be addressed.
>
> (p. 117)

The concept of 'upstream social marketing', which can be viewed as the contribution that social marketing can make to policy selection and refinement, has been used extensively in recent years. The 'dangerous stream' metaphor was originally adapted from a story told by Irving Zola (cited in McKinlay, 1986). The analogy is that a person witnesses a fast flowing and dangerous stream with lots of people in it, with many of the people drowning. Public servants are deployed to dive in and rescue people or pull them to the bank of the stream and revive them. The punch line is that it would be better to focus upstream to see what was causing people to be in the water in the first place (some may have jumped in for fun; others might have been pushed in or stumbled in) and do something about it. This metaphor is often used in appeals to use a more strategic and or preventive approach in social programme delivery, especially emphasising the need for preventive action.

The concept of upstream social marketing emerged as a response to calls to focus action beyond the confines of individual behaviour change (Wallack, 1990; Novelli, 1996). During the 1990s there were also calls for a shift in emphasis within social marketing towards a focus on policy applications of social marketing (Wells, 1993; Andreasen, 1995; Goldberg, 1995). Social marketers acknowledged that rather than solely focus on individual behaviour, social marketing could influence behaviour upstream, by influencing decision makers, policy makers, service providers, and regulators (Newton, Newton, & Rep, 2016; French & Gordon, 2015). Operating upstream often involves research to inform regulation and policy and involvement in media advocacy and lobbying (Saunders, Barrington & Sridharan, 2015). Yet despite increasing recognition of the importance of moving beyond a focus on individual behaviour (Wymer, 2010; Hoek & Jones, 2011), many social marketing interventions remain focused on downstream issues. However, recent work attempting to drive forward the concept of upstream social marketing and its application (French, 2011a; Gordon, 2013; French & Gordon, 2015; Hastings & Domegan, 2018) has continued. This understanding has been further strengthened to some extent by Brychkov, Domegan (2008, 2017) and also by Kennedy and Parsons (2012). Examining upstream social marketing in the context of what they term 'macro-social marketing', Kennedy and Parsons contend:

> if the macro-social marketing of a government is a part of a long-term strategy of social change which includes other means of behaviour change, and is trying to shape the context in which the behaviour is undertaken (a systems approach), it is actually part of a positive social engineering intervention.
>
> (p. 38)

By evoking macroeconomic considerations, these authors have made explicit the interconnectedness of the application of social marketing with economic policy and in so doing have opened the way for a broader discussion and examination of the links between social marketing and what are fundamentally political and philosophical considerations. Rather than just perpetuating debates about the technical aspects of ensuring interventions at all levels of policy formulation via the 'stream' metaphor or by making the case for 'strategic social marketing', which is an appeal for technical completeness (French & Gordon, 2015), the evocation of macro-social marketing locates the key debate within government and political/economic decision making. In this sense, the concept of macro-social marketing is distinct from upstream social marketing as it is about developing the context in which individuals and groups exercise choice and preferences as well as direct attempts to influence such choices and preferences through the development of integrated social policy informed by social marketing principles. This economic focus, as stated previously, necessarily engages social marketing in the business of political/economic choice and the actions that flow from it. It should also be noted that additional work focused on exploring the importance of action at what has been termed 'midstream social marketing' or meso-level social marketing (Brennan & Fry, 2016) has also been completed in recent years. The exact nature of what constitutes midstream social marketing has been used to describe elements including:

1. The co-creation and the delivery of citizen orientated social services (Russell-Bennett, Wood, & Previte, 2013)
2. The process of influencing environmental and social conditions that impact on behaviour (Swinburn, 2009)

3. Co-ordination and value creation through managing differing conceptions of value and available resources in community-based social marketing practices, including providing professionals with role support (Luca, Hibbert, & McDonald, 2016)
4. Influencing and changing the social welfare service environment to make it more responsive (Wood, 2016)

This increasing clarity about what constitutes midstream action coupled with a great deal of understanding about downstream issues focused on how to design and deliver social marketing programmes directed at influencing individual behaviour, when coupled with greater awareness about the need for and how to deliver upstream social marketing contributions, indicates that we now have the tools to develop successful interventions at multiple levels of influence. A key theoretical and practical challenge facing social marketing now is not to make the case for upstream social marketing or to develop better ways to do this; rather we need to develop better understanding about how and when social marketing can be integrated within differing economic, political, and policy contexts.

The Fundamentals, Social Marketing and Macroeconomic Philosophy

Whilst social marketing is ostensibly an ideologically neutral set of concepts and principles, it is clearly focused on promoting social good. In 2013, the first consensus definition of social marketing was developed by the International Social Marketing Association together with its federated national and regional associations. These organisations defined social marketing as:

> Social Marketing seeks to develop and integrate marketing concepts with other approaches to influence behaviours that benefit individuals and communities for the greater social good.

This focus on 'influencing behaviours that benefit individuals and social good' is clearly pertinent to the first three of the fundamental questions posed previously in this chapter; what are appropriate social goals? Who decides what social goals are appropriate? And what level should social action be directed at along the spectrum of individual choice through to macroeconomic and environmental context?

Contrary to the aspirations of those who support the previous definition, critics have argued (Kelly & Charlton, 1995; Raftopoulou, 2003) that social marketing is in fact a stalking horse for uncontrolled free market economics to be applied to the supply and consumption of social goods (Buchanan, Reddy, & Hossain, 1994; Langford & Panter-Brick, 2013). However, others (French & Gordon, 2015) have argued that rather than positioning social marketing as a free market adjunct, those who apply social marketing are more communitarian in outlook believing that three fundamental human characteristics signify social marketing interventions, these being mutuality, co-operation, and reciprocity. These three fundamental characteristics can be used as powerful drivers to promote social development, and for most of human history they have been. Ever since groups of humans have existed, they have tried to influence each other, and as argued by Ridley (2012), trade and exchange via mutually beneficial markets are fundamental aspects of what it is to be human. Exchange and trade are part of the social fabric of reciprocity that characterises human behaviour and motivation. These behaviours have enabled humans to flourish as a species. It could be argued that we are in fact '*Homosociomarketus*', so deep rooted are the instincts to trade and exchange within the human psyche and social bonding rituals and practices. It is through these processes that we develop individual and collective good. The realisation that social marketing is fundamentally about enhancing the positive consequences of mutuality, co-operation, and reciprocity can often come as a surprise to people who erroneously believe marketing is merely about advertising and communication in relation to the sale of goods and services in the pursuance of one-sided gain/profit. The key difference between commercial marketing and social marketing is that in the commercial world the core objective of marketing is to deliver value to the owners and/or shareholders of a firm and their customers, with a secondary but highly important objective of creating general social value (Porter & Kramer, 2011). In social marketing, the core objective is to support the development and or continuation of social good, through creating individual and social value. This in turn makes a valuable contribution to macroeconomic value and general wealth creation through mechanisms such as reducing economic drag factors associated with poor health, crime, and energy waste, and contributions to positive economic multipliers such as encouraging the uptake of education and training, recycling, and saving. The pervasive nature of marketing and how it is woven through both the for-profit and not-for-profit sectors has been outlined by Dibb, Simkin, Pride, and Ferrell (2012).

Markets and marketing are also increasingly being used to deliver social goals and programmes. Social marketing is often used to guide and inform the development of such social markets and goods, for example, social marketing's contribution to creating sustainable markets for products such as condoms and anti-malarial bed nets. Social marketing is also used alongside social franchising to increase the spread and quality of health services. Encouraging the uptake of social investment bonds, the development of social enterprises, and the marketing of their services all apply social marketing principles. Other forms of cross-over and application of social marketing include public/private partnerships and for-profit led social marketing programmes and other forms of corporate social value creation such as support for exercise promotion, reducing harmful drinking, and the promotion of cleaner cooking fuels in developing countries. As French, Russell-Bennett, and Mulcahy (2017) have articulated, there are significant benefits in terms of social value creation to be had from fostering such co-operative arrangements.

Markets and marketing are then fundamental to human nature, they are pervasive, and there are strong and growing connections and interconnectedness between for-profit and social good applications of marketing principles and market mechanisms. As discussed at the beginning of this chapter, we now also know a lot about how to influence people and systems. However, all this understanding is influenced by fundamental assumptions about what constitutes social good, who gets to decide, and what are appropriate mechanisms in pursuit of these ends.

Without clarity about the ideological assumptions driving social policy, we are not able to understand and justify why and how social marketing should be applied. This necessarily brings us to a consideration of fundamental macroeconomic policy, how it has a direct effect on what policies are selected, how they are delivered, and how they are assessed.

There are two main domains of economics: macroeconomics and microeconomics. Macroeconomics is concerned with understanding what is going on and what is likely to happen in the economy of a country, region, and/or globally and how to influence the many forces that drive the economy. In macroeconomics, analysis and research are focused on analysing how an economy is performing, including variables such as employment, GDP, money supply, investment rates, and inflation. Governments use this assessment to help develop their economic policies, including fiscal and monetary policies to keep the economy growing (assuming growth is a strategic objective as it is for most modern states). Macroeconomic analysis and the mechanisms used by states to influence the economy have a direct effect on a wide range of issues, such as wealth creation and distribution, employment, wages, poverty and equality. Action to address these issues clearly also has a substantial impact on and is consequently influenced by social solidarity, health—physical and mental, environmental conditions, crime, and general wellbeing.

Microeconomics by contrast is focused on factors in an economy such as confidence, buying and selling behaviour, supply and demand issues, within particular contexts or settings. There are also many developing theories about the nature and focus of Mezzo economics (Mann, 2011) focused on intermediary factors between micro and macroeconomic consideration such as local community resilience. Economic considerations are not however purely technical. How economics and in fact society is perceived is informed by the particular economic philosophy adopted. If we leave aside Marxism due to the fact there are no purely Marxist states in the world today, two main economic philosophies compete to inform most economic policy; Keynesian and Hayekian Hayek (1944). It could be argued that centralised state-controlled capitalism exemplified by the People's Republic of China represents a third way, but for the purposes of this chapter it will be viewed as an extreme example of a Keynesian planned economy.

We do not have space in this chapter for a full description of Keynesian and Hayekian doctrine, but for the sake of clarity a brief (and necessarily incomplete) description of these two dominant conceptions of what constitute economic responsibility follows. Keynesian economics is named after its chief proponent, John Maynard Keynes. Keynesian economics as set out in *The General Theory of Employment, Interest, and Money* (1936) and expanded on in numerous other texts is driven by the need to avoid the social catastrophe that results when economic systems crash and the need to provide viable and sustained alternatives to unfettered laissez-fair private enterprise or disasters brought about by socialism, revolution, and counter revolution witnessed between the 1920s–1960s. Keynesians believe that governments and international institutions have a key role to play in economic management. Through mechanisms such as state driven spending in times of less demand, governments can smooth out extremes in economic cycles. One of Keynes' key solutions to economic downturns and rising unemployment was that the state should step in and invest to create jobs. Famously Keynes argued that America could, in the Depression, spend its way to prosperity. Governments should also use tools such as money supply, interest rates, and taxes in an active way to act as incentives for growth or to cool down economies that are overheating. So, Keynes advocated governments adopting an active role in influencing the economy, but he and his advocates are also dedicated supporters of market capitalism and liberal democracy as the best way of ensuring sustainable wellbeing.

In contrast to Keynes, Friedrich Hayek, in his famous book *The Road to Serfdom*, published in 1944, along with other liberal thinkers such as Joseph Schumpeter and Karl Popper, developed an alternative set of social and economic recommendations for liberal democratic economic policy also designed to prevent a repetition of any of the twentieth century's great tyrannies. For Hayek and like-minded liberals, planned and managed economics and notions of collective purpose are misguided and dangerous to personal liberty. Such attempts can result in short-term benefits, but borrowing to spend in the short-run has to be repaid at some point, leading to intergenerational indebtedness and weaker economic performance. Hayek emphasises the need for competition and decentralisation of power to the lowest levels possible, and the power of markets, as the best way to ensure efficient distribution of wealth, personal liberty, and long-term sustained prosperity for all. Governments should avoid the use of top down economic and social policies that are coercive; rather they should act as enablers of individual choice and free-market capitalism, using laws and other forms of central planning minimally to ensure that legal frameworks are in place to facilitate a creative wealth generating dynamic.

The two competing macroeconomic philosophies set out here have a profound influence on global and national social policy. Social marketing as an approach to developing and delivering effective and efficient social policy is likewise directly influenced by these competing economic approaches.

When a commitment to a planned and managed economy is adopted and this is coupled with an interventionist mind-set (Keynesian), it is more probable that an individualistic, persuasive, and formulaic conception of social marketing will tend to be preferred and applied. In centrally planned and managed states, social marketing can be conceived as an important tool of state influence and control that can be used to influence people as a legitimate means for maximising productivity and state defined wellbeing. For example, if in a country, an international agency or an NGO were seeking to bring about high rates of immunisation, social marketing interventions could include both voluntary changes based on education and communication, and also coercive interventions such as compulsory vaccination programs and the use of Nudges and state sponsored incentive systems. Such programs would be centrally planned and delivered. They would also be driven and evaluated based on centrally set goals and objectives. Alternatively, when a more liberal, enabling, and less directive conception of the state and its purpose is adopted (Hayekian), a more community oriented, market, facilitatory, and voluntary conception of social marketing practice will be more likely to be adopted and applied. For example, the same kind of immunisation programme in this context might be characterised by community focused interventions supported by the development of some kind of social market. Interventions would focus on engaging individuals and families in considering the issue and information dissemination to aid personal decision making rather than any form of compulsion or non-rational interventions such as default schemes. Such programmes would be evaluated against more extensive success criteria, including rates of community engagement, trust, and individual perception of control and empowerment as well as up-take rates.

This example hopefully illustrates that macroeconomic policy has a direct and profound influence on what kind of social marketing interventions are selected and how they are applied. The issue of at what level of influence is the focus of the intervention, e.g., up, middle, or downstream, is an important but secondary consideration. How social marketing is conceived by those who fund it and those who deliver it is directly influenced by political and economic preferences. For example, in a country that embraces free market principles and the primacy of individual responsibility, social marketing will tend to focus on persuading and supporting individuals to make good choices and making those choices as attractive and easy as possible. In countries where a more collective and managed market philosophy prevails, social marketing will tend to emphasise action focused on determinants, collective action, and behaviour change. These issues are not trivial or marginal. Lack of clarity and congruency between underlying fundamental philosophy will lead to conflict between providers and sponsors of programmes and potentially citizens as well as suboptimal programme management and evaluation. For example, an NGO such as UNICEF, which could be described as being aligned with a Keynesian view of the world, may well clash in its application of social marketing with a state government in a country that holds a more free market individual responsibility set of convictions.

Mapping the Interdependencies Between Social Marketing and Macroeconomic Policy

Figure 8.1 sets out some of the main issues that need to be understood if confusion and potential conflict are to be avoided when considering how social marketing can be integrated with social policy selection, delivery, and evaluation. The assumption of this map is that governments seek to influence citizens, groups, and organisations to behave in ways that are both individually and collectively beneficial. The map's central elements relate to what economic philosophy underpins a state's beliefs and preferred economic philosophy for promoting/facilitating and spreading

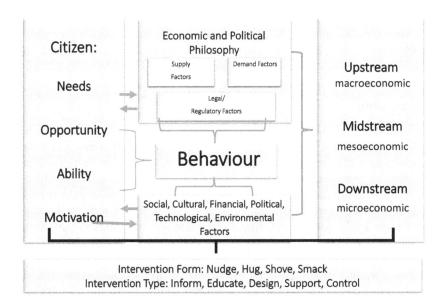

Figure 8.1 Social Marketing Systems Map

wellbeing. As discussed earlier, clarity regarding this will dictate how social marketing can be applied in support of these objectives. The central elements of the map also highlight the importance of understanding market factors, such as demand and supply of both commercial products and services, as well as social assets and needs and the regulatory and legal protections that should be in place to ensure relevant protections exist to enable whatever system is desired to operate fairly.

The influences of social, cultural, financial, fiscal, political, technological, and environmental factors also need to be addressed, as all of these will influence the nature of any social marketing contribution. On the left of the map, citizens' needs, opportunity, ability, and motivations are included. Governments need deep understanding of all these elements if they are to support citizens to adopt positive social behaviours. Social marketing can assist with the gathering and interpretation of this data, including the development of segmentation models and citizen insights, which can be fed into developing optimal strategies and tactical interventions. On the right of the map, different levels of social marketing intervention are indicated. As discussed earlier, the utility of identifying different levels of intervention is helpful. Those considering commissioning and/or applying social marketing as part of social policy selection, development, or delivery also need to consider what tactics they should employ to deliver social policy. The bottom box of the map outlines the selection of interventions 'Types' and 'Forms' of social marketing (French, 2011a) that can be used in combination to deliver an effective intervention mix. Most importantly, however, as stated earlier, there is a need for explicit understanding and agreement about what social and economic philosophy is driving the selection of interventions at each level and how the selected intervention Types and Forms will aid and fit with the strategic goals of the social program.

Conclusion

This chapter has sought to draw out some of the key issues and features associated with the development of more effective social policy and how social policy can be enhanced and informed by the application of social marketing principles and other forms of social influence such as behavioural sciences. Social marketing has and can further assist in developing coordinated and sustained social programmes at down-, mid-, and upstream levels. Social marketing has a contribution to make at all these levels of social programme selection, design, and delivery. Important work has been completed in advancing social marketing theory and practice as it applies to influencing and supporting up, mid, and downstream social marketing over recent years. More examples and methodologies about how social marketing is being used to influence policy and policy makers and deliver contributions that go beyond a focus on individual responsibility are also now emerging, as are hybrid models between for-profit and not-for-profit organisations and coalitions that all, to some extent, apply marketing and market principles to promote social good.

What underpins the selection and application of social marketing at any level of social policy influence or contribution, however, is the fundamental macroeconomic philosophy that predominates in any given state or organisation. To date there has been little overt consideration of this issue. One possible reason for a lack of exposition of the issues associated with clarifying fundamental macroeconomic policy considerations and social marketing is what we could call the technical conversion retreat. It is easier to focus on technical issues, such as the level of social policy that social marketing should seek to influence and how this should be done, than focusing on the nature of the fundamental ideology that underpins the systems and how or if social marketing principles can or should be applied in support of the goals of the system. Focusing on fundamental principles means clarifying the ideology that informs policy and its implementation. Such a focus can be uncomfortable, as it exposes individual and group core values, assumptions, and views about the nature of society, the people who represent it, and what constitutes the most efficient but also ethical intervention approach to take in any given situation. For a deeper discussion of this issue, see the chapter by Eagle, Dahl, and Low in this volume.

This chapter has explored the challenges for governments and social institutions when seeking to develop social policy focused on influencing behaviour for social good. The web of influences on behaviour and the complexity associated with developing systemic interventions is clear. As globally citizens become more educated, wealthy, and empowered, governments and other national and international organisations will increasingly be driven by people's expectations and needs. This shift in emphasis signals an inevitable and fundamental change in the power relationship between states and public organisations and the citizens they seek to serve. This shift necessitates the integration of social marketing as an embedded and consistent feature of social policy development and delivery because it is the discipline that is focused on developing understanding of citizens and how they can be influenced and engaged in delivering solutions to social challenges. Social marketing principles have the potential to positively inform and enhance all levels of economic policy and policy enactment. As we enter this new era of civic development and as we begin to redefine the nature of the state, that of commercial interests, and the rights, responsibilities, and roles of citizens, the creation of citizen defined value sits at the heart of future social policy development. A new paradigm for social programme design is inevitable because we are now at a point in human history where a confluence of factors is coming together that mean that existing approaches to social policy selection, design, and application are no longer tenable.

In most circumstances, to succeed in designing optimally effective, efficient, and acceptable social programmes, the marketing concepts of value creation, mutually beneficial exchange, and relationship building will all need to be used to design future social programmes. These core marketing concepts focus on building social policy and intervention strategies through collaboration and consensus building, incorporating effort aimed at the genuine engagement and empowerment of citizens in the policy selection and implementation process. The development of social strategy based on both value creation and citizen engagement also leads to the application of a longer-term strategic approach and a more diverse range of interventions being applied. This is because when citizens are engaged and if listened to, they often generate policy responses and intervention solutions that go beyond the narrow confines of legislation enforcement and information provision.

However, as discussed in some detail in this chapter, social programmes have to be developed on the basis of their fit with the prevailing political, economic, ideological, and moral sensibilities of societies as well as considerations of science, evidence, and what we know about cost-effective programme implementation. To develop such efficient, effective, and ethically sound programmes, we need a deep pool of understanding about how to craft, design, and deliver such interventions. Social marketing represents a pool of such understanding and a set of organising principles based on a great deal of evidence and experience. Social marketing can, however, be applied in a variety of ways in support of very different social and economic goals. A more detailed consideration of how social marketing can and should be applied in a congruent way with the prevailing macroeconomic and policy imperatives in any given situation has to date been under emphasised in the literature, and needs more consideration, research, and application if we are to maximise social marketing's potential economic and social utility in a variety of different social and economic contexts around the world.

References

Andreasen, A. (1995). *Marketing social change*. San Francisco: Jossey-Bass.

Biroscak, B. (2018). Policy, systems and environmental change; reflections and suggestions for social marketers. *Social Marketing Quarterly*, 24(3), 127–131.

Borden, S., Cohn, S., & Gooderham, C. (2018). Transitioning upward when "downstream" efforts are insufficient. *Social Marketing Quarterly*, 24(3), 151–163.

Brennan, L., & Fry, M. (2016). Guest editorial. *Journal of Social Marketing*, 6(3), 214–218.

Brychkov, D., & Domegan, C. (2017). "Social marketing and systems science: past, present and future", *Journal of Social Marketing*, Vol. 7 No. 1.

Buchanan, D., Reddy, S., & Hossain, Z. (1994). Social marketing: A critical appraisal. *Health Promotion International, 9*(1), 49–57.

Dessart, F., & van Bavel, R. (2017). Two converging paths: Behavioural sciences and social marketing for better policies. *Journal of Social Marketing, 7*(4), 355–365.

Dibb, S, Simkin, L., Pride, W., & Ferrell, O. (2012). *Marketing: Concepts and strategies.* London: Cengage.

Domegan, C. T. (2008). Social marketing: Implications for contemporary marketing practices classification scheme. *Journal of Business and Industrial Marketing, 23*(2), 135–141.

French, J. (2011a). Business as unusual: The contribution of social marketing to government policy making and strategy development. In G. Hastings, K. Angus, & C. Bryant (Eds.), *The Sage handbook of social marketing.* London: Sage Publications.

French, J. (2011b). Why nudging is not enough. *Journal of Social Marketing, 1*(2), 154–162.

French, J., & Gordon, R. (2015). *Strategic social marketing.* London: Sage Publications.

French, J., Russell-Bennett, R., & Mulcahy, R. (2017). Travelling alone or travelling far? Meso-level value co-creation by social marketing and for-profit organisations. *Journal of Social Marketing, 7*(3), 280–296.

Goldberg, M. (1995). Social marketing: Are we fiddling while Rome burns? *Journal of Consumer Psychology, 4*(4), 347–370.

Gordon, R. (2013). Unlocking the potential of upstream social marketing. *European Journal of Marketing, 47*(9), 1525–1547.

Hastings, G., & Domegan, C. (2018). *Social marketing, rebels with a cause* (3rd ed.). London: Routledge.

Hayek, F. (1944). *The road to serfdom.* Routledge Classics (2001). London: Routledge.

Hoek, J., & Jones, S. (2011). Regulation, public health and social marketing: A behaviour change trinity. *Journal of Social Marketing, 1*(1), 32–44.

House of Lords, Science and Technology Select Committee. (2011). *Behaviour change.* London: Authority of the House of Lords. Retrieved from www.publications.parliament.uk/pa/ld201012/ldselect/ldsctech/179/179.pdf

Kahneman, D. (2011). *Thinking fast and slow.* Oxford: Oxford University Press.

Kelly, M., & Charlton, B. (1995). The sociology of health promotion. In R. Bunton, S. Nettleton, & R. Burrows (Eds.), *The sociology of health promotion: Critical analysis of consumption, lifestyle and risk.* London: Routledge.

Kennedy, A-M., & Parsons, A. (2012). Macro-social marketing and social engineering: A systems approach. *Journal of Social Marketing, 2*(1), 37–51.

Keynes, J. (1936). *The general theory of employment, interest and money.* Retrieved from https://cas2.umkc.edu/economics/people/facultypages/kregel/courses/econ645/winter2011/generaltheory.pdf

Langford, R., & Panter-Brick, C. (2013). A health equity critique of social marketing: When interventions have impact but sufficient reach. *Social Science and Medicine, 83*, 133–141.

Luca, N., Hibbert, S., & McDonald, R. (2016). Midstream value creation in social marketing. *Journal of Marketing Management, 32*(11–12), 1145–1173.

Mann, S. (2011). *Sectors matter! Exploring macroeconomics.* New York, NY: Springer.

McKinlay, J. (1986). A case for refocusing upstream: The political economy of illness. In P. Conrad & R. Kern (Eds.), *The sociology of health and illness: Critical perspectives* (2nd ed., pp. 484–498). St. Martin's Press.

Newton, J., Newton, F., & Rep, S. (2016). Evaluating social marketing up stream metaphor; Does it capture the flows of behavioural influence between upstream and downstream actors? *Journal of Marketing Management, 32,* 1103–1122.

Novelli, W. (1996, April 24). *Class presentation on the campaign for smoke-free kids.* Washington, DC: School of Business, Georgetown University.

Oliver, A. (2013). *Behavioural public policy.* Cambridge: Cambridge University press.

Porter, M., & Kramer, M. (2011). Creating shared value. *The Big Ideas Harvard Business Review, 89*(1–2), 62–77.

Raftopoulou, E. (2003). *The captured citizen- a critique of social marketing.* Stream 23: Critical Marketing: Visibility, Inclusivity, Captivity. Manchester School of Management UMIST. Retrieved from www.mngt.waikato.ac.nz/ ejrot/cmsconference/2003/proceedings/criticalmarketing/Reftopoulou.pdf

Ridley, M. (2012). *The rational optimist.* London: Harper Collins.

Rubenstein, L., Dukes, S., Fearing, C., Foster, B., Painter, K., Rosenblatt, A., & Rubin, W. (2018). Case study for social marketing: Key strategies for transforming the children's mental health system in the United States. *Social Marketing Quarterly, 24*(3), 132–150.

Russell-Bennett, R., Wood, M., & Previte, J. (2013). Fresh ideas: Services thinking for social marketing. *Journal of Social Marketing, 3*(3), 223–238.

Saunders, S., Barrington, D., & Sridharan, B. (2015). Redefining social marketing beyond behavioural change. *Journal of Social Marketing, 5,* 160–168.

Shafir, E. (Ed.). (2013). *The behavioural foundations of public policy.* Princeton and Oxford: Princeton University Press.

Sunstein, C., & Thaler, T. (2003, Fall). Libertarian paternalism is not an oxymoron. *The University of Chicago Law Review, 70*(4).

Swinburn, B. (2009). Commentary: Closing the disparity gaps in obesity. *International Journal of Epidemiology, 38,* 509–511.

Thaler, R., & Sunstein, C. (2008). *Nudge: Improving decisions about health, wealth and happiness.* New Haven, CT: Yale University Press.

Wallack, L. (1990). Media advocacy: Promoting health through mass communication. In K. Glanz, F. Marcus Lewis, & B. K. Rimer (Eds.), *Health behaviour and health education* (pp. 370–386). San Francisco: Jossey-Bass.

Wells, W. (1993). Discovery-oriented consumer research. *Journal of Consumer Research, 19*(4), 489–504.

Wood, M. (2016). Midstream social marketing and the co-creation of public services. *Journal of Social Marketing, 6*(3), 277–293.

Wymer, W. (2010). Rethinking the boundaries of social marketing: Activism or advertising? *Journal of Business Research, 63*(2), 99–103.

9 Co-Creating Social Change Using Human-Centred Design

Anne Hamby, Meghan Pierce, and Kim Daniloski

Introduction

Poverty, addiction, pollution, and many forms of exploitation are instances where the market system plays a role in creating or facilitating problems, and an emphasis on individual behaviour change alone is unlikely to fully address these problems. Macro-social marketing tackles wicked problems through applying social marketing principles to a system of organisations and institutions rather than to individuals (Domegan, 2008; Kennedy & Parsons, 2012) to create social change. Due to the complex nature of social problems, Kennedy and Parsons (2012) argue that this top-down approach, typically characterised by targeting government-level change, is uniquely positioned to allow for 'trickle down' effects throughout the system. More recent work in the macro-social marketing literature has acknowledged that change can take place at the macro, as well as meso and micro levels, of a marketing system (Kemper & Ballantine, 2017). While the downstream flow of change in the marketing system is broadly acknowledged, there has been less direct discussion regarding *how* this change can move through the multiple levels of a marketing system (Kemper & Ballantine, 2017).

Work from other traditions of social change has embraced a co-creative approach to collaboratively develop solutions (e.g., social entrepreneurship—Dees, 1998) and social marketing (Kotler & Zaltman, 1971). In this chapter, we argue that macro-social marketing should embrace this common foundation to emphasise not simply the consideration of stakeholders, but the inclusion of stakeholders in the social change process; that is, rather than a more passive, 'trickle down' approach, the active development of solutions with other stakeholders is not only more likely to produce change, but to create change that sustains over time.

Extant work on macro-social marketing suggests that targeting the different parts of the network (upstream and downstream) is important to address 'wicked problems' (Domegan et al., 2016). We expand upon this description to suggest that efforts in different parts of the network should adopt a *co-creative approach*. Given the network is an inherent part of the macro-social marketing perspective, we believe macro-social marketers are especially in a position to leverage the co-creation process at various levels of the marketing ecosystem. In the first part of this chapter, we describe human-centred design (HCD) as a way to structure macro-social marketing approaches; many of the principles of HCD are implicit in scholarship on macro-social marketing, and we highlight conceptual linkages which can be used to explicitly guide macro-social marketing efforts. Then, we describe a case study of a partnership between a U.S. university and an East African nonprofit, which illustrates the co-creation framework.

Macro-Social Marketing

Many modern 'wicked' problems are systemically entrenched. Recognising the need for a holistic, systemic approach to address such problems, recent work describing a macro-social marketing approach to social change has flourished (Dibb, 2014; Kennedy, 2017), targeting institutional norms that perpetuate the problems (Domegan, 2008). This approach represents an innovation on (micro) social marketing by taking the marketing ecosystem into account. Kennedy (2016, p. 358) notes,

> where regular micro-social marketing seeks to create behavior change in individuals, macro-social marketing seeks to institutionalize long-term societal behavioral change, that is, macro-social marketing seeks to create different system wide normative frameworks.

While the emphasis on differences in outcome scope (systemic vs. individual) is clearly relevant in contrasting micro- and macro-social marketing, an inherent distinction between the two also lies in the starting point of each approach. Traditional social marketing activity begins with downstream individuals, whereas macro-social marketing activity begins with upstream actors, such as government (Wymer, 2011) or nonprofit groups (Huff, Barnhart, Mcalexander, & Mcalexander, 2017). Scholarly work on macro-social marketing emphasises change in public and business policy as one way to create macro-level change (Carrigan, Moraes, & Leek, 2011).

The idea that macro-social marketing efforts should be directed towards upstream actors is well accepted; most recent work acknowledges that upstream changes play an important role in shaping the market ecosystem and facilitate institutionalisation of changes (Domegan et al., 2016). This past work has characterised macro-social change as a process through which the upstream changes flow through the system to end-users: "*Change at a broader conceptual level . . . trickles down to individual organizations within the marketing system*" (Kennedy, 2016, p. 354). This view likens change to a diffusion process in which norms and structures passively, organically occur.

Macromarketers do not restrict their efforts solely to upstream actors: Dibb (2014) describes how down-, mid-, and upstream efforts are needed for social change to be effective, and recent work has elaborated on how agents desiring to create macromarketing change can direct their efforts to different levels of the system. For example, Huff et al. (2017) describe the efforts of gun violence prevention groups directed towards upstream (policy makers), midstream (community leaders and service providers), and downstream (current and potential gun users) members of the market system. Kemper and Ballantine (2017) describe how a multi-level perspective on a market system can help to first identify actors at the different stages in the market system, and then guide upstream, midstream, and downstream actions. This work largely focuses on targeting the various levels in the system with different message strategies.

The general approach adopted by past work involves directing effort towards the entities that reside within the various portions of the market system and focuses less on the interactions between the entities themselves (that is, the macro-social marketer may target efforts to public policy makers and service providers, but does not consider the exchange between those two entities). Yet more recent scholarly work has petitioned for the inclusion of various levels of stakeholders when creating or implementing solutions (Lefebvre, 2012).

Answering this call, more macro-social marketing researchers have considered how cross-sector (micro/meso/macro) collaboration can occur as an approach to institutionalise change (Kennedy, 2016). Domegan et al. (2016, p. 1135) contend, *"when working with government, NGOs, regulators, experts and citizens in diverse, non-rational and dynamic circumstances, we believe social marketing progresses when it facilitates joint actions with actors across and between micro, meso and macro levels"*. Getting 'all eyes on the problem' (Hastings & Domegan, 2013) can foster a more profound understanding of the problem and build consensus around solutions. In one notable example, Domegan et al. (2016) invited various stakeholders in a marine ecosystem to develop a cartography of the down-, mid-, and upstream causes of the problem using interactive management software (IM; Warfield & Cárdenas, 1994). This mapping allowed the 'whole-system-in-the-room' stakeholders to build a common understanding of the problem and view the linkages (and lack thereof) within the system.

It is also worth noting that Domegan and colleagues (2016) highlight the importance of co-creation in systems-thinking social marketing through communicating *with* (bidirectional) rather than *to* (unidirectional) stakeholders but do not articulate *how* actors within a system may facilitate co-creation across levels (i.e., as this chapter describes through HCD). They propose one approach to co-creation in which stakeholders from the various parts of the ecosystem are gathered together. This process is not always feasible. In the current work, we propose a complementary perspective: co-created efforts between individual stakeholders at different levels in the stream or network. We respond to their call for research to *"examine [the] co-creation process as [it] pertain[s] to social marketing and systems thinking"* (Domegan et al., 2016, p. 1139).

In the current work, we focus on the exchanges between agents at different levels of the market system. While it is possible that upstream change may indeed 'trickle down' and cumulatively create change through the market system, we propose that active co-creation of change between the different members of the market system increases the likelihood of institutionalisation, or sustained change. The importance of actions that are jointly developed or co-created has been occasionally acknowledged in the macro-social marketing literature—for example, Kennedy (2016) discusses the importance of partnerships to create institutionalisation of social change, and Domegan et al. (2016), as aforementioned, demonstrated how generating a common understanding of the problem across stakeholders can facilitate efforts to change the system—but there has not been, to our knowledge, consideration of how a co-creative approach to social change in a macro-social marketing context (co-creation at multiple levels of the network) differs from the approach discussed in (micro) social marketing (co-creation of marketing intervention efforts with a community, for example). Adopting a macro-level focus, the current work outlines how a series of co-creative actions at the various levels of a marketing ecosystem can *actively* create sustained social change. A contribution of the current chapter is thus to make explicit the importance of co-creation to macro-social marketing, to introduce a process that macro-social marketers can apply to facilitate this co-creation (human-centred design), and to outline a systems structure of co-creation: That is, it can occur at multiple levels throughout the network. Sustained systematic change is accomplished through the co-creation of solutions at these various points in the market system.

Co-Creation and Human-Centred Design

In the service marketing literature, the central tenets of co-creation entail directly involving the end-user or beneficiary in the product or service value creation (Grönroos, 2012) whereby both (or multiple) stakeholders contribute to the process of value creation (Normann & Ramirez, 1993) such that all stakeholders may receive value from the process itself (Vargo & Lusch, 2008). This value comes in the form of increased satisfaction for end-users and competitive advantage for the firms involved (Grissemann & Stokburger-Sauer, 2012). The traditional marketing principles of conducting extensive market research, focusing on the customer, and considering the customer as 'king' recognise the importance of the end-user but are not forms of co-creation (Prahalad & Ramaswamy, 2004). Specifically, *"the firm and the customer act together in a merged, coordinated, dialogical, and interactive process that creates value for the customer, and for the firm as well"* (Grönroos, 2012, p. 1522). This definition and the practice thereof are employed using various levels of involvement of the beneficiary in co-creation.

Human-centred design (HCD) formalises the concept of co-creation further by articulating an iterative process that can guide co-creative efforts (Buchanan, 2011). Human-centred design, a process that has been developed in the design literature (Rowe, 1991) and popularised by IDEO and the Stanford D. school (Brown, 2009; Martin, 2009), recognises that beneficiaries or end-users should be at the core of and included throughout any value creation process. End-users are not only included, but central to each component of design thinking. HCD works under the *"presumption that people are competent interpreters of their own lives and competent solvers of their own problems"* (Mulgan, 2006, p. 150) and removes the focus on technological or organisational prowess (Kimbell, 2011). The emphasis here is that the beneficiary will not be simply a collaborator in value creation, but is the most important partner in defining the problem, generating ideas, testing, and implementing solutions.

We view the principles of HCD as a process for co-creation, rather than a discipline, that can help structure interactive efforts within a system to create social change. HCD is multidisciplinary in nature, purposively including diverse collaborators (Brown & Wyatt, 2010), borrowing concepts from anthropology, psychology, and education (Dorst, 2011) to develop a *process* which can be applied, broadly, by entities seeking to resolve wicked problems. In this sense, HCD is a tool that can be applied by macro-social marketers to interactions with their stakeholders (and can be taught to stakeholder groups to apply in their own separate interactions) to contribute to a shared social change goal. We next describe the three nonlinear feedback loops—inspiration, ideation, and implementation (Brown & Wyatt, 2010) of HCD—and discuss how macro-social marketers can adopt an HCD perspective and potential benefits of this approach in order to provide a framework for collaboration across levels of the system.

Phase One: Inspiration

Generally, the first stage focuses on the problem or opportunity as a source of inspiration. Design problems have been described similarly to macro-social problems in that they are 'indeterminate' or 'wicked' (Buchanan, 2011) and require *"systemic solutions grounded in the clients' or customers' needs"* (Brown & Wyatt, 2010, p. 32). During this phase, 'designers' immerse themselves in the field of the problem to live with and learn from individuals experiencing the problem, partnering with locals who may serve as *"interpreters and cultural guides"* to make connections in the community and to appropriately contextualise observations (Brown &

Wyatt 2010, p. 33). Designers work to remove their biases and preconceived notions to take on the positionality and the perspective of the beneficiaries (Brown & Wyatt, 2010) using ethnography-aligned methods to develop an understanding of the local context (Brown, 2009).

In application of the inspiration phase for macro-social marketers, up or midstream actors (described as 'designers' in the HCD process) become embedded in the local context of downstream stakeholders or the focal community (described as end-users or beneficiaries in the HCD process) to better understand the needs of the community. Up and downstream stakeholders (designers and end-users) co-discover (Domegan, Collins, Stead, McHugh, & Hughes, 2013) a common understanding of the systemic social problem or opportunity. This process has the potential to reveal misunderstandings about the problem on the part of the designers. For example, an environmental organisation may believe that lower rates of recycling among consumers may be due to a lack of knowledge about the importance of recycling. In fact, consumers may believe in the benefits of recycling, but simply lack the infrastructure to support their recycling efforts. Analogously, past research on macro-social marketing highlights the importance of developing an understanding of the network surrounding a problem to identify problematic linkages as well as connections that are needed; according to Kennedy, Kapitan, Bajaj, Bakonyi, and Sands (2017, p. 53),

> these influences need to be identified and mapped so that the structure of the system that perpetuates the problem can be understood, along with the interplay between actors at multiple levels simultaneously.

Phase Two: Ideation

Ideation is the process of brainstorming, elaborating, and experimenting with possible solutions with the goal of generating many ideas rather than perfect ideas. In this phase, designers work with the beneficiaries to synthesise a user-based understanding of the problem, develop themes and insights from this understanding, and to produce ideas for solutions that range from the simple to radical. For example, ideas are narrowed down by grouping those that are similar, voting, and selecting those that are seemingly the most likely to succeed or are innovative. These remaining ideas are further conceptualised and prototyped.

In application of the ideation phase, stakeholders in the macro-social system jointly generate ideas to address the problem defined in the first phase; one of which might include, for example, petitioning the government for involvement (e.g., providing recycling services). The co-design (Domegan et al., 2013) of potential solutions has the benefit of developing buy-in from the initial stages of action discussion. Co-creation during the ideation phase thus has the potential dual benefit of generating solutions that are more likely to be *effective* (i.e., vetted by stakeholders with diverse perspectives on the problem) as well as *accepted* (i.e., potential disagreements or reservations about a solution can be discussed prior to implementation—Cronin & Mccarthy, 2011; Gebauer, Füller, & Pezzei, 2013).

Phase Three: Implementation

Implementation occurs through a more formal testing among stakeholders. Prototypes of solutions are created and shared with the beneficiary community, who then provide iterative feedback. Solutions are refined based on the feedback and re-tested with the beneficiary community. At any point, designers and beneficiaries may have to redefine the problem, generate additional ideas for solutions, or reiterate solutions based on feedback.

In application of the implementation phase, macro-social marketers employ the proposed solution (i.e., co-delivery—Domegan et al., 2013). Joint creation during the prior inspiration and ideation phases of the process reduces the friction often experienced by actors attempting to enact social change, particularly relative to social change actors who may try to influence decisions or changes while simultaneously trying to develop buy-in for these changes (Luca, Hibbert, & Mcdonald, 2016). A shared decision-making process is likely to enhance motivation among stakeholders such that entities will persist through the difficulties encountered during the implementation phase.

Inherent in a human-centred design approach is the idea that these three phrases are not necessarily to be taken sequentially, but rather followed in a cyclical fashion. Feedback loops are embedded in each phase, which may result in a re-conceptualisation of the problem itself. Similarly, Kennedy (2017) points out that macro-social marketing efforts need not be linear, but should take a more iterative or adaptive approach. Checkland (2000) describes the development of a learning system whereby there are constant interactions among stakeholders to listen to and learn from each other as a means to achieve social change.

Co-Creation, Alternative Approaches to Social Change, and Macro-Social Marketing

The concept of co-creation has been applied in several social change literatures. Design thinking has recently been applied to social innovations (Mulgan, 2006) and highlighted in social marketing (Lefebvre, 2012), social entrepreneurship (Fleischmann, 2013), and community action (Fuad-Luke, 2013) disciplines. For example, (micro) social marketers develop an understanding of and test their campaign with their downstream target audience (Leathar & Hastings, 1987). These points map onto elements of the co-creative nature of HCD by including the beneficiaries during both the problem definition and implementation of the programme. Lefebvre (2012) describes the role of the social marketer as a facilitator of co-creation, instead of viewing beneficiaries as target audiences. There is also evidence that social programmes "*designed and directed by community members, are far more likely to succeed than those planned and executed exclusively by outsiders*" (Bryant et al., 2007, p. 61). Brown and Wyatt (2010) contend that design thinking is particularly useful for social change agents given their common intersection of human centricity. As opposed to user-centred design, where the end-user is observed (Sanders & Stappers, 2008), Fleischmann (2013) asserts that through co-creation, the social change agent considers the end-user as an equal, giving them 'expert status'.

Work in the field of social entrepreneurship also suggests that, to be most effective, it is "*collaborative and collective, drawing on a broad array of support, cooperation and alliances to build awareness, gain resources and, ultimately, make change*" (Montgomery, Dacin, & Dacin, 2012, p. 376). Montgomery and colleagues (2012) describe this embeddedness through the concept of 'collective social entrepreneurship' whereby same sector and cross-sector organisations pool and trade resources. To accomplish this collaboration, collective social entrepreneurs build a consensus towards a common understanding of the problem (Benford & Snow, 2000) and convene to share intellectual resources (Svendsen & Laberge, 2005). These points map on to the co-creative nature of HCD in that social entrepreneurs are including beneficiaries and other stakeholders in their understanding of the problem, their creation of the opportunity, and the sustained business in a community.

While macro-social marketing can and has drawn insights from these other approaches to social change (Hamby, Pierce, & Brinberg, 2017), a main innovation supplied by the macro-social marketing perspective is the embedded nature of such problems; that is, a network level perspective. Past work applying the HCD process has primarily examined the interactions at one level of a network. We propose that the systematic application of the HCD co-creation process can occur at multiple levels within the network in order to produce and sustain change; that is, co-created change enacted by the various stakeholders in a network is more likely to develop the institutionalised change described by Kennedy et al. (2017).

The 'network' has been implicitly viewed in hierarchical terms by past work on macro-social marketing. For example, Huff et al. (2017) describe the efforts of gun violence prevention groups directed towards upstream (policy makers), midstream (community leaders and service providers), and downstream (current and potential gun users) members of the market system. Actors may engage with and influence other actors at the same level (i.e., members of a government agency and industry lobbyists;

different groups of downstream consumers) or at different hierarchical levels (retailers and final consumers). We suggest that co-creation ideally occurs at both a vertical level (with up or downstream actors) and horizontal level (with actors at the same position of the 'stream') within an ecosystem to create and sustain social change. For example, at the vertical level, a macro-social marketer can apply the HCD process with actors further downstream to develop ideas for a solution to the social problem that will form the basis of a policy proposal to be implemented downstream. For example, Truong (2017) describes a macro-social marketing effort in Vietnam coordinated by the government whereby the National Institute of Nutrition involved food producers and other stakeholders in the development of interventions. At the horizontal level, a macro-social marketer must engage in coalition building with organisations with similar goals in order to enact the policy-level change co-created with vertical-level stakeholders. For example, Huff et al. (2017) describe a process of internal marketing within gun violence prevention groups to build a sense of community, motivate volunteers, and prevent burnout as they advocate for change.

In the next section, we discuss an extended case example where the HCD process was used to structure and facilitate relationships at vertical (across organisations to beneficiaries) and horizontal (across organisations and, separately, across beneficiaries) levels to create social change, followed by a discussion of the elements of macro-social marketing that are key to each phase of the HCD process. In the final section, we describe how the case illustrates key themes articulated in the macro-social marketing literature and the form they take in the HCD process.

The Linking Lives Programme: A Case Study in Human-Centred Design at Multiple Levels of an Ecosystem

The Linking Lives programme is a transdisciplinary, experiential learning opportunity for undergraduate students at Virginia Tech. The programme combines nine weeks of coursework related to social change in Europe with four weeks of human-centred design and service-learning projects with nonprofit organisations in Africa. The programme provides a unique experience for students to develop skills related to international social impact work through placement with one of Linking Lives' five nonprofit partner sites in Ethiopia and Rwanda for four weeks.

The following structure of the case study provides an overview of a network where goals are coordinated (inspiration), resources are pooled (ideation), and communication is inclusive and iterative (implementation), and ultimately contributes to downstream change in the context of gender equity and education. This perspective illustrates the complexity of actors in a network with distinct goals, co-creating at each level of a system to accomplish their overlapping goals. We describe the goals and interactions of partners at different stages in the 'stream': as aforementioned, social marketing can be classified by macro (up), meso (mid), and micro (downstream) level activities. Table 9.1 depicts the relationships between the different actors in the ecosystem. A *vertical* interaction depicts the interaction of partners at different stages in the stream and can be conceptualised in terms of micro-social marketing (where an entity further up in the stream attempts to create a change in the partner further down in the stream). A *horizontal* interaction depicts the interaction of entities at the same level in the stream (where organisations or entities interact to pursue mutually beneficial goals).

We next describe the interactions between 'upstream' entities (as is the focus of macro-social marketing) and focus less on interactions with final beneficiaries.

Horizontal 1: University to NGO

Huff et al. (2017) contend that NGOs with shared goals may work together to achieve 'complementary' social change efforts. This is conceptualised as macro-level, or upstream, social change, which can be co-created using the three phases of human-centred design, as described in what follows.

Inspiration

Linking Lives (a university programme) aims to provide undergraduate students with a transformative experience that gives them both the drive and the tools to become agents of sustainable, social change. One way

Table 9.1 Relationships Between Actors in the Ecosystem

	Vertical 1	Vertical 2
Horizontal 1 *Macro Level*	Organisation 1: University Linking Lives Programme & Faculty	Organisation 2: Rwandan Nonprofit
	Goal: create experiences to educate undergraduate students and cultivate responsible citizens	*Goal: obtain funding to further the organisational mission of creating gender equity among Rwandan youth and create cultural change through sport*
Horizontal 2 *Meso Level*	University Students	Rwandan Teachers/Coaches
	Goal: learning, collecting experiences, engaging with other cultures	*Goal: obtain tools that will enhance their ability to educate and improve the wellbeing of Rwandan youth*
Micro Level	Beneficiaries (Rwandan youth)	

this university-based entity aims to do this is to develop long-term relationships with established nonprofit partners implementing projects for social change. The program's process of developing a relationship with nonprofit partners starts with an examination of shared values.

Linking Lives identified a Rwandan nonprofit organisation that teaches gender equity to children through an after school sport programme as a potential partner. Among their values are the beliefs that the best way to create change is through young people and that engaging within a community over an extended period of time is the path to create sustainable change. These values map on to the Linking Lives program's belief in the power of educating the next generation to tackle social issues and the importance of engaging in lasting relationships with organisations dedicated to social change.

Once an organisation with shared values has been identified, the next step in developing a relationship with a nonprofit partner involves discussing possible projects. The Linking Lives staff spends at least a year learning about the organisation, making site visits, and talking with staff about their needs and different ways the programme might co-create value.

Ideation

One project that emerged as a good fit was a monitoring and evaluation (M&E) study. The Rwandan nonprofit identified a need to collect data to present to external organisations to assist in funding for its programming. Resources were identified that both teams could bring to the table to make this project a reality. The Linking Lives programme brought faculty with expertise in research methods and incorporated a research methods course and training on M&E procedures as part of the Linking Lives coursework. The Rwandan nonprofit team brought knowledge of their annual grant goals, current programming initiatives, the outcomes they'd like to investigate in their beneficiaries, and an awareness of how questions should be translated and procedures should be revised for the cultural context.

During the ideation phase, the Linking Lives and Rwandan nonprofit teams planned the M&E through a collaborative process that involved multiple iterations of generating, revising, and adapting content for the data collection materials, procedures, and logistics. The process involved input and buy-in from team members of both organisations at multiple levels.

Implementation

In the months preceding data collection, the Linking Lives and Rwandan nonprofit teams were in contact at least once a week to finalise and translate all M&E materials. During the month the Linking Lives students were on site, their data collection work was supervised by the cultural ambassadors, the Rwandan nonprofit staff, and Linking Lives staff. All groups had daily, face-to-face communication to ensure the project was running smoothly and adapted the process as needed.

Once the data were collected, the information was sent to Virginia Tech faculty with expertise in data analysis and reporting. Again, there was an iterative process between the Linking Lives and Rwandan nonprofit teams. After a first round of data analysis was completed, there was discussion of follow up questions (e.g., examining different segments of the sample), the understanding of M&E results, and the creation of appropriate visual aids. The final report was developed over a period of several months, with weekly contact via email and Skype between the Linking Lives and Rwandan nonprofit teams.

Vertical 1: University to Students

Each macro-level actor in the network seeks to influence the behaviour of actors further down in the stream in ways that take into account the goals of their target. For example, Virginia Tech's primary goal is to educate university students and cultivate responsible citizens. Students may have a goal of learning, collecting experiences to share with friends or future employers, or interacting with other cultures. The service-learning projects developed by Virginia Tech are one way for the organisation to create the desired change in their target beneficiary group (students).

Inspiration

An important component of the Linking Lives programme is to facilitate experiential learning. The semester before students participate, they are enrolled in a one-credit course called "Ut Prosim Abroad" ("Ut Prosim" is the motto of Virginia Tech and translates to "That I may serve"). The course is intended to facilitate conversations before living and engaging in service-learning experiences abroad and focuses on the attitudes (i.e., open-mindedness, curiosity, respect, and empathy), skills (i.e., interpersonal communication, self-care, planning, and debriefing), and knowledge (i.e., intercultural awareness, privilege, intersectionality, and professional standards) needed to engage in service-learning across cultures. During this course, students spend time thinking about their intentions behind enrolling in the programme and their learning goals while in the program. The Linking Lives staff then works with its nonprofit partners to identify and develop projects that match the organisation's needs with the students' self-identified skill sets and interests. Students are placed with organisations and projects that provide the best fit.

Ideation

Students spend time preparing for specific projects for the organisation they will visit. As an example, the Rwanda nonprofit requested the students lead morning camp sessions for kids who attend the nonprofit's after school sport programming. The Linking Lives' staff described the general parameters of the project (based on interactions with the Rwandan nonprofit and an understanding of their goals) and provided feedback on the content (lectures, discussion topics, and activities) generated by the students. These materials were then shared with the Rwandan nonprofit staff for their feedback and revised in a continuous iterative process until consensus on a final product was reached.

Implementation

Reflection is a critical component of the students' experiential learning while implementing their service-learning projects; it is through this process, in particular, that the university's goal of creating change in their downstream target (students) is achieved. Students are required to journal and engage in bi-weekly facilitated reflection discussions with the Linking Lives staff. One purpose of these discussions is for the students to investigate their feelings and spend time thinking about what their experience means to them in a larger sense. Another purpose is to reflect on the activities they are participating in with the organisation and ensure the organisation's needs are being met. A third purpose is for students to identify ways in which the programme could be improved for both the students' and the program's nonprofit partners (ultimately contributing to achieving the university's goal of creating a more enriching experience for university students). In essence, multiple forms of communication are employed to reinforce the creation of value for both parties engaged in the exchange and inform both parties' future actions. For example, former students who articulated a desire for more up-front course content that addressed privilege and intersectionality shaped the content that was included in the "Ut Prosim Abroad" course.

Vertical 2: NGO—Rwandan Coaches and Teachers

As aforementioned, in vertical interactions, the upstream partner in the network seeks to influence the behaviour of actors further down in the stream in ways that take into account the goals of their target and achieve their organisational goals. The Rwandan nonprofit has multiple downstream targets, but the actors most proximal to them are the coaches that deliver the programming to the youth. That is, to achieve their organisational mission of transforming socio-cultural gender norms through sport (and a more concrete objective of obtaining funding to do so), the nonprofit seeks to change the behaviour of coaches to maximise their effectiveness in delivering content. Coaches may desire capacity building activities designed to improve their effectiveness in delivering the content to help them achieve their professional goals. The three phases of human-centred design, outlined in what follows, were used to approach the goal of developing coach-delivered programs sponsored by the Rwandan non-profit organisation.

Inspiration

The Rwandan nonprofit's vision is to use the power of sport to challenge and shift inequitable gender norms and promote gender equity. The initial inspiration for the organisation's programme was based on input from one child in the community who said, "I see now that girls can play too". The common understanding became that girls can 'play' or contribute when given equal opportunities, though opportunities in the community were lacking.

Ideation

In the process of creating the structure and content for a gender equity program, sport was identified as an approachable medium for reaching children in the community. The Rwandan nonprofit team brought expertise in sport programming and gender equity curriculum for youth. The local community brought an understanding of the cultural norms, language, and local sport and customs, thus representing a pooling of resources. After school was identified as the best time to make programming accessible. Through conversations with community leaders, teachers from the local schools were identified as the best candidates to serve as coaches. In an ongoing, iterative process, the Rwandan nonprofit team and coaches work together to develop an after school sport programme for boys and girls that uses sport as a way to reach gender equity and provide a space for boys and girls to play together in an environment that fosters fairness and mutual respect.

Implementation

The Rwandan nonprofit began implementing its programme in the local community in 2012. To ensure the programme meets the needs of the community, the nonprofit team collects data to look at the outcomes of its participating youth, has weekly meetings with its coaches, and talks semi-annually with parents and community members to assess the impact of its programming on the local community. Based on the communicated feedback, the team makes changes to best serve the community's needs. Over the last six years, the nonprofit's work has evolved to include a weekly community day with programming to include parents and local community members, additional training for coaches, and an additional all-female camp to provide additional support and resources for local female youth.

Horizontal 2: Students—Rwandan Coaches and Teachers

The interaction between entities at the same level in the 'stream' can occur further upstream (as described in the context of the university partner and NGO) or further downstream (closer to the final beneficiaries) where the interacting entities collaborate to achieve mutually beneficial goals. In this system, the interaction between the university students and Rwandan teachers (employed by the NGO as coaches) can be considered as the meso level. Their interaction was shaped through the three phases of human-centred design, as described in the following.

Inspiration

The collaborative projects that place students working directly with the nonprofit's key stakeholders are a cornerstone of the Linking Lives program. These projects provide Linking Lives students the opportunity to learn about their nonprofit organisation's efforts directly from those involved in implementation and provide the folks involved in implementation opportunity to provide insight on the programs and services the nonprofit delivers, as well as identify areas for growth. For example, students recently engaged in a project aimed at identifying top priority teacher training needs for the Rwandan nonprofit. The Rwandan nonprofit sought to develop a training programme to help its coaches (all local teachers) implement a new policy of the Rwandan government (i.e., curriculum changes focusing on competency-based outcomes). Mutual interest and shared goals guided this phase: The Linking Lives programme students were interested in getting a first-hand account of the change in the Rwandan educational system from local teachers, and the local teachers were interested in sharing their feedback and experiences with the new curriculum and their challenges implementing these changes in the classroom.

Ideation

During the interview process with Linking Lives students, the teachers were able to identify their needs to support their work in the classroom. For example, teachers felt they lacked sufficient training and resources to plan lessons in a way that was learner-centred and lacked confidence in practices they could use to create gender-inclusive classroom environments.

The information the students collected was then communicated to the Rwandan nonprofit team, who used the information to help inform a three-day gender inclusive training programme for teachers based on best practice models for eliminating gender disparities. A programme was developed which was then vetted by local education government leaders and the Rwandan Ministry of Education.

Implementation

A first round of teacher training sessions took place last spring. This year, another project is planned with attendees of the training. Linking Lives students will engage directly with attendees of this programme to learn how the tools they learned in the training are being used in the classroom and whether the teachers perceive them as effective (i.e., communication to reinforce the creation of value for both parties engaged in the exchange and inform both parties' future actions). This will begin another cycle of iterations to provide teachers with the tools they need to successfully implement the new curriculum in the classroom.

Discussion: Combining Human-Centred Design and Systems Thinking

Multiple themes illustrated in the Linking Lives case study have been articulated in the macro-social marketing literature as important to consider in designing macro-social marketing efforts. Specifically, the consideration of goals/mission, resources to create action, and interpersonal communication processes are key in developing macro-social efforts. In this final discussion, we describe how these criteria can be considered at each step in the human-centred design process, bridging the literatures on HCD and macro-social marketing, and highlight elements to consider as best practices.

Shared Goals and Inspiration

Each inspiration phase described in the Linking Lives case study highlighted the importance of shared goals. Past research in macro-social marketing and the institutional theory literature has identified the importance of working with partners who share a mission or goal (in the context or organisations) or values (in the context of individuals or groups of individuals). For example, Huff et al. (2017) describe how groups of non-governmental organisations opposed to gun violence joined forces to create a political action committee to generate and support political influence. While some organisations could be interested in reducing gun violence through discrediting the Second Amendment, this coalition shared the perspective that attacking the Second Amendment would be a conversation ender rather than starter (Huff et al., 2017). The common goal and approach enabled collaboration. Articulating a shared understanding of an overarching goal or mission will facilitate the inspiration phase, in which two entities work together to develop a common understanding of a problem. For example, an organisation that promotes vegetarianism as a way to reduce one's carbon footprint and an organisation that encourages the use of public transit may share the goal of environmental conservation; this shared set of beliefs about what is important in the abstract allows both entities to come together to have a conversation to approach a more concrete problem.

Resources and Ideation

The ideation phases in the Linking Lives case study illustrates the importance of shared resources. Past research in macro-social marketing, social entrepreneurship, and the institutional theory literature has also identified the importance of a resource-based approach to developing partnerships that leverage each entity's distinct set of resources (Oliver, 1997; Luca et al., 2016; Stead, Arnott, & Dempsey, 2013). The resource-based view conceptualises capabilities as a pool of internal resources (Wernerfelt, 1984), and past work suggests that collaboration between organisations is most fruitful when it capitalises on synergies between the organisations' resources (Hardy, Phillips, & Lawrence, 2003). These resources can take the form of financial, knowledge, human capital, social capital, and infrastructure-based resources, among others. During the ideation phase of co-creation, entities brainstorm a wide range of ideas to address a problem, implicitly considering resources as a constraining as well as facilitating factor for what can be enacted. The past research on the resource-based view would suggest that brainstorming could entail an explicit delineation of the resources each organisation has to contribute, facilitating conversation about how to develop solutions that make best use of the available resources. In the gun violence prevention group example, a group of organisations pooled resources from each entity bringing something different to the table, as described in the following quote (Huff et al., 2017, p. 399).

> Each group has something to offer. Smart Action has the experience. We've been in this game a long time. Marco's organization [Sensible Gun Owners]: they know guns, inside and out. They're all gun owners. Safe And Sound: they've got the numbers. We need 80,000 people at a rally? They get involved, and they also have the resources to do [safe gun storage] training at the local level, to change how people are actually being safer with their guns. If we need data, research, that comes from Take Action. They have the people on that. It's all a big team. We all know what the other [GVPGs] are up to, and then we can bring it all together when we need to.
>
> (Patricia, the leader of Smart Action)

Implementation and Communication Process

Finally, the Linking Lives case study illustrates the importance of the communication process during the implementation phase. Past research on institutional communication has identified the importance of the communicative process to successfully implement the jointly developed solutions (Gustafsson, Kristensson, & Witell, 2012). Facets of communication entail frequency (amount of continuous inter-organisational feedback), direction (democratic communication, or extent to which one party exerts power over the other and whether both parties take equal initiative to interact and assume approximately the same workload), modality (how communication is transmitted; face to face or via mediated channels), and content (what is focused on during communication; such as current problems and what is going well—Mohr, Fisher, & Nevin, 1996). A consideration of the communication process is particularly important during the implementation phase, where the solution is enacted. Ideally, communication will be enacted at a level that is mutually agreed upon in terms of frequency, will be shared (in terms of initiation and workload), will be conducted through a mutually decided upon modality, and will feature content that is helpful in addressing problems that arise but also bolster morale and develop the relationship between entities. Communication between the organisations takes place before and during the implementation of the jointly developed solution, and a breakdown in the communication process will forestall the successful accomplishment of the desired social change.

References

Benford, R. D., & Snow, D. A. (2000). Framing processes and social movements: An overview and assessment. *Annual Review of Sociology, 26*(1), 611–639.

Brown, T. (2009). *Change by design: How design thinking transforms organizations and inspires innovation* (1st ed.). New York, NY: Harper Business.

Brown, T., & Wyatt, J. (2010). Design thinking for social innovation. *Development Outreach, 12*(1), 29–43.

Bryant, C. A., Mccormack Brown, K. R., Mcdermott, R. J., Forthofer, M. S., Bumpus, E. C., Calkins, S. A., & Zapata, L. B. (2007). Community-based prevention marketing. *Health Promotion Practice, 8*(2), 154–163.

Buchanan, R. (2011). Human dignity and human rights: Thoughts on the principles of human-centered design. *Design Issues, 17*(3), 35–39.

Carrigan, M., Moraes, C., & Leek, S. (2011). Fostering responsible communities: A community social marketing approach to sustainable living. *Journal of Business Ethics, 100*(3), 515–534.

Checkland, P. (2000). Soft systems methodology: A thirty year retrospective. *Systems Research and Behavioural Science, 17*(Suppl 1), S11–S58.

Cronin, J. M., & Mccarthy, M. B. (2011). Preventing game over. *Journal of Social Marketing, 1*(2), 133–153.

Dees, J. G. (1998). Enterprising nonprofits. *Harvard Business Review*, 76, 54–69.

Dibb, S. (2014). Up, up and away: Social marketing breaks free. *Journal of Marketing Management*, 30(11–12), 1159–1185.

Domegan, C., Collins, K., Stead, M., McHugh, P., & Hughes, T. (2013). Value co-creation in social marketing: Functional or fanciful? *Journal of Social Marketing*, 3(3), 239–256.

Domegan, C., McHugh, P., Devaney, M., Duane, S., Hogan, M., Broome, B. J., . . . Piwowarczyk, J. (2016). Systems-thinking social marketing: Conceptual extensions and empirical investigations. *Journal of Marketing Management*, 32(11–12), 1123–1144.

Domegan, C. T. (2008). Social marketing: Implications for contemporary marketing practices classification scheme. *Journal of Business & Industrial Marketing*, 23(2), 135–141.

Dorst, K. (2011). The core of 'design thinking and its application. *Design studies*, 32(6), 521–532.

Fleischmann, K. (2013). Social entrepreneurs and social designers: Change makers with a new mindset? *International Journal of Business and Social Science*, 4(16), 9–17.

Fuad-Luke, A. (2013). *Design activism: Beautiful strangeness for a sustainable world*. London: Routledge.

Gebauer, J., Füller, J., & Pezzei, R. (2013). The dark and the bright side of co-creation: Triggers of member behaviour in online innovation communities. *Journal of Business Research*, 66(9), 1516–1527.

Grissemann, U. S., & Stokburger-Sauer, N. E. (2012). Customer co-creation of travel services: The role of company support and customer satisfaction with the co-creation performance. *Tourism Management*, 33(6), 1483–1492.

Grönroos, C. (2012). Conceptualising value co-creation: A journey to the 1970s and back to the future. *Journal of Marketing Management*, 28(13–14), 1520–1534.

Gustafsson, A., Kristensson, P., & Witell, L. (2012). Customer co-creation in service innovation: A matter of communication? *Journal of Service Management*, 23(3), 311–327.

Hamby, A., Pierce, M., & Brinberg, D. (2017). Solving complex problems: Enduring solutions through social entrepreneurship, community action, and social marketing. *Journal of Macromarketing*, 37(4), 369–380.

Hardy, C., Phillips, N., & Lawrence, T. B. (2003). Resources, knowledge and influence: The organizational effects of interorganizational collaboration. *Journal of Management Studies*, 40(2), 321–347.

Hastings, G., & Domegan, C. (2013). *Social marketing*. London: Routledge.

Huff, A. D., Barnhart, M., Mcalexander, B., & Mcalexander, J. (2017). Addressing the wicked problem of American gun violence. *Journal of Macromarketing*, 37(4), 393–408.

Kemper, J. A., & Ballantine, P. W. (2017). Socio-technical transitions and institutional change. *Journal of Macromarketing*, 37(4), 381–392.

Kennedy, A-M. (2016). Macro-social marketing. *Journal of Macromarketing*, 36(3), 354–365.

Kennedy, A-M. (2017). Macro-social marketing research. *Journal of Macromarketing*, 37(4), 347–355.

Kennedy, A-M., Kapitan, S., Bajaj, N., Bakonyi, A., & Sands, S. (2017). Uncovering wicked problem's system structure: Seeing the forest for the trees. *Journal of Social Marketing, 7*(1), 51–73.

Kennedy, A-M., & Parsons, A. (2012). Macro-social marketing and social engineering: A systems approach. *Journal of Social Marketing, 2*(1), 37–51.

Kimbell, L. (2011). Rethinking design thinking: Part I. *Design and Culture, 3*(3), 285–306.

Kotler, P., & Zaltman, G. (1971). Social marketing: An approach to planned social change. *Journal of Marketing, 35*(3), 3–12.

Leathar, D. S., & Hastings, G. B. (1987). Social marketing and health education. *Journal of Services Marketing, 1*(2), 49–52.

Lefebvre, R. C. (2012). Transformative social marketing: Co-creating the social marketing discipline and brand. *Journal of Social Marketing, 2*(2), 118–129.

Luca, N. R., Hibbert, S., & Mcdonald, R. (2016). Towards a service-dominant approach to social marketing. *Marketing Theory, 16*(2), 194–218.

Martin, R. L. (2009). *The design of business: Why design thinking is the next competitive advantage*. Boston: Harvard Business Press.

Mohr, J. J., Fisher, R. J., & Nevin, J. R. (1996). Collaborative communication in interfirm relationships: Moderating effects of integration and control. *Journal of Marketing, 60*(3), 103–115.

Montgomery, A. W., Dacin, P. A., & Dacin, M. T. (2012). Collective social entrepreneurship: Collaboratively shaping social good. *Journal of Business Ethics, 111*(3), 375–388.

Mulgan, G. (2006). The process of social innovation. *Innovations: Technology, Governance, Globalization, 1*(2), 145–162.

Normann, R., & Ramirez, R. (1993). From value chain to value constellation: Designing interactive strategy. *Harvard Business Review, 71*(4), 65–77.

Oliver, C. (1997). Sustainable competitive advantage: Combining institutional and resource-based views. *Strategic Management Journal, 18*(9), 697–713.

Prahalad, C. K., & Ramaswamy, V. (2004). Co-creation experiences: The next practice in value creation. *Journal of Interactive Marketing, 18*(3), 5–14.

Rowe, P. G. (1991). *Design thinking*. Cambridge, MA: MIT Press.

Sanders, E. B-N., & Stappers, P. J. (2008). Co-creation and the new landscapes of design. *Co-Design, 4*(1), 5–18.

Stead, M., Arnott, L., & Dempsey, E. (2013). Healthy heroes, magic meals, and a visiting alien. *Social Marketing Quarterly, 19*(1), 26–39.

Svendsen, A. C., & Laberge, M. (2005). Convening stakeholder networks. *Journal of Corporate Citizenship, 19*, 91–104.

Truong, V. D. (2017). Government-led macro-social marketing programs in Vietnam. *Journal of Macromarketing, 37*(4), 409–425.

Vargo, S. L., & Lusch, R. F. (2008). Service-dominant logic: Continuing the evolution. *Journal of the Academy of Marketing Science, 36*(1), 1–10.

Warfield, J. N., & Cárdenas, A. R. (1994). *A handbook of interactive management*. Ames: Iowa State University Press.

Wernerfelt, B. (1984). A resource-based view of the firm. *Strategic Management Journal, 5*(2), 171–180.

Wymer, W. (2011). Developing more effective social marketing strategies. *Journal of Social Marketing, 1*(1), 17–31.

10 Collaborative Systems Thinking for Social Change

Josephine Previte and Liam Pomfret

Introduction

Systems thinking social marketing has evolved in response to critiques and concerns about individual-level social marketing. Concerns raised about micro-focused social marketing point out that interventions designed to create exchanges with targeted individuals underestimate the complexity, or 'wicked', nature of some social problems (Brennan & Parker, 2014; McHugh & Domegan, 2013; Rittel & Webber, 1973). These problems are wicked because they are hard to define; and some problems in society make it difficult to 'pin-point' the network of power and influence from multiple actors and stakeholders that make the problem intractable to achieving positive social change outcomes (Hastings & Domegan, 2017). For example, the well-used case of obesity is often discussed by 'systems thinkers' to identify why it is not solely up to the individual to engage in healthy living and physical activity. Given the range of different stakeholders connected to the obesity problem—food producers, manufacturers, marketing and advertising decision makers, business, and government policy decision makers—the potential for the interpretation of what the problem *is*, how to deal with it, and in which order of priority encapsulates the challenge. This challenge cannot be successfully resolved with traditional linear and analytical approaches (Kennedy, 2016; McHugh & Domegan, 2013). For example, information and awareness campaigns, such as the controversial Australian 'Toxic Fat' campaign that used mass media to graphically depict visceral fat of an overweight individual (Morley, Niven, Coomber, Dixon, & Wakefield, 2013), leverage the resources of the marketing systems to create awareness of the problem in targeted 'at-risk' groups. Other social change advocates argue the case for legislative responses such as a proposed 'fat tax', or introduction of 'sugar taxes' on soft drinks. Yet the socially complex nature of the obesity problem means that responsibility and power are more distributed—not simply 'upstream' or 'downstream'—in finding solutions based on the allocation of social change resources. Thus, systems thinkers argue that to achieve long-term change it is important to embrace a deeper understanding and *coordination* of a broader system of influences (Kennedy & Parsons, 2012; Roberts, 2000).

This social marketing discussion of the forces and factors that influence behaviour reveals marketing itself as a form of social behaviour (Dixon, 1984). In fact, social marketing brings to the forefront the positive and negative consequences that evolve from the interactions between marketing and society. These interactions are shaped and influenced by the interactions of a range of actors and market interactions that demonstrate different explanations of system influences. For example, in defining macro-social marketing, Kennedy and Parsons (2012) clearly articulated how social marketing techniques used in a holistic way can effect systemic change. In explaining how this is achievable, Kennedy (2016) more recently argued that macro-social marketing seeks to change institutional norms, which requires a holistic, system-wide view of the issue, particularly where social marketing techniques are deployed to 'solve' wicked problems. When further explicating the influence of marketing systems, Layton (2015, p. 305) discussed social marketing as a type of marketing system involving "*a network of individuals, groups and/or entities, embedded in a social matrix*" that exploits tangible and intangible resources for "*initiating, supporting, or countervailing issues of community concern*". What is implicit, but not explicitly explained nor defined in these theories and conceptualisations of how to achieve systemic change, is the required action of collaboration. In this chapter, we aim to explore the marketing meaning of collaboration, to further guide social marketers towards collaborative systems thinking to inform social marketing theory and practice. Our starting point to achieve this aim was to turn to the broader marketing literature to seek insight about the meaning of collaboration.

The Meaning of Collaborative Thinking

Collaboration and collaborative thinking have been investigated in the marketing literature substantially through discussions of collaborative consumption. The earliest uses in the literature of the term 'collaborative consumption' refer to the consumption of goods or services as part of one or more consumers engaging in joint activities with one or more others (Felson & Spaeth, 1978). More recent authors have, however, criticised this early perspective as being overly broad, lacking sufficient focus on the acquisition and distribution of economic resources by and between collaborators (Belk, 2014). Drawing on Hawley's (1950) human ecological theory, this perspective of collaborative consumption places emphasis on the interdependent relationships between people, other living creatures, and the physical environment, as well as on spatial and temporal aspects of community and community activities. This human ecological theory shares many similarities with recent work on behavioural ecological systems and systems thinking in social marketing (Brennan, Previte, & Fry, 2016; Brychkov & Domegan, 2017; Domegan et al., 2016). In the marketing literature, however, this initial conceptualisation of collaborative consumption manifested primarily in research concerned with consumption at small social distances, such as by family groups towards collective goals (e.g., Hamilton & Catterall, 2007), rather than investigations exploring collaborations taking place within broader social systems.

Felson and Spaeth (1978) used Hawley's (1950) spatio-temporal structures to break collaborative consumption down into three basic categories: 1) 'Direct-contact collaboration', when the consumption occurs without any physical or temporal separation of collaborators; 2) 'System-hookup collaboration', when collaborators are physically but not temporally segregated; and 3) 'Segregated collaboration', when collaborators are both physically and temporarily separated. Though missing from their framework, we can also readily conceptualise a fourth basic category, where collaborators consume in the same location, but not at the same time. For instance, a community garden would involve the collective contributions over time of a group of collaborators, whose efforts build off of and support one another.

Felson and Spaeth (1978) argued changes to the spatio-temporal structure of community activities would impact on the structure of collaborative consumption, and on what particular types of collaborative consumption would be generated. For instance, while Felson and Spaeth (1978) would have conceptualised the spatial as referring exclusively to physical separation, modern examples of collaborative consumption include behaviours such as sharing on social media (Belk, 2014), where collaborators share a single digital space despite any physical or temporal separation which may exist. In reframing Felson and Spaeth's (1978) categories for modern consumption behaviours, we therefore must necessarily adopt a broader understanding of what it means to consume 'in the same place' to incorporate digital environments. Similarly, Felson and Spaeth's (1978) categories simplistically assume that all collaborations happen only within a single mode. This is a limiting factor for understanding collaborations between networks of actors each with differing degrees of spatio-temporal separation from one another, such as where multiple teams spread across multiple locations might all collaborate on a single collective task. It also fails to recognise that collaborations may be ongoing processes rather than individual time-delimited events, and that such activity may involve collaboration over multiple modes over time.

In the more recent marketing literature, collaborative consumption is frequently conflated with the internet-facilitated consumer-producer networks known collectively as the 'sharing economy' (e.g., Ertz, Durif, Lecompte, & Boivin, 2018; Wahlen & Laamanen, 2017), to the extent that authors such as Belk (2014, p. 1595) have described collaborative consumption and sharing as 'phenomena born of the Internet age'. The term collaborative consumption itself is, however, poorly defined in both the academic and professional literature, with no common agreement as to a clear classification for what it involves (Botsman, 2013; McArthur, 2015). The conflation of collaborative consumption with sharing appears to originate with Botsman and Rogers' (2010, p. xv) definition of collaborative consumption as the "*rapid explosion in swapping, sharing, bartering, trading and renting being reinvented through the latest technologies and peer-to-peer marketplaces in ways and on a scale never possible before*" while also encompassing "*traditional sharing, bartering, lending, trading, renting, gifting, and swapping*". This definition has attracted critiques for being too broad, conflating collaborative consumption with prototypical marketplace exchanges (Belk, 2014; Ertz, Durif, & Arcand, 2018). Though previously Belk (2010) originally discussed how sharing behaviours could also be examples of collaborative consumption, in later work Belk (2014) instead framed these as more separate and distinct concepts, albeit with collaborative consumption demonstrating some elements of sharing. Wahlen and Laamanen (2017) have recently described collaborative consumption as being embedded within the sharing economy.

Table 10.1 illustrates how definitions of collaborative consumption have evolved over time in the literature. Evidenced in these definitions is the shifting role of the consumer, and the changing nature of consumers' relationships with firms and with co-consumers. Whereas the early perspective on collaborative consumption implicitly assumed that collaboration took place only between consumers, we now recognise that consumers in these collaborative consumer-producer networks do not merely act as joint receivers of economic resources, but instead may also shift roles to "*engage in embedded entrepreneurship and collaborate to produce and access resources*" (Scaraboto, 2015, p. 166), acting with the same agency typical of the producer, and creating new forms of consumption and consumers, as well as new forms of business activity (Wahlen & Laamanen, 2017). Similarly, early views of collaborative consumption were focused more on collaborations in familial and household settings, often in dyadic exchanges, with collaborators who could be characterised by their mutual dependency and functional similarity (Wahlen & Laamanen, 2017). Newer perspectives of collaborative consumption instead open up discussions about different types of relationships, incorporating a stronger focus on and understanding of facilitated and/or mediated extra-familial collaborations with broadly distributed networked actors, including with random strangers (Arnould & Rose, 2015; Ertz et al., 2018; Figueiredo & Scaraboto, 2016).

Modern perspectives on collaborative consumption describe dynamic, self-adjusting networks of actors (Akaka, Vargo, & Lusch, 2012; Vargo &

Table 10.1 Changing Definitions of Collaborative Consumption and Sharing Over Time

Author & Year	Concept	Definition
Felson & Spaeth, 1978, p. 614	Collaborative Consumption	"Those events in which one or more persons consume economic goods or services in the process of engaging in joint activities with one or more others."
Belk, 2007, p. 126	Sharing	"The act and process of distributing what is ours to others for their use and/or the act and process of receiving or taking something from others for our use."
Botsman & Rogers, 2010, p. xv	Collaborative Consumption	"The rapid explosion in swapping, sharing, bartering, trading and renting being reinvented through the latest technologies and peer-to-peer marketplaces in ways and on a scale never possible before . . . traditional sharing, bartering, lending, trading, renting, gifting, and swapping."
Botsman, 2013	Collaborative Consumption	"An economic model based on sharing, swapping, trading, or renting products and services, enabling access over ownership."
Belk, 2014, p. 1597	Collaborative Consumption	"People coordinating the acquisition and distribution of a resource for a fee or other compensation."
McArthur, 2015, p. 239	Collaborative Consumption	"People sharing goods and services with other people."
Wahlen & Laamanen, 2017, p. 94	Collaborative Consumption	"A form of economic collaboration where idling resources are made available – shared – with others in a larger community – the sharing economy/"
Wahlen & Laamanen, 2017, p. 97	Sharing	"The acts and practices through which people gain access to resources, both material and immaterial, in a given (virtual) network, group, or community . . . sharing can be understood not only as a mode of exchange or transfer of ownership, as in commercial exchange, but also as a form of co-ownership."
Ertz et al., 2018	Collaborative Consumption	"The set of resource circulation schemes that enable consumers to both receive and provide, temporarily or permanently, valuable resources or services through direct interaction with other consumers or through an intermediary."

Lusch, 2011). Within these networks, disparate and diverse actions for collective outcomes, including the integration and exchange of resources, allow for a systemic process of value co-creation through circulation (Figueiredo & Scaraboto, 2016). From this process, collaborators receive both individual and collective benefits. With those forms of collective consumption where the focus of the behaviour is on the broader and/or long-term collective benefits, such as where collaborative consumption is used as a vehicle to contribute to sustainable consumption (de Burgh-Woodman & King, 2013; Luchs et al., 2011), these can represent new kinds of socially responsible behaviour and consumer activism (Ertz et al., 2018). These understandings of collaborative consumption, however, display a strong focus on micro, individual-level considerations of social behaviour. While acknowledging the role played by meso-level actors in the process of collaborative consumption, these actors are narrowly framed as mere service providers or market intermediaries. Rather than being active participants engaging in the collaborative sharing of resources, they are typically positioned as co-operators who enable or facilitate consumers' collaborative consumption processes.

Approaches for social marketing based on systems thinking offer substantial potential for shaping and effecting change. While complex, wicked problems are beyond the resources of a single marketplace actor to impact, they can be addressed through collaboration of multiple stakeholders (Levine & Prietula, 2014; McArthur, 2015). Our review of marketing's collaborative consumption definitions raises interesting questions for us to consider when conceptualising the meaning and application of collaboration for social marketing theory and practice. Collaborative consumption implies interactions and sharing of resources *between* actors in the market, as well as the longer-term investment or exploitation of resources to seek *collective benefits* for the stakeholders involved. We decided to closely examine the systems literature in social marketing to identify how the notions of interactions between actors across multiple layers of influence within a system are discussed. We also wondered if the emerging systems thinking literature was reflective of the general collaborative marketing literatures, in that it also maintained a myopic consumer framing of the market interactions (Brennan et al., 2016).

Analysing the Social Marketing Systems Literature

Within the emerging social marketing systems literature, notions of collaboration, relational influences, and the interactions between actors and systems is yet to be more extensively developed. McHugh and Domegan (2013, p. 89) started this examination when they identified collaborative system indicators to inform how social marketers examine interrelationships and interconnections between elements, processes, and outcomes within a social marketing system. In extending this early discussion, we turned to an analysis of the existing social marketing systems literature to inform and identify the core concepts used when explicating social marketing systems thinking. This analysis is then applied to guide and inform our understanding of collaborative systems thinking.

Method and Approach

A systematic scoping review was conducted to identify literature relating to systems thinking in social marketing. In adopting this scoping review approach, we directed our attention towards the key features of published research across the full scope of available articles (Grant & Booth, 2009). During this initial phase of our inquiry, our objective was to capture the breadth of systems research, identifying those key features which characterise research in this domain. The initial search strategy involved keyword searches for 'systems' (and variations thereof) in the abstracts of papers published in the *Journal of Social Marketing* and in *Social Marketing Quarterly*, as well as keyword searches for 'systems' and 'social marketing' (and variations thereof) in the *Journal of Macromarketing*. The abstracts of each paper identified were read to filter for work relevant to systems thinking. Where this was unclear from the abstract, we read the paper to see if systems thinking was a focus of the paper.

Following from this first stage, a broader search was then conducted using a combination of EBSCO Business Source Complete, a database of over 1,200 academic journals in business (EBSCO Industries, 2018) which indexes all of our explicitly targeted journals along with a large number of generalist marketing journals which typically publish articles relating to social marketing (Dahl, 2010); ProQuest ABI/Inform Global, which includes over 4,500 academic peer-reviewed titles (ProQuest, 2018); and the large multi-disciplinary databases of Scopus and the Web of Science. These searches, which were not restricted by date, involved keyword searches for 'systems' and 'social marketing' (and variations thereof) in the abstracts and keywords of scholarly journals. Specifically for Web of Science, which does not support abstract-only search, we performed a full keyword search and then manually examined the abstracts for our desired keywords. In total, we found 40 articles that met our selection criteria across 8 marketing journals. In addition to the three journals listed above, this included articles from the *Journal of Marketing Management, Marketing Theory, Australasian Marketing Journal, Journal of Consumer Marketing*, and *Journal of Nonprofit and Public Sector Marketing*. While the multi-disciplinary databases also returned several articles in non-marketing journals, we excluded these as we desired to focus on how the topic has been dealt with specifically within the marketing discipline.

To examine the large corpus of data generated from the selected 40 papers, we used the Computer Assisted Qualitative Data Analysis Software (CAQDAS) program, Leximancer (Version 4.5). Using this tool guided our 'deep dive' into an interpretive examination of how social marketing scholars are conceptualising and applying systems thinking, and identification of where in these discussions they had also explicated notions of collaboration and relationships between stakeholders and systems. We took this approach because we wanted to closely align our conceptualisation of collaborative systems thinking within the current social marketing approach, and to also ensure that our conceptualisation was emergent from the central notions that define social marketing systems thinking.

We followed a typical Leximancer (2018) text-mining analysis, which included a three-step interpretive process in managing and analysing the data. Our first data management step involved automatically processing the data to create a unique thesaurus of terms generated from the social marketing articles; this stage resulted in concept selection (Smith & Humphreys, 2006). This initial step generated 139 concepts from the data, which indicated the most frequent concepts (words) generated from Leximancer's grounded-like content analysis. Next, we manually seeded the data, which engaged us in reviewing the concepts and the associated text sections in the data corpus. This phase of the analysis focused on exploring, refining concepts, and the textual data. For example, we reviewed text segments linked to the concepts of **systems** and **system**, deciding to leave both concepts individually represented on the data map to demonstrate the breadth of meaning communicated through social marketers' discussions of system analysis and mapping, and systems theory. Some concept words were merged, simply because they were nouns or verbs with plural forms, e.g., 'group' and 'groups', and 'behaviour' and 'behaviours'. However, we did not merge 'behavioural' with these other behaviour concepts. This is because 'behavioural' was linked to explanations of **behavioural influences** of various 'upstream actors' (Newton, Newton, & Rep, 2016), or discussions about behavioural ecology (Brennan et al., 2016), whereas 'behaviour' was integrated into discussions about **problem** and **individual behaviour**(s) as key focal concepts used in micro-level social marketing discussions.

Following the seeding, our new concepts thus reflect our interpretation of social marketing systems meaning being evidenced in the data, and resulted in a final list of 97 concepts. Finally, we explored the clustering of concepts into higher-level themes to further refine our interpretation of the data by grouping the clusters of concepts, and visualising their interrelationships in an illustrative thematic map (see Figure 10.1). In the following discussion, we reflect on four orienting themes from the social marketing systems literature; these are: social, value, consumers, and systems.

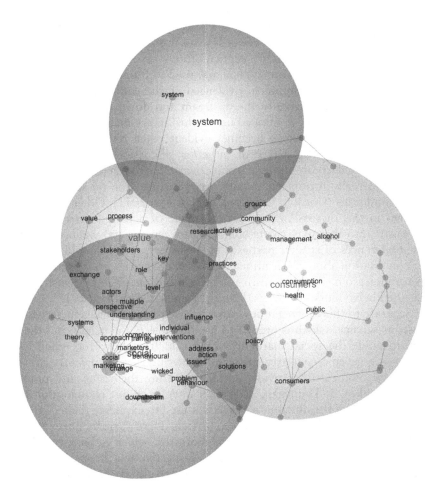

Figure 10.1 Social Marketing Systems Thematic Map

Findings: Reflections on Social Marketing Systems Thinking

The Social Framing of Marketing Systems

Given that our analysis was concerned with discussions of systems linked to social marketing, it was no surprise that the concepts of social (100% relevance; 5501 mentions) and marketing (99% relevance; 4978 mentions) were identified as highly relevant concepts in the literature. Other concepts most connected to **social** were 'change' (31% relevance; 1567 mentions), 'system' (25% relevance; 1249 mentions), 'systems' (20% relevance; 1021 mentions), and 'problem' (20% relevance; 992 mentions).

These concepts are clearly aligned with the foundation principles of what is social marketing, and therefore expected to be frequently used concepts when engaging in discussions about systems thinking in social marketing.

Of more interest to our conceptualisations of collaborative systems thinking is how **systems** are applied and used to frame discussion about the social marketing approach. Evidenced on the data map is the commonly used nomenclature of the **upstream** and **downstream** metaphor. The implication of the continued use of this binary metaphor in discussions of systematic change becomes evident when reviewing the data extracts, which reveals a type of 'either/or' discussion. Typically, these discussions reflect on shifting from downstream targeted approaches to the upstream in response to calls for more attention on social structural conditions (Gordon, Carrigan, & Hastings, 2011). Other common themes in this discussion consider the range of actors—upstream and downstream—that may create conflicts between societal wellbeing and the preferences of specific parties (Luca, Hibbert, & McDonald, 2016); or contestation about the legitimacy of social change efforts based on the perception from either the upstream, institutional actors, or downstream targeted behaviours of citizens (Hamby, Pierce, & Brinberg, 2017).

Separate to this upstream/downstream discussion is engagement with **systems science,** which is argued to provide selected concepts and **theory** to guide the social marketing approach. It is, however, noted as being a more emergent area in social marketing that is currently gaining some momentum in wider social marketing theorising and practice (Brychkov & Domegan, 2017). Of interest to our examination is identification of the different **perspectives** used to explicate the meaning of **systems** in a social marketing approach. Here there is an explicit identification with the notion of **collaborative,** which is linked to the adoption of a Service-Dominant logic perspective which espouses collaborative approaches to *value* creation, especially if social marketing programs are to accommodate action at the downstream, midstream, and upstream levels (Luca et al., 2016). May and Previte (2016), in their study of cat overpopulation, noted **collaborative** *approaches* are needed when a complex network of stakeholders is involved, starting with a community mindset. In the literature, being collaborative is aligned frequently with notions of operating in a 'network of networks' mode (Luca et al., 2016).

Other interesting perspectives informing systems thinking in social marketing are: **service, value,** and **stakeholders.** Discussion of **service** and **systems** draws upon the theory of 'service ecosystems' as a means to reconceptualise relationships (Johansson, Bedggood, Farquharson, & Perenyi, 2018), map service systems, and examine their nature (Luca et al., 2016). It also indicates engagement with the **multiple** meanings of **value,** and **collaborative** activities, which are needed when diverse actors are involved in finding beneficial social and health outcomes (French,

Russell-Bennett, & Mulcahy, 2017). These discussions frequently identify the role of **stakeholders** as a means to find solutions to complex problems. Venturini (2016) notes, however, when governments do social marketing, and shift focus from mass media and paid communications, the challenge becomes attempting to service a multitude of different priorities and multiple **stakeholders** in the face of budgetary restrictions. The concept of **stakeholders** brings forward other challenges, including the actual maintenance of wicked problems, as stakeholder participation can create resistance to enduring solutions (Kennedy & Parsons, 2012), and the formation of greater complexity, which is complicated by **stakeholder** efforts that also require their cooperation, expertise, and skills (Parkinson et al., 2017). Inherent to the concept of stakeholders then is a relational logic implied in interactions between stakeholders (or other actors).

That said, stakeholders at multiple **levels** are integral to systems thinking social marketing. Specifically, Hamby et al. (2017) argue that to change institutional norms, stakeholder buy-in is a necessary condition, requiring **multiple levels** of an institution to effect change. The notion of **level** is also meaningful in its connection in systems social marketing discussions about value.

Value Perspective in Social Marketing Systems

Discussions of value in social marketing systems literature are strongly influenced by service theory, value co-creation, and the underlying logic of resource integration between actors (McColl-Kennedy, Vargo, Dagger, Sweeney, & van Kasteren, 2012). When specifically examining the value theme, the concepts that were revealed to be most connected to **value** were 'service' (42% relevance to value), 'resources' (33% relevance to value), 'organisation' (32% relevance to value), 'collaboration' (29% relevance to value), 'actors' (28% relevance to value), and collaborative (23% relevance to value). Figure 10.1 illustrates the intersection of themes 'social' and 'value', highlighting the integration of service thinking and value meanings to the social marketing systems approach.

Value is embedded in **stakeholders** and **organisations**, which are identified as *"pools of **resources**, expertise and information"*, which are able to be *"diffused and shared, allowing coordination for value co-creation as these influence the facilitation of resource integration and service for service exchange"* (Johansson et al., 2018, p. 163). Integral to this notion of diffusing and sharing is the **value** co-creation **process**, which engages organisations in *"developing value propositions with the customer or beneficiary determining value upon consumption"* (Westberg et al., 2017, p. 105). Significantly, **process** is noted as being *"inherently collaborative and co-creative, although this does not always lead to agreement, consensus and equality"* (Nolan & Varey, 2014, p. 444). Evident in the Leximancer analysis is a predominant service perspective (Vargo & Lusch, 2016), and discussions of value co-creation as the lens through which interactions and network-based processes are explained. Service thinking also guides additional insight into the *"role of social context, configurational fit and resource integration of actors involved"* (Luca et al., 2016, p. 1165).

Importantly, this **value** discussion identifies the **resources** that are available or required, which *"are not static but change, evolve and devolve"* (Luca et al., 2016, p. 1150). Resources have a breadth of meaning, based on the system, or context, through which the social marketing study has been conducted. Resources can include monetary inputs, from one organisation to another for the purpose of co-production, but also as economic resources provided by commercial organisations to social marketing organisations at the meso level (French et al., 2017). Polonsky (2017, p. 271) notes that, despite some negative association, *"businesses can play an important role in solutions to complex problems"* and that social marketers should be leveraging resources in the private sector. **Value, resources,** and **process** are key concepts to the systems thinking literature, and as Fry, Previte, and Brennan (2017, p. 128) note,

> rather than considering value as an entity that is presented to the market by producers. . . [value is a] process which is continuous and which evolves through the actions and interactions that occur between actors and the sharing of resources.

A Consumer Lens to Social Marketing Systems Thinking

It is not surprising that a continued focus on consumers, consumer orientation, and consumer interests motivate social marketers in applying systems thinking. Figure 10.1 shows the integrated and expected close alignment between social marketing systems thinking and the study of **consumers**. In the social marketing systems literature, consumption by consumers is a key motivator for social marketers to examine the market and the layers of interactions between actors, which is indicated by the connected concepts of 'alcohol' (33% relevance to consumption), 'responsible' (28% relevance to consumption), 'sport' (27% relevance to consumption), 'food' (22% relevance to consumption), and 'management' (20% relevance to consumption). The consumer theme therefore explains how the context, or the identified social problem, motivates social marketers' examination and considerations of the **multiple** level interactions required to find solutions to a wicked problem.

Social marketing is entrenched in studies of **health**; it is frequently used as a context to demonstrate the complexity and intractability of 'wicked problems' involving consumer abuse/misuse of food and alcohol. That said, alternative contexts such as fast fashion (Kennedy, 2016) and sustainable lifestyle (Newton et al., 2016) have started to inform understanding of the systems approach. Research about **health,** however, continues to provide a rich context to examine social change. This is evidenced in the discussions about health contexts in the systems literature as social marketers focus attention on the explication and implication of how system levels, or external factors, shape and influence individual consumer behaviour. Therefore, Figure 10.1 illustrates the network of concepts—**health, public, government,** and **policy**—which inform the consumer theme. This theme identifies that in the systems literature policy influences are examined from multiple perspectives; from the influence of government institutions *doing* social marketing, to the governance of influences in other settings, such as clubs that may shape the **advertising** and marketing of **products** and **services** that impact consumer wellbeing. A study of community sporting by Thompson and colleagues (Thompson et al., 2017) is an interesting example that demonstrates how interactional mechanisms, such as club administrators, who set strategic directions on a sport club's culture, are also influenced by the sporting community, team members, and local individuals, which combine to shape the alcohol culture in a club. Additionally, they identified other system influences, inclusive of influential actors at the macro level, such as public authorities and local community authorities, which combine to influence the available alcohol **management** options. Thus, the realm of systems thinkers is to reflect on the consumer and to explore and explain the systematic factors that influence and change a system. As Kemper and Ballantine (2017, p. 386) argue, theoretical developments that embrace systems thinking, such as macro-social marketing, *"offe[r] public health and social marketing the opportunity to truly integrate both environmental and individual behaviour change perspectives"*. Applying a different marketing lens, but sharing a similar motivation to explain the role of wider systems influences, Venturini (2016, p. 1195) notes in his discussion about the specific health enterprise communicated through the 'The Healthy Together Victoria brand' (in Australia) that success was achievable because the brand embraces and connects *"with a variety of different audiences – government, the prevention and public health sector, business and industry, and the biggest audience of all – each and every Victorian"*.

In further demonstrating how systems thinking social marketers engage with studies of, or about consumers, systems thinkers discuss how their studies extend to membership **groups** and **community**. Some recent meso-level studies that indicate this shift in social marketing studies are Luca et al.'s (2016) study of a Smokefree programme in England and May and Previte's study of animal welfare in Australia. Luca et al. (2016, p. 1145) studied how the service interactions embedded in a smoke-free homes and cars programme allowed for the identification of *"customer-centred cues for action"*. In conducting their stated 'midstream (meso) level' research, they interviewed a breadth of consuming publics (smokers and non-smokers), Smokefree programme staff, and professionals (e.g., teachers, hospital staff). Taking a similar meso-level approach, May and Previte's (2016, p. 266) study involved interviewing veterinarians to gather evidence that could answer questions about their power and influence in a social marketing system that is attempting to change the individual behaviour of a specific consumer group.

Yes, systems thinking social marketers remained strongly focused on a consumer inquiry trajectory. However, their social change questions and approaches undertake to extend the lens of social marketing thinking to *"include 'experts' such as legislators, policy makers, influencers, mediators, service providers, community leaders, media executives, corporate managers and health professionals"* (Nolan & Varey, 2014, p. 434). In doing so, systems thinkers initiate reflection and discussion about the multi-level influence of actors and stakeholders in the social marketing system.

Social Marketing System Thinking

Systems thinking extends social marketing theory and practice, which is represented in Figure 10.1 as an emergent theme, connected to social marketing theory and practice through engagement with new theory and literatures—Service-Dominant logic and system theory. Whilst not represented to 'intersect' with the earlier terminology evidenced by the 'social' theme in Figure 10.1, the discussion of a system perspective is connected most frequently in social marketing literature to the concepts: 'complex' (20% relevance to system), 'wicked' (18% relevance to system), 'outcomes' (17% relevance to system), 'actors' (15% relevance to system), and 'multiple' (15% relevance to system).

The system theme in the literature reveals how this emerging approach to studying solutions to wicked problems involves the study of **complex** adaptive systems—which require social marketers to act and think differently (Venturini, 2016). Or, as Kennedy (2016) suggests, to consider different types of very **complex**, system-wide issues. Biroscak (2018, p. 129) points out that when social marketers increase their systems thinking skills, they increase their *"ability to see the world as a **complex** system"*.

In developing system knowledge and skills, the literature addresses the importance of **participants,** which are integral to both relationship building for successfully engaging all parties in a social marketing project (Johansson et al., 2018) and as a resource within organisations to build and maintain relationships. Relationships are a type of resource that can influence stakeholder 'buy-in', which Hamby et al. (2017, p. 370) argue signify commitment from interested stakeholders, as well as being a *"necessary condition to changing norms in a system"*. In explaining the influence of systems, Kennedy (2016) also points out that the *"marketing system creates cultural inputs . . . and is also governed by the social* *institutions within the cultural system for behaviour, interaction, labour, and remuneration expectations"*. This discussion of systems points to reflection about multiple systems—social systems, economic systems, social marketing systems, and more. The key, however, is to bring forward 'joined up thinking', which also considers *"how the barriers, options and benefits connect to each other and where one could intervene to change behaviours"* (Domegan et al., 2016, p. 1129). Addressing barriers is important to engagement, which Parkinson et al. (2017) argue is required when a range of stakeholders across a sector are involved to create traction around a wicked problem.

This Leximancer analysis reveals the theoretical influences informing social marketing systems thinking. First, there is a strong service perspective (Vargo & Lusch, 2016), and discussions of value-co-creation as the lens through which interactions and network-based processes are explained (Luca et al., 2016). Second, social marketers (e.g., Domegan et al., 2016; Kennedy, 2016) also establish strong linkages to Layton's (2015) discussions of mechanisms, actions, and structure theory. To this discussion we add collaborative consumption meanings, to inform further understanding of the collaborative actions of *all* people (actors)—consumers, legislators, policy makers, online/offline influencers, mediators, service providers, community leaders, media executives, corporate managers, and professionals—who have resource potential—material and immaterial—to exchange, transfer ownership, or share in a given system (Nolan & Varey, 2014; Wahlen & Laamanen, 2017). This explanation of collaborative consumption provides a richer view of consumer participation and resources, which is important given the continued influence and focus of consumers in social marketing systems thinking.

In our conceptualisation of collaborative systems thinking, we further draw from Layton's (2015) conceptualisation of social marketing as a form of marketing system to add refinements to our interpretation of collaboration. What is missing from collaborative consumption that Layton (2015) provides is an understanding of the broader social spaces generated by networks, and in which these networks are embedded. It is through the interplay of processes that the micro level of individual interactions, relationships, and transactions of and between consumers, as described in collaborative consumption, is linked with meso-level market structures, functions, and institutions, such as those of service providers and intermediaries; and with broader macro-level patterns and systems. From within these systems, collaborative systems form from emergent boundary spanning collaborations across micro, meso, and macro levels, with the co-evolution of shared values and meanings. In the context of social marketing systems, these would take the form of boundary spanning collaborations specifically addressing issues of collective concern for actors at multiple levels. Based on these multiple perspectives, we outline a typology of collaborative systems thinking for social change.

The Social Marketing System Logic
of Collaborative Actions

Our analysis of the social marketing systems literature has identified system logics to guide conceptualisation of collaborative systems thinking for social change. The seven logics we outline in Table 10.2 are based on the analysis and integration of a wide-ranging set of prior social marketing systems studies and conceptualisations that are strongly influenced by Service-Dominant (S-D) logic (Vargo & Lusch, 2004, 2017) and Layton's marketing systems (2007). The explanation of these influential logics is framed for the purpose of social marketing theory and practice, which can be responsive to the challenges inherent in addressing and designing solutions to wicked social problems. A fundamental systems theory perspective guiding our conceptualisation of these logics is that *"the whole is greater than the sum of its parts"* (Dixon, 1984, p. 7); therefore we do not prioritise any logic over the other, but rather consider the interactional and dynamic aspects of systems to inform our thinking about social change processes and outcomes.

In extending current social marketing systems thinking, we embrace and draw upon existing system logics, and add two collaboratively oriented notions—these are the logic of *collaborative consumers* and *shared value*. In defining the logic of *collaborative consumers*, we integrated insights from the collaborative consumption literature, with the S-D logic purview of consumers as proactive co-creators of resources. Our shift in perspective argues that consumers are enabled to receive and provide valuable resources or services through interactions with a range of multiple stakeholders (or actors) in the social marketing system. Therefore, we maintain the view of consumers as fundamental actors and social influencers who also identify and participate in wicked problem solutions or social change outcomes. Furthermore, by situating consumers as resource collaborators, there are explicit actions grounded in relational logics that can and will involve multiple actors in responding to social change solutions. This shift in perspective moves beyond notions of dyadic exchange based on social marketers designing interventions to complete and create individual level change, towards the involvement of multiple stakeholders participating in solutions to complex problems. The reciprocity inherent in this relational view of multiple stakeholder engagement also highlights the view of consumers and other stakeholders in the system engaging in *resource integration*. The notion of resource integration is typically focused on the empowered role of the consumer. Here, we extend this notion to all stakeholders who can participate in reshaping the value created, received, and afforded to others in the social marketing system.

In fact, we envision that the shift to collaborative systems thinking may well involve system solutions that will not require explicit behaviour change from consumers, or for them to initiate new behaviours (Newton

Table 10.2 Social Marketing System Logics

Collaborative System Logics	Implications for Social Marketing
Collaborative consumers	Consumers continue to be an important focus in social marketing solutions. However, successful social marketing outcomes will not be easily measured against individual behaviour change in targeted consumers. Rather, new metrics, that consider a breadth of consumers' resources, will need to be identified. This will need to include how the resources that are both received and provided by consumers influence and shape other actors in the social marketing system.
Multiple stakeholders engagement	Multiple stakeholders and actors are identified and have a role in effecting social change outcomes. This means stakeholders are a means to finding solutions to complex problems. These collaborative actions require engagement with institutions to discuss and engage with the design products and services that can have positive outcomes for community good. As well as engaging in critiques, or mobilisation against institutions and organisations that destroy community value and have negative influences (acting as a detractor) to positive social change outcomes. Thus destroy shared value and reducing social change outcomes.
	To effect system-wide change—contemporary social marketing, influenced by knowledge from systems theory, purposefully engages in theorisation and practice—planning and implementing programs for change—that rely on influencing multiple levels of organisational and institution resources.
'Network of network' mode engages with a process dynamic perspective of social change	The network view of markets has a central focus on the relational ties between actors as the fabric of social structure. This requires social marketers to examine the social structures in relational data, not simply the underlying relationships and the mechanisms they represent. When operating in a 'network of networks' mode (Vargo & Lusch, 2014), social marketers will engage with reciprocal value propositions, framing various engagement with stakeholders to co-create with all social change actors (Luca et al., 2016).

(*Continued*)

Table 10.2 (Continued)

Collaborative System Logics	Implications for Social Marketing
Multiple systems of actions	The perspective of 'systems of action' (Dixon, 1984) focuses on the multiple systems within which behaviour change and social change take place. Multiple systems consideration and planning require: *within* system thinking involving the multiple levels of structures within a system at the micro, meso and macro levels. Additionally, consideration of the multiple system effects—the interaction between the social and cultural systems within the material environment—will further require reflection and management of the flow of resources and interactions between stakeholders.
Resource integration	Institutional and organisational resources are diffused in the *doing* of resource integration to influence value co-creation (co-destruction) between stakeholders. This influential shift in the thinking engages social marketers in the exploitation of resources to seek *collective benefits* for the stakeholder involved. *Collaborative consumers* can participate in process of change, as consumer can also deploy their resources as they undertake 'bundles of activities' that create value directly or that will facilitate subsequent consumption or use from which they will derive value. Complexity is embraced and managed.
Relational logic	Logics have within and between mechanisms that influence social change outcomes. Stakeholder considerations, or the design of partnerships within communities, are important but needed to engage deeper analysis of effects and consequences. Relational logic perspective brings to the forefront of social marketers thinking about how the underlying processes—mechanisms and triggers for change—can impact (for positive or negative reasoning) the outcomes of social change.
Shared value	The policies and operating practices that enhance the competitiveness of a company and efficiencies of government services, while simultaneously advancing the economic and social conditions in the communities in which they operate.

et al., 2016). Rather, it may be the actions and interactions of other actors—institutions and/or organisations—within the system who enact the social change. Whilst consumers' behaviour remains an important focus (e.g., encouraging consumers to reduce purchasing of fast fashion garments so as to reduce landfill and other environmentally damaging factors), the range of strategic opportunities to achieve a social change goal may not require a specific planned behaviour from targeted consumers. In considering the role and influence of multiple actors in the 'network of network mode', we consider how the process of value creation can also influence wider stakeholder 'buy-in' to social change agendas. We therefore argue that a logic of *shared value* is important to achieving positive social change outcomes.

The logic of *shared value* is proposed to extend systems to collaborative systems thinking by drawing upon two complementary, but different notions of value. First, as we have identified, S-D logic has had a strong influence on current thinking in social marketing—both at a systems and micro-system level. Our purview of collaborative systems thinking continues to leverage co-creation theory, which informs important meanings about the actions and interactions between consumers and the market in 'service-for-service' exchanges (Vargo & Lusch, 2017). In extending and integrating a value framework for multiple stakeholders, beyond the consumer-focused view of S-D logic, we draw on the notion of *shared value* as a contributing logic in collaborative systems thinking. Porter and Kramer (2011, p. 65) coined the term 'shared value', defining it as *"policies and operating practices that enhance the competitiveness of a company while simultaneously advancing the economic and social conditions in the communities in which it operates"*. The concept of shared value considers both the economic needs and the societal needs of businesses. Their argument, however, is not about sharing value already created by an organisation, which simply involves redistributing resources to others in the community. Rather their view is to expand *"the total pool of economic and social value"* by making connections between societal and economic progress (Porter & Kramer, 2011, p. 67).

Specifically, adopting this 'shared value' logic in collaborative systems thinking brings forward the influence of both the overlapping economic and social system forces that shape and influence stakeholder participation in social change solutions. Thus, when designing solutions, social marketers and other stakeholders can work *with* companies and firms; in doing so firms are encouraged to reset boundaries between market actors—specifically between organisation resources and the community—to find alternative product and service solutions that can have outcomes for multiple beneficiaries. In our conceptualisation of shared value logic, we extend this notion of shared value beyond business to also include government and other social service institutions. This is appropriate because governments are increasingly involved in doing business through service provision. In doing so, government services need to manage economic efficiencies so that they can continue to provide services to their constituents and communities.

Conclusion

In this chapter, we have undertaken to further develop a social marketing purview of collaborative systems thinking to guide theory and practice when considering the wider system level impacts that influence social change design and outcomes. Our approach has brought together historical insights on collaboration from the broader marketing literature, and insights on the theoretical influences informing social marketing systems thinking from a Leximancer analysis of current, social marketing systems research. Taken together, these insights illustrate how collaborative systems form from emergent boundary spanning collaborations across micro, meso, and macro levels, with a co-evolution of shared values and meanings between stakeholders. Building off of this analysis, we outline a typology of collaborative systems thinking for social change, integrating logics from past work on S-D logic (Vargo & Lusch, 2004, 2017), and marketing systems (Layton, 2007), together with logics of collaborative consumers and shared value. In this set of seven logics, we extend the notion of resource integration to situate all stakeholders as proactive co-creators of resources and active participants in the reshaping of value created, received, and afforded to others in the social marketing system. This shift from the typical dyadic exchange perspective of traditional social marketing interventions opens pathways for further engagement with the systems literature. Specifically, this shift may facilitate the identification of methods by which social change may be enacted within a system to shifts in considering the actions, interactions, and shared values of system actors other than consumers.

References

Archpru Akaka, M., Vargo, S. L., & Lusch, R. F. (2012). An exploration of networks in value cocreation: A service-ecosystems view. Special Issue – *Toward a Better Understanding of the Role of Value in Markets and Marketing*, 13–50.

Arnould, E. J., & Rose, A. S. (2015). Mutuality: Critique and substitute for Belk's "sharing." *Marketing Theory*, 16(1), 75–99.

Belk, R. W. (2007). Why Not Share Rather Than Own? *The ANNALS of the American Academy of Political and Social Science*, 611(1), 126–140.

Belk, R. W. (2010). Sharing. *Journal of Consumer Research*, 36(5), 715–734.

Belk, R. W. (2014). You are what you can access: Sharing and collaborative consumption online. *Journal of Business Research*, 67(8), 1595–1600.

Biroscak, B. J. (2018). Editorial: Policy, systems, and environmental change: Reflections and suggestions for social marketers. *Social Marketing Quarterly*, 24(3), 127–131.

Botsman, R. (2013, November 21). *The sharing economy lacks a shared definition*. Retrieved October 23, 2018, from www.fastcompany.com/3022028/the-sharing-economy-lacks-a-shared-definition

Botsman, R., & Rogers, R. (2010). *What's mine is yours: The rise of collaborative consumption*. London: Collins.

Brennan, L., & Parker, L. (2014). Editorial: Beyond behaviour change: Social marketing and social change. *Journal of Social Marketing*, 4(3), 1.

Brennan, L., Previte, J., & Fry, M-L. (2016). Social marketing's consumer myopia: Applying a behavioural ecological model to address wicked problems. *Journal of Social Marketing*, 6(3), 219–239.

Brychkov, D., & Domegan, C. T. (2017). Social marketing and systems science: Past, present and future. *Journal of Social Marketing*, 7(1), 74–93.

Dahl, S. (2010). Current themes in social marketing research: Text-mining the past five years. *Social Marketing Quarterly*, 16(2), 128–136.

de Burgh-Woodman, H., & King, D. (2013). Sustainability and the human/nature connection: A critical discourse analysis of being "symbolically" sustainable. *Consumption Markets and Culture*, 16(2), 145–168.

Dixon, D. F. (1984). Macromarketing: A social systems perspective. *Journal of Macromarketing*, 5(2), 4–17.

Domegan, C. T., McHugh, P., Devaney, M., Duane, S., Hogan, M., Broome, B. J., . . . Piwowarczyk, J. (2016). Systems-thinking social marketing: Conceptual extensions and empirical investigations. *Journal of Marketing Management*, 32(11–12), 1123–1144.

EBSCO Industries. (2018). Business Source Complete. Retrieved October 24, 2018, from https://www.ebsco.com/products/research-databases/business-source-complete

Ertz, M., Durif, F., & Arcand, M. (2018). A conceptual perspective on collaborative consumption. *AMS Review*. https://link.springer.com/article/10.1007%2Fs13162-018-0121-3

Ertz, M., Durif, F., Lecompte, A., & Boivin, C. (2018). Does "sharing" mean "socially responsible consuming"? Exploration of the relationship between collaborative consumption and socially responsible consumption. *Journal of Consumer Marketing*, 35(4), 392–402.

Felson, M., & Spaeth, J. L. (1978). Community structure and collaborative consumption: A routine activity approach. *American Behavioral Scientist*, 21(4), 614–624.

Figueiredo, B., & Scaraboto, D. (2016). The systemic creation of value through circulation in collaborative consumer networks. *Journal of Consumer Research*, 43(4), 509–533.

French, J., Russell-Bennett, R., & Mulcahy, R. (2017). Travelling alone or travelling far? Meso-level value co-creation by social marketing and for-profit organisations. *Journal of Social Marketing*, 7(3), 280–296.

Fry, M. L., Previte, J., & Brennan, L. (2017). Social change design: Disrupting the benchmark template. *Journal of Social Marketing*, 7(2), 119–134.

Gordon, R., Carrigan, M., & Hastings, G. (2011). A framework for sustainable marketing. *Marketing Theory*, 11(2), 143–163.

Grant, M. J., & Booth, A. (2009). A typology of reviews: An analysis of 14 review types and associated methodologies. *Health Information and Libraries Journal*, 26(2), 91–108.

Hamby, A., Pierce, M., & Brinberg, D. (2017). Solving complex problems: Enduring solutions through social entrepreneurship, community action, and social marketing. *Journal of Macromarketing, 37*(4), 369–380.

Hamilton, K., & Catterall, M. (2007). Love and consumption in poor families headed by lone mothers. In G. Fitzsimons & V. Morwitz (Eds.), *NA advances in consumer research* (vol. 34, pp. 559–564). Duluth, MN: Association for Consumer Research. Retrieved from www.acrwebsite.org/volumes/12588/volumes/v34/NA-34

Hastings, G., & Domegan, C. T. (2017). *Social marketing: Rebels with a cause* (3rd ed.). London: Routledge.

Hawley, A. H. (1950). *Human ecology: A theory of community structure.* New York, NY: Ronald Press.

Johansson, C., Bedggood, R., Farquharson, K., & Perenyi, A. (2018). Shared leadership as a vehicle to healthy service eco-systems: Practical or fanciful? *Journal of Social Marketing, 8*(2), 159–181.

Kemper, J. A., & Ballantine, P. W. (2017). Socio-technical transitions and institutional change: Addressing obesity through macro-social marketing. *Journal of Macromarketing, 37*(4), 381–392.

Kennedy, A-M. (2016). Macro-social marketing. *Journal of Macromarketing, 36*(3), 354–365.

Kennedy, A-M., & Parsons, A. (2012). Macro-social marketing and social engineering: A systems approach, 2(1), 37–51.

Layton, R. A. (2007). Marketing systems – A core macromarketing concept. *Journal of Macromarketing, 27*(3), 227–242.

Layton, R. A. (2015). Formation, growth, and adaptive change in marketing systems. *Journal of Macromarketing, 35*(3), 302–319.

Levine, S. S., & Prietula, M. J. (2014). Open collaboration for innovation: Principles and performance. *Organization Science, 25*(5), 1414–1433.

Leximancer Pty Ltd. (2018). *Leximancer user guide: Release 4.5.* Retrieved July 8, 2018, from https://doc.leximancer.com/doc/LeximancerManual.pdf

Luca, N. R., Hibbert, S., & McDonald, R. (2016). Midstream value creation in social marketing. *Journal of Marketing Management, 32*(11–12), 1145–1173.

Luchs, M., Naylor, R. W., Rose, R. L., Catlin, J. R., Gau, R., Kapitan, S., . . . Weaver, T. (2011). Toward a sustainable marketplace: Expanding options and benefits for consumers. *Journal of Research for Consumers, 19*(19), 1–12.

May, C., & Previte, J. (2016). Understanding the midstream environment within a social change systems continuum. *Journal of Social Marketing, 6*(3), 258–276.

McArthur, E. (2015). Many-to-many exchange without money: Why people share their resources. *Consumption Markets and Culture, 18*(3), 239–256.

McColl-Kennedy, J. R., Vargo, S. L., Dagger, T. S., Sweeney, J. C., & van Kasteren, Y. (2012). Health care customer value cocreation practice styles. *Journal of Service Research, 15*(4), 370–389.

McHugh, P., & Domegan, C. T. (2013). From reductionism to holism: How social marketing captures the bigger picture through collaborative system indicators. In K. Kubacki & S. R. Rundle-Thiele (Eds.), *Contemporary issues in social marketing* (pp. 78–95). Newcastle: Cambridge Scholars Publishing.

Morley, B., Niven, P., Coomber, K., Dixon, H., & Wakefield, M. (2013). Awareness and impact of the LiveLighter "toxic fat" obesity prevention campaign. *Obesity Research and Clinical Practice*, 7, e8.

Newton, J. D., Newton, F. J., & Rep, S. (2016). Evaluating social marketing's upstream metaphor: Does it capture the flows of behavioural influence between 'upstream' and 'downstream' actors? *Journal of Marketing Management*, 32(11–12), 1103–1122.

Nolan, T., & Varey, T. (2014). Re-cognising the interaction space: Marketing for social transformation. *Marketing Theory*, 14(4), 431–450.

Parkinson, J., Dubelaar, C., Carins, J., Holden, S., Newton, F., & Pescud, M. (2017). Approaching the wicked problem of obesity: An introduction to the food system compass. *Journal of Social Marketing*, 7(4), 387–404.

Polonsky, M. J. (2017). The role of corporate social marketing. *Journal of Social Marketing*, 7(3), 268–279.

Porter, M. E., & Kramer, M. R. (2011). Creating shared value. *Harvard Business Review*, 89(1–2), 62–77.

ProQuest. (2018). ABI/INFORM Global. Retrieved from https://search.proquest.com/abiglobal/index

Rittel, H. W. J., & Webber, M. M. (1973). Dilemmas in a general theory of planning. *Policy Sciences*, 4(2), 155–169.

Roberts, J. H. (2000). Developing new rules for new markets. *Journal of the Academy of Marketing Science*, 28(1), 31–44.

Scaraboto, D. (2015). Selling, sharing, and everything in between: The hybrid economies of collaborative networks. *Journal of Consumer Research*, 42(1), 152–176.

Smith, A. E., & Humphreys, M. S. (2006). Evaluation of unsupervised semantic mapping of natural language with Leximancer concept mapping. *Behavior Research Methods*, 38(2), 262–279.

Thompson, H. M., Previte, J., Kelly, S., & Kelly, A. B. (2017). Examining alcohol management practices in community sports clubs: A systems approach. *Journal of Social Marketing*, 7(3), 250–267.

Vargo, S. L., & Lusch, R. F. (2004). Evolving to a new dominant logic for marketing. *Journal of Marketing*, 68(1), 1–17.

Vargo, S. L., & Lusch, R. F. (2011). It's all B2B and beyond: Toward a systems perspective of the market. *Industrial Marketing Management*, 40(2), 181–187.

Vargo, S. L., & Lusch, R. F. (2014). Inversions of service-dominant logic. *Marketing Theory*, 14(3), 239–248.

Vargo, S. L., & Lusch, R. F. (2016). Institutions and axioms: An extension and update of service-dominant logic. *Journal of the Academy of Marketing Science*, 44(1), 5–23.

Vargo, S. L., & Lusch, R. F. (2017). Service-dominant logic 2025. *International Journal of Research in Marketing*, 34, 46–67.

Venturini, R. (2016). Social marketing and big social change: Personal social marketing insights from a complex system obesity prevention intervention. *Journal of Marketing Management*, 32(11–12), 1190–1199.

Wahlen, S., & Laamanen, M. (2017). Collaborative consumption and sharing economies. In M. Keller, B. Halkier, T. A. Wilska, & M. Truninger (Eds), *Routledge handbook on consumption* (pp. 94–105). Abingdon, Oxon: Routledge.

Westberg, K., Stavros, C., Smith, A. C. T., Newton, J., Lindsay, S., Kelly, S., . . . Adair, D. (2017). Exploring the wicked problem of athlete and consumer vulnerability in sport. *Journal of Social Marketing*, 7(1), 94–112.

11 Ethical Dimensions of Social Marketing and Social Change

Lynne Eagle, Stephan Dahl, and David Low

Introduction

The fact that social marketing and related fields such as health promotion have significant ethical dimensions (Eagle, Dahl, & Low, 2017; Rossi & Yudell, 2012; Tengland, 2016) may surprise many, given the aim to improve the lives of individuals, communities, and society as a whole. At their broadest, ethical issues start with who has a mandate to determine what behaviour is deemed to be problematic, what action should be taken, and whether interventions that may restrict individual freedoms are justified (Eagle & Dahl, 2015; Lefebvre, 2011; Polonsky, 2017). More specific issues arise in relation to targeting decisions, especially in regard to which sectors of a population should be the primary focus of activity and whether excluding some sectors is discriminatory (Eagle, Dahl, Hill, Bird, Spotswood, & Tapp, 2013; Peattie, Peattie, & Newcombe, 2016), together with issues relating to equity (Langford & Panter-Brick, 2013). Also problematic is the issue of whether strategies may result in unintended outcomes such as anxiety or distress, stigmatising individuals or groups, creating, or unfairly blaming individuals whose desired actions may be hampered by wider social or environmental issues (Bombak, 2014; Byers & Gilmer, 2018; Carter, Mayes, Eagle, & Dahl, 2017; Cherrier & Gurrieri, 2014; Coleman & Hatley Major, 2014). In this chapter, we examine several of these issues in detail, analysing how they are impacted by decisions taken at a macro level and discussing potential strategies to minimise negative impacts.

Part 1: Ethical and Social Issues Within Macro-Social Marketing

The need to move beyond a micro (individual) focus to wider macro perspectives does not mean ignoring the former and thus the ethical issues identified earlier. Many of the problems social marketers are tasked to address are readily classifiable as 'wicked' (Domegan, McHugh, Biroscak, Bryant, & Calis, 2017), such as obesity and environmental degradation

(Kennedy, Kapitan, Bajaj, Bakonyi, & Sands, 2017). There is therefore a need to consider the impact of activity, including ethical issues, at any level, be it micro, meso, or macro on the other levels. Also recognised is the need to take an integrated approach to both strategy and tactics at all levels (Hoek & Jones, 2011) and to recognise the interconnectedness and potential synergies between the levels (Domegan et al., 2016; Gordon, 2013; Hamby, Pierce, & Brinberg, 2017). Coupled with this is the need to consider the *"different forces that shape social change processes"* (Brychkov & Domegan, 2017, p. 75).

In addition to examining the social and economic pressures, it is suggested that a legitimate focus on macro issues includes examining *"the social consequences of commercial marketing activity in order to determine whether there is a need to amend policies, regulations or legislation"* (Cherrier & Gurrieri, 2014, p. 610). Examples will be discussed in more detail in later sections of this chapter.

There are a range of stakeholders, such as policy makers, regulators, and the media, with a mapping of stakeholders advocated as an integral part of deciding on strategy options (Gordon, 2013). The relative influence of different stakeholders will vary across specific issues. Further, within these groups, a number of competing influences such as lobbyists and pressure groups will be evident (Jacobs, 2015). Also to be considered is the impact of social movements—groups united by a focus on a specific issue such as reducing harm from gambling—whose strategies may cover micro to macro perspectives, and whose influence may be positive or negative, given that their objectives may not be societal benefits (Daellenbach & Parkinson, 2017). Further, the media are not themselves necessarily neutral, being influenced by *"powerful societal interests that control and finance them"* (Herman & Chomsky, 2010 [updated from1988 edition], p. xi). The actual or potential involvement of the commercial sector in social marketing is also seen as unethical, given the likely conflicting interests (Polonsky, 2017), being seen by some as akin to *"sleeping with the enemy"* (Cherrier & Gurrieri, 2014, p. 610).

Macro-Level Ethics: Unaware or Unconsidered?

We have identified a number of concerns among social marketing practitioners relating to the actions of upstream stakeholders. For example, from rounds of data collection at consecutive social marketing conferences from 2014 to 2018 and also at specific social marketing ethics workshops conducted at the 2016 and 2018 International Social Marketing Conference, several severe criticisms were levelled at policy makers and funders. For example: wanting to *"appear to do something"*, only wanting to *"spend their advertising budget and not change the issue"*, *"wanting research to justify continuing on with existing strategy even though that was not effective"*, *"client accepted research indicated new approaches to problems but determinedly clung to existing practices"*.

In recent work in the area of environmental degradation, we have identified ethical issues relating to a lack of cooperation between different levels of government, and government-funded organisations liaising with agricultural land managers. This lack of a *"system wide focus for strategy development and implementation for complex issues has been identified as a long standing problem for which no workable solution has yet been found"* (Dale et al., 2016, p. 712). A second issue relates to a refusal by government organisations to convert highly complex and technical material into more 'reader friendly' formats. This occurs even though there is an acknowledgement that the material, based on the type of information deficit assumptions discussed in the next section, is beyond the comprehension ability of the 'average farmer', often requiring reading levels at a post graduate degree level in order to be able to comprehend it (Hay & Eagle, 2016).

A further concern is the continued use of an information deficit approach, with the assumption that information provision is all that is necessary to change behaviours, ignoring the complex interaction of factors impacting on behavioural decisions and the well-recognised disconnect between awareness, attitudes, and actual behaviours (Byers & Gilmer, 2018; Claudy, Peterson, & O'Driscoll, 2013; Simis, Madden, Cacciatore, & Yeo, 2016), influenced at least in part by group norms (Smith & Louis, 2009).

Another area for concern is the increasing use of online platforms to provide information, such as for health-related issues. A number of assumptions are apparent in this strategy. The first is that patients attempting to access online information have the ability to do so (Peters, Hibbard, Slovic, & Dieckmann, 2007), and that they are able to distinguish between high and low quality information. There is a body of evidence indicating that this assumption is incorrect (Fiksdal et al., 2014). Low quality information use may actually result in harm if inaccurate information is used (Hu, Bell, Kravitz, & Orrange, 2012). A related issue is the readability of information provided. Multiple studies have found that online health information is written well above the ability of the general population to comprehend it (Dahl, Eagle, & Souza, 2017; Eagle & Dahl, 2016). As noted earlier, similar issues are evident in relation to environmental management (Hay & Eagle, 2016).

Another assumption is that information provision alone will lead to better patient outcomes (Ricciardi, Mostashari, Murphy, Daniel, & Siminerio, 2013), but this assumes that people are sufficiently engaged with the relevant issues to undertake information searches. This is certainly not the case for young age groups who appear to be unconcerned about possible future adverse health (Brennan, Dahl, & Eagle, 2010). Correct interpretation of retrieved information and action as a result of it are also assumed (Agree, King, Castro, Wiley, & Borzekowski, 2015). Ignored are the complex combinations of social, environmental, structural, and institutional factors, which may be significant barriers to successfully undertaking the desired behaviour change (Walach & Loef, 2014).

Socio-economic or environmental factors may also impact on equity issues due to the limitations they place on possible behaviour change (Stephens, 2014), such as the lack or affordability of exercise facilities—or public transport to get people to those facilities in some areas which may be targeted for fitness and weight reduction interventions (Crawshaw, 2012). A more extreme example of the impact of external factors is the futility of working in low socio-economic areas such as slums to encourage hand-washing or other personal hygiene actions if the target groups do not have adequate water supplies or other necessary infrastructure (Langford & Panter-Brick, 2013).

These examples raise the question of whether policy makers and funders understand the ethical issues that may arise as a result of their decisions and, if not, what action might be appropriate to address this. Even a basic understanding of commonly cited ethical frameworks and their inherent different values and potential outcomes (Carter et al., 2011) could be useful in sensitising these stakeholders. For example, commonly cited frameworks are Deontology, Teleology, and Utilitarianism. Deontology (from the Greek word for 'obligation' or 'duty') focuses on intentions, whereas Teleology (from the Greek word for 'ends'). focuses on consequences or outcomes. A subset of Teleology is Utilitarianism, under which behaviour is seen as ethical if it results in the greatest good for the greatest number, even if some groups may not benefit or may even be disadvantaged (Andreasen, 2001; Eagle et al., 2013). For a critique of Utilitarianism in the context of strategies used to encourage healthier lifestyles, see Bouman and Brown (2010).

Space prohibits a detailed discussion of the ethics of marketing across a wide range of sectors (instead see the text edited by Eagle & Dahl, 2015, for more depth). In the following sections, we explore ethical issues in relation to specific areas within social marketing. Of particular interest here is the relatively recent dimension of corporate social marketing (CSM) within wider corporate social responsibility initiatives. CSR itself is a contested concept, with multiple (in excess of 30) definitions identified, all variations around a central theme of whether and how commercial organisations can voluntarily integrate positive social and environmental activities into the organisation's business activity (Dahlsrud, 2008). CSM is regarded by its promotors as a form of CSR with a specific focus on using commercial resources to positively influence individual and community wellbeing (Jones, Wyatt, & Daube, 2016). As such, it has been criticised by some authors for the use of questionable tactics due to an inherent conflict between commercial and societal objectives (see, for example, Polonsky, 2017). This criticism also applies to the self-regulatory systems that apply to advertising and some other forms of promotional activity in many countries, with the key issue being identified as relating to balancing the interests of markets with those of their targets (Feenstra & Esteban, 2017). These contradictions present challenges in addressing complex problems such as those outlined in the examples that follow, as it is desirable from a macro perspective to involve all stakeholders in harm minimisation strategies (Lefebvre, 2013).

Example 1: Integrated Micro- to Macro-Strategies to Reduce Tobacco Use

The harm caused by tobacco is no longer disputed, and the magnitude of costs associated with smoking is recognised. It is estimated that the healthcare expenditure worldwide exceeds US$422 billion and productivity losses exceeds US$1,000 billion, "*equal to 1.8% of the world's annual gross domestic product (GDP). Almost 40% of this cost occurred in developing countries, highlighting the substantial burden these countries suffer*" (Goodchild, Nargis, & d'Espaignet, 2017, p. 58).

In a seminal paper, Rothschild (1999) advocates considering education, marketing, and legislation, individually or in combination, depending on the specific behaviour change objective. The use of all three has been seen in sustained efforts to reduce cigarette smoking rates in developed countries, with restrictions placed on advertising, event sponsorship, product placements, and retail displays, coupled with restrictions on places where smoking is permitted and health warnings on cigarette packaging, more recently plain packaging (Hoek, Gifford, Pirikahu, Thomson, & Edwards, 2010). These moves have been coupled with extensive educational programmes to communicate the harm not only to smokers but also those exposed to 'passive' smoke (Bedford, Wen, Hua, Kehoe, & Rissel, 2003) and attempts via health promotion and social marketing to help smokers to quit the habit or, in the case of young adults, to not commence smoking at all (Eagle, Bird, Spotswood, & Tapp, 2015). Legislation aimed at preventing exposure of non-smokers to cigarette smoke was deemed necessary to ensure that those who resisted behaviour change were forced to do so, leading to complaints regarding restrictions on individual rights (Satterlund, Cassady, Treiber, & Lemp, 2011).

Such moves are ongoing as the industry seeks new platforms such as digital media forms to promote their products and countries with weak regulation and legislation (BinDihm, Freeman, & Trevena, 2012; Coombs, Bond, Van, & Daube, 2011; Forsyth & Malone, 2010; Freeman & Chapman, 2009). The industry has moved from a long history of denial of harm to attempting to position themselves as actively committed to 'harm reduction' as part of attempts to improve their reputation and regain lost influence over future policy development, a move condemned as opportunistic (Peeters & Gilmore, 2015). The marketing of e-cigarettes as a healthy alternative to conventional cigarettes and an aid to helping people quit smoking altogether has proven contentious, with some researchers claiming that the marketing of these products is actually intended to re-normalise smoking behaviours (Dawson & Verweij, 2017; Fairchild, Bayer, & Colgrove, 2014).

Example 2: Suboptimal Strategies: The Example of Alcohol

The potentially harmful results of excess alcohol consumption are underestimated (Kubacki, Rundle-Thiele, Pang, & Buyucek, 2015), especially among younger age groups where it has long been regarded as the "*drug of choice*" (Mart, 2011, p. 889), and where consumption is integrated into the social life of young adults in many countries (Wettlaufer, Cukier, Giesbrecht, & Greenfield, 2012). A summary of the magnitude of the impact of alcohol misuse and excess consumption follows:

- Alcohol misuse accounts for approximately 2.5 million annual deaths globally
- Of these deaths, over 300,000 are young people between 15 and 29 years of age (World Health Organisation, 2010)
- Alcohol's impact in terms of disability-adjusted life years shows alcohol contributed 4.5% of the total, exceeding that of both tobacco (3.7%) and illicit drugs (0.9%) (Donovan, Fielder, & Jalleh, 2011)
- There are further societal costs in terms of reduced workplace productivity and alcohol-fueled violence (Manning, Smith, & Mazerolle, 2013)

In the context of attempts to minimise harm from excessive alcohol consumption, policy makers have been criticised for ignoring research indicating potentially effective strategies when framing policy (Aspara & Tikkanen, 2017). There has long been considerable scepticism about industry's social responsibility initiatives, such as the insertion of drinking moderation messages, given that they require no substantive amendment to overall marketing strategies and are primarily attempts to ward off any attempts to increase regulation of all forms of promotion (Babor & Robaina, 2013). CSM initiatives such as 'responsible drinking' campaigns have been specifically criticised for ambiguous messages, such as reducing harmful levels of alcohol consumption while at the same time "*promoting drinking as sophisticated and stylish*" (Jones et al., 2016, p. 269).

Warning labels have been specifically criticised due to their lack of demonstrable effectiveness (Scholes-Balog, Heerde, & Hemphill, 2012). Critics suggest that the use of warnings on labels is a largely symbolic strategy, requiring minimal change in marketing activity in return for positive public relations value in claiming responsiveness to societal concerns (Jessop & Wade, 2008). Warning messages such as the link between alcohol consumption and cancer have been shown to be met with scepticism and resistance to altering consumption habits on the basis of "*everything causes cancer*" (May, Eliott, & Crabb, 2017, p. 419). However it is noted that part of their appeal lies in their being both "*inexpensive and politically acceptable*" (Louise, Eliott, Olver, & Braunack-Mayer, 2015, p. 3) compared to other empirically supported strategies such as setting a minimum unit price (Gordon, 2013). Similarly, calorie labelling on fast food menus is also suggested as ineffective (Elbel, Kersh, Brescoll, & Dixon, 2009).

Example 3: Provision of Personal Financial Incentives (PFI)

Provision of financial incentives to influence behaviour change has been used across a wide range of areas including smoking cessation, HIV prevention, physical activity, a range of health screening programmes, and environmental protection programmes such as recycling (Heise, Lutz, Ranganathan, & Watts, 2013; Lavack, Watson, & Markwart, 2007; Lynagh, Sanson-Fisher, & Bonevski, 2013). The concept of paying people to change behaviours has been criticised for a lack of evidence of effectiveness and also for not addressing wider equity issues. The limited evidence available indicates that behaviour is not changed in the long term. Once incentives cease, people tend to revert back to previous behaviours (Iyer & Kashyap, 2007). There is also the danger of people misusing the system to gain incentives to which they are not entitled (Giles, Sniehotta, McColl, & Adams, 2016).

In terms of whether equity-related issues are relevant, critics of PFIs question whether it is equitable to pay some people to change their behaviours when others do so without any form of reward (Lynagh et al., 2013). Additionally, these types of incentives may inadvertently penalise people with poor health or disabilities who may be willing but unable to change behaviours (Schmidt, Asch, & Halpern, 2012). A further concern relates to situations where intrinsic (internal) motivations, such as a sense of social obligation, may be replaced by extrinsic (financial reward) factors. In the case of blood donations, payment of PFIs has been shown to negatively impact on future donations once incentives are withdrawn (Mortimer, Ghijben, Harris, & Hollingsworth, 2013).

As noted earlier, for an in-depth discussion of other areas in which ethical issues arise, see Eagle and Dahl (2015).

Unintended Effects

While there is some evidence of social marketing having unintended positive benefits (Peattie et al., 2016), there is a considerable body of evidence of the counter-productive effects of negative unintended effects (Gordon & Gurrieri, 2014; Key & Czaplewski, 2017)

Strategies such as taxes on foods deemed to be unhealthy, while claimed to be potentially effective in encouraging healthier food choices (Sacks, Veerman, Moodie, & Swinburn, 2011), have been shown to have regressive effects, i.e., they have a disproportionate impact on those in low socio-economic groups with limited financial resources (Eagle, Bulmer, De Bruin, & Kitchen, 2006; Powell & Chaloupka, 2009). This is especially true when access to healthier options may be hampered by lack of food outlets offering healthier food and/or transport to these outlets, raising questions regarding the role of governments at all levels in ensuring equality of access to nutritious food (Burns & Inglis, 2007; Murphy, Koohsari, Badland, & Giles-Corti, 2017). Other unintended effects include inadvertent stigmatisation, discussed in the next section.

Stigma

In the context of obesity, obese people are reported as feeling stigmatised (Kemper & Ballantine, 2017), and there is evidence that even inadvertent stigmatising of the obese in behaviour change interventions actually decreases their motivation to adopt actions such as dietary changes and commencing or increasing exercise (Vartanian & Smyth, 2013). These effects have been found in other sectors where guilt and shame lead to inaction rather than desired actions (Key & Czaplewski, 2017). For example, anti-smoking activity, particularly where fear-based messages are used, has been shown to stigmatise people with smoking-related illnesses such as lung cancer (Riley, Ulrich, Hamann, & Ostroff, 2017).

Assumptions Regarding Food Labelling

There is a large and growing body of literature exploring the way that nutritional information is presented on product packaging, ranging from debates over which form of on-pack labelling of nutrition information is the most effective (Siegrist, Leins-Hess, & Keller, 2015), through to whether symbols such as stars or colour codes are effective (see, for example, Hamlin & McNeill, 2016; Julia et al., 2015; VanEpps, Downs, & Loewenstein, 2016). Much of the debate to date is underpinned by the information deficit assumptions discussed earlier and presuppose that consumers are interested in the information and are able to correctly interpret it. Prior research has indicated that some consumer segments, such as young adults, are simply not interested (Brennan, Dahl, & Eagle, 2010). 'Halo effects' have also been found, whereby packaging with eco-labels or products from companies with positive social reputations are (often wrongly) perceived as being healthier (Peloza, Ye, & Montford, 2015; Sörqvist et al., 2015). Missing from much of the debate is the interaction between words and visuals, together with the impact of colours and the best way to help consumers interpret information (Hieke & Harris, 2016).

Part 2: Potential Ethical Solutions to Issues

The ethical issues discussed in the preceding sections are complex because the problems that lead to them are complex. We cannot assume a simple linear relationship between cause and effect and thus cannot assume simple solutions will be effective. Indeed, as other authors in this text have discussed, the nature of complex 'wicked' problems includes multiple interdependencies and multiple causation (see also Head & Alford, 2015).

Adopting the calls noted earlier for integrated approaches to solving complex issues and the involvement of multiple stakeholders across all social levels, we now address potential strategies to solve some of the ethical dilemmas that may arise. A number of strategies require training and upskilling. For example, strategies are needed to raise awareness among stakeholders that ethical issues may arise and that they are important. We have noted elsewhere (Eagle, Dahl, & Low, 2015) a failure to understand the 'value-laden-ness' inherent in many social marketing decisions (see also Rossi & Yudell, 2012). Similar strategies are needed to raise awareness of the value of research in framing policy, and the dangers inherent in ignoring relevant research findings (Aspara & Tikkanen, 2017). Coupled with this is the need to raise awareness of the value of theory. Unfortunately, the legacy of a founder of modern psychology, Kurt Lewin, who is widely quoted as having claimed that there is nothing so practical as a good theory (Bargal, Gold, & Lewin, 1992), appears to have weakened over time, yet his claim is valid today.

There is *"increasing evidence . . . that public health and health-promotion interventions that are based on social and behavioural science theories are more effective than those lacking a theoretical base"* (Glanz & Bishop, 2010, p. 399). We know, however, that practitioners report finding theory confusing and intimidating: Whereas there are many different theories to choose from (Chatterton & Wilson, 2014; Gainforth, West, & Michie, 2015), there is little guidance on how to select and use appropriate theory. This is coupled with a lack of appreciation of the value theory can add. It has been noted that if practitioners *"want theory at all, it is for its potential in helping them design and implement interventions with the greatest possible impact in their particular context, which is often small and local"* (Davidoff, Dixon-Woods, Leviton, & Michie, 2015, p. 1). There is little practical guidance available. For example, suggestions such as *"from initial 'customer insight' [look] at what theory can best inform intervention option selection"* (French & Blair-Stevens, 2007, p. 77), while correct, are not helpful.

The need for non-linear solutions to complex problems has been noted by others (see, for example, Domegan, McHugh, Biroscak, Bryant, & Calis, 2017). This type of approach will require upskilling of social marketers and also those that fund their activity. Simple linear interventions may be based on a restricted perception of a community that might form the basis for an intervention. We have found that, in areas such as environmental protection, the definition of community among target groups is not immediate geographic proximity but rather a complex network of contacts who may share common cultural heritage and kinship ties that may have evolved over a century or more (Eagle, Hay, & Farr, 2016). Hence social networks rather than conventional communities may be more applicable. The use of techniques such as social network analysis (SNA) to analyse the social and informational contacts between individuals and their relative influence on behavioural choices (Dempwolf & Lyles, 2012) would again require upskilling within the social marketing community.

Communication

The form and nature of communication should also be considered. The tendency to equate social marketing with social advertising has been noted by many authors (see, for example, French & Gordon, 2015), presumably driven by the information deficit assumptions noted earlier. Ethical issues that need to be addressed in the context of communication include communicating complex information to the surprisingly large number of people who have some degree of literacy limitations (Eagle, Hawkins, Styles, & Reid, 2006), message framing, and imagery.

These issues need to be considered in the light of increasing use of computer-generated messages, particularly as the 'semantic web' (where computers are able to read and respond to textual information) continues to evolve (Casanovas, 2015). Depending on the algorithms used for computer-generated activity, behaviour change messages may lack the subtle nuances that may impact on message effectiveness across different population segments. A failure to develop and deliver messages tailored for specific population segments may result in messages being counter-productive (Eagle et al., 2015; Soraghan, Thomson, & Ensor, 2016).

Message Framing and Trust

Message framing evolved from extensive research into responses to people's perceptions of the prospect of positive (gain) or negative (loss) outcomes stemming from specific behaviours, now referred to as 'Prospect Theory' (Rothman & Salovey, 1997). Message framing in the context of social marketing generally refers to decisions regarding whether to present messages in positive or negative ways and how messages should be structured: i.e., the message can either emphasise the advantages of doing a certain action (e.g., losing weight or participating in health screening programmes), or it can emphasise the negative consequences of not taking a specific action (e.g., having a higher likelihood of cardiovascular disease as a result of not taking regular exercise, smoking, or consuming excessive amounts of alcohol). No framing approach is applicable across all intervention types: Effectiveness is influenced by a number of factors, including perceived susceptibility to negative outcomes, the level of personal motivation in relation to the behaviour, and the level of certainty that undertaking the action will result in the desired outcome (Borah, 2011). Additional factors influencing effectiveness include the perceived expertise, trustworthiness, and reputation of the message sponsor and spokesperson (Rucker & Petty, 2006).

Imagery

The importance of visual communication in helping people to process complex information has only recently been recognised in the academic literature (Thomsen, 2015). There are three main benefits to including visuals such as diagrams, pictograms, cartoons, or photos. First, they may help gain attention and thus encourage investment of time and effort in written material (Lazard & Atkinson, 2014). Secondly, noting the largely unrecognised problem of functional literacy levels discussed earlier, visuals can help clarify the meaning of text-based information (Altinay, 2015), expand on the persuasive component of a written message (Seo, Dillard, & Shen, 2013), or draw attention to key aspects of the message (Altinay, 2015). Visuals may also communicate key messages more effectively than words alone (Lazard & Atkinson, 2014).

The selection of images is not straightforward—the message that is intended to be sent may not be the message received. For example, in the context of environmental impacts (including the impact of climate change), the use of iconic images such as polar bears on melting ice floes or other images that are not seen by the message recipient as personally relevant are likely to be ineffective (Thomsen, 2015). In the health context, the use of graphic 'harm' images may attract the attention of some segments of the target but be resisted by others. For example, plain cigarette packaging appears to be ineffective in influencing the smoking behaviours of heavy smokers (Munafò, Roberts, Bauld, & Leonards, 2011), whereas the impact of graphic pictorial warnings varies across segments depending on the level of 'graphic' harm portrayed (Davis & Burton, 2016). All visuals should be pre-tested with members of key segments of the target group to ensure that the message intended is delivered (Dowse, 2004).

Competition Including News Media

Social marketing activity does not operate in a vacuum and there are multiple influences, both commercial and social, competing for attention and acceptance. The impact of competing forces has been recognised for well over a decade (Grier & Bryant, 2005; Peattie & Peattie, 2003; Wettstein & Suggs, 2016), but the impact of competition is frequently underestimated, although this issue is gradually being recognised (Dibb, Carrigan, Zainuddin, Russell-Bennett, & Previte, 2013; Schuster, 2015). This has led to a greater focus on understanding the perceived value of undertaking behaviour change (Gordon, Dibb, Magee, Cooper, & Waitt, 2018). A recent text discusses the impact of actual and potential actions that might compete with, or be used as substitutes for, behaviours being planned (Lefebvre, 2013); other texts discuss the need for formal analysis of competition and ongoing monitoring of its impact (Eagle et al., 2013)

Engaging with Targets and Countering Dissenting Views

Previous studies (see, for example, Eagle & Dahl, 2016; Low & Eagle, 2017) have demonstrated that scientists and policy makers tend to communicate in a manner that lay people with average levels of literacy and numeracy competence cannot access. This remains a significant stumbling block for attempts to progress macro-social marketing initiatives.

The assumption that additional knowledge and information will result in the person acting in the desired way is far too commonly evoked, especially by those commissioning social marketing activity. This ignores additional factors which influence behavioural choices, such as attitudes, values, and trust (Kraft, Lodge, & Taber, 2015; Simis, Madden, Cacciatore, & Yeo, 2016). As repeatedly stated, when trying to change misconceptions, *"being right is not enough"* (Camargo & Grant, 2015, p. 2). Rather, communication skills (Seiler, Engwall, & Hollert, 2013) and open dialogue with stakeholders and all sectors of the public are essential for scientists to influence behaviour appropriately (Lee & VanDyke, 2015). This issue is further intensified by the noted hesitancy of some scientists to engage in science communication beyond their community and through academic journals, while simultaneously *"lamenting that the public just does not understand"* (Mikulak, 2011, p. 202).

Communication skills and open dialogue beyond the scientific community are particularly important in cases of well-meaning campaigns, which aim to 'correct' misinformation: Engaging in one-sided information provision has been found to reinforce existing beliefs rather than change them (Hart & Nisbet, 2012). Strength of preexisting attitudes are a major factor in whether corrective messages are accepted (Lewandowsky, Ecker, Seifert, Schwarz, & Cook, 2012). As an unintended consequence, 'correctional' campaigns may produce a 'boomerang effect' where people's world views are challenged (Cook, Lewandowsky, & Ecker, 2017). Moreover, mistrust of science and scientists *"has produced a paralyzing form of skepticism that empowers scientific popularism"* (Camargo & Grant, 2015, p. 232), increasing receptiveness to misinformation, for example as seen in the case of anti-vaccination advocates (Goldenberg, 2016).

One Off vs Ongoing Dialogue

A compounding issue is the tendency to use social marketing campaigns as a one off, sporadic tool to address issues, rather than as a means to open and ongoing dialogue. Such concerns are not new (Hastings & Saren, 2003; Wakefield, Loken, & Hornik, 2010), yet despite these repeated cautions, concerns about sporadic use remain current (Kelly & Barker, 2016). Such usage can result in the efforts made being lost or may even have a validating effect on dissenting views, where the withdrawal of the campaign can be construed as an admission of negative effects.

Example 4

During an outbreak of Hepatitis A in the 'men who have sex with men' (MSM)-community in Lisbon, the Portuguese health ministry initiated a laudable campaign to increase vaccination rates. The message was being communicated through press engagements, and health care workers were motivated to provide 'on the spot' vaccination in the Barrio Alto area of Lisbon, targeting visitors of gay bars in the area. During the two-week campaign, around 1100 vaccines were administered (Esteves, 2017). While the campaign was certainly worthwhile, there has been no further follow up from this campaign. Thus, this incident represented a missed opportunity to engage in a wider dialogue with the MSM community, and specifically to converse more openly over the need for vaccinations.

Summary

Policy makers would benefit from increased sensitivity to the ethical dimensions of behaviour change, particularly in the context of complex multifaceted issues. No two issues are likely to have the same types of behavioural drivers or potential solutions, and the issues themselves may change over time. Further, complex problems will not have a simple single solution (Kennedy, Kemper, & Parsons, 2018), adding to the potential for unintended issues to arise. Policy makers may need assistance in developing sensitivity to the ethical issues that may arise and in the range of techniques available to reframe policy problems to minimise any potential negative impacts. In doing this, they may also encourage the engagement of those whose behaviours are targeted in order to present behaviour change options in ways that are compatible with the targets' perceptions and priorities (Arklay, van Acker, & Hollander, 2018). A particular issue needing focus at a macro level is the development of strategies for engaging those who are disengaged or disagree with the issues underpinning policy, driving macro-social marketing interventions.

References

Agree, E. M., King, A. C., Castro, C. M., Wiley, A., & Borzekowski, D. L. (2015). "It's got to be on this page": Age and cognitive style in a study of online health information seeking. *Journal of Medical Internet Research*, 17(3), online edition e79.

Altinay, Z. M. (2015). *Communicating sustainability with visuals: Issue perception and issue engagement* (PhD), Louisiana State University.

Andreasen, A. R. (Ed.). (2001). *Ethics in social marketing*. Washington, DC: Georgetown University Press.

Arklay, T., van Acker, E., & Hollander, R. (2018). Policy entrepreneurs searching for the open-minded skeptic: A new approach to engagement in difficult policy areas. *Policy Design and Practice*, 1(2), 103–114.

Aspara, J., & Tikkanen, H. (2017). Why do public policy-makers ignore marketing and consumer research? A case study of policy-making for alcohol advertising. *Consumption Markets and Culture*, 20(1), 12–34.

Babor, T. F., & Robaina, K. (2013). Public health, academic medicine, and the alcohol industry's corporate social responsibility activities. *American Journal of Public Health*, 103(2), 206–214.

Bargal, D., Gold, M., & Lewin, M. (1992). Introduction: The heritage of Kurt Lewin. *Journal of Social Issues*, 48(2), 3–13.

Bedford, K., Wen, L. M., Hua, M., Kehoe, P., & Rissel, C. (2003). 'Smoke near me and I smoke too': Evaluation of a smoke-free homes program in central Sydney, NSW. *Health Promotion Journal of Australia*, 14(2), 108–113.

BinDihm, N. F., Freeman, B., & Trevena, L. (2012). Pro-smoking apps for smartphones: The latest vehicle for the tobacco industry? *Tobacco Control*, 1(4), 11–15.

Bombak, A. E. (2014). The contribution of applied social sciences to obesity stigma-related public health approaches. *Journal of Obesity*, 104, 60–68.

Borah, P. (2011). Conceptual issues in framing theory: A systematic examination of a decade's literature. *Journal of Communication*, 61(2), 246–263.

Bouman, M. P., & Brown, W. J. (2010). Ethical approaches to lifestyle campaigns. *Journal of Mass Media Ethics*, 25(1), 34–52.

Brennan, R., Dahl, S., & Eagle, L. (2010). Persuading young consumers to make healthy nutritional decisions. *Journal of Marketing Management*, 26(7–8), 635–655.

Brychkov, D., & Domegan, C. (2017). Social marketing and systems science: Past, present and future. *Journal of Social Marketing*, 7(1), 74–93.

Burns, C., & Inglis, A. (2007). Measuring food access in Melbourne: Access to healthy and fast foods by car, bus and foot in an urban municipality in Melbourne. *Health and Place*, 13(4), 877–885.

Byers, V., & Gilmer, A. (2018). Developing a unified approach to sustainable consumption behaviour: Opportunities for a new environmental paradigm. *European Journal of Sustainable Development, 7*(1), 1–16.

Camargo, K. J., & Grant, R. (2015). Public health, science, and policy debate: Being right is not enough. *American Journal of Public Health, 105*(2), 232–235.

Carter, S. M., Mayes, C., Eagle, L., & Dahl, S. (2017). A code of ethics for social marketing? bridging procedural ethics and ethics-in-practice. *Journal of Nonprofit and Public Sector Marketing, 29*(1), 20–38.

Carter, S. M., Rychetnik, L., Lloyd, B., Kerridge, I. H., Baur, L., Bauman, A., . . . Zask, A. (2011). Evidence, ethics, and values: A framework for health promotion. *American Journal of Public Health, 101*(3), 465–472.

Casanovas, P. (2015). Semantic web regulatory models: Why ethics matter. *Philosophy and Technology, 28*(1), 33–55.

Chatterton, T., & Wilson, C. (2014). The 'Four Dimensions of Behaviour' framework: A tool for characterising behaviours to help design better interventions. *Transportation Planning and Technology, 37*(1), 38–61.

Cherrier, H., & Gurrieri, L. (2014). Framing social marketing as a system of interaction: A neo-institutional approach to alcohol abstinence. *Journal of Marketing Management, 30*(7–8), 607–633.

Claudy, M. C., Peterson, M., & O'Driscoll, A. (2013). Understanding the attitude-behaviour gap for renewable energy systems using behavioural reasoning theory. *Journal of Macromarketing, 33*(4), 273–287.

Coleman, R., & Hatley Major, L. (2014). Ethical health communication: A content analysis of predominant frames and primes in public service announcements. *Journal of Mass Media Ethics, 29*(2), 91–107.

Cook, J., Lewandowsky, S., & Ecker, U. K. (2017). Neutralizing misinformation through inoculation: Exposing misleading argumentation techniques reduces their influence. *PLoS One, 12*(5), online edition e0175799.

Coombs, J., Bond, L., Van, V., & Daube, M. (2011). "Below the Line": The tobacco industry and youth smoking. *The Australasian Medical Journal, 4*(12), 655–673.

Crawshaw, P. (2012). Governing at a distance: Social marketing and the (bio) politics of responsibility. *Social Science and Medicine, 75*(1), 200–207.

Daellenbach, K., & Parkinson, J. (2017). A useful shift in our perspective: Integrating social movement framing into social marketing. *Journal of Social Marketing, 7*(2), 188–204.

Dahl, S., Eagle, L., & Souza, V. (2017). Oi! Estás a ouvir-me? An exploration of health information seeking and likely comprehension of internet-based health information in Portuguese and English. *Revista de Gestão dos Países de Língua Portuguesa (Journal of Management of Portuguese-Speaking Countries), 16*(3), 44–58.

Dahlsrud, A. (2008). How corporate social responsibility is defined: An analysis of 37 definitions. *Corporate Social Responsibility and Environmental Management, 15*(1), 1–13.

Dale, A. P., Vella, K., Pressey, R. L., Brodie, J., Gooch, M., Potts, R., & Eberhard, R. (2016). Risk analysis of the governance system affecting outcomes in the great Barrier Reef. *Journal of Environmental Management, 183*, 712–721.

Davidoff, F., Dixon-Woods, M., Leviton, L., & Michie, S. (2015). Demystifying theory and its use in improvement. *BMJ Quality and Safety, 24*(3), 228–238.

Davis, C., & Burton, S. (2016). Understanding graphic pictorial warnings in advertising: A replication and extension. *Journal of Advertising, 45*(1), 33–42.

Dawson, A., & Verweij, M. (2017). No smoke without fire: Harm reduction, E-Cigarettes and the smoking endgame. *Public Health Ethics, 10*(1), 1–4.

Dempwolf, C. S., & Lyles, L. W. (2012). The uses of social network analysis in planning: A review of the literature. *CPL Bibliography, 27*(1), 3–21.

Dibb, S., Carrigan, M., Zainuddin, N., Russell-Bennett, R., & Previte, J. (2013). The value of health and wellbeing: An empirical model of value creation in social marketing. *European Journal of Marketing, 47*(9), 1504–1524.

Domegan, C., McHugh, P., Biroscak, B. J., Bryant, C., & Calis, T. (2017). Non-linear causal modelling in social marketing for wicked problems. *Journal of Social Marketing, 7*(3), 305–329.

Domegan, C., McHugh, P., Devaney, M., Duane, S., Hogan, M., Broome, B. J., . . . Piwowarczyk, J. (2016). Systems-thinking social marketing: Conceptual extensions and empirical investigations. *Journal of Marketing Management, 32*(11–12), 1123–1144.

Donovan, R. J., Fielder, L., & Jalleh, G. (2011). Alcohol advertising advocacy research no match for corporate dollars: The case of Bundy R Bear. *Journal of Research for Consumers, 20*, 1–13.

Dowse, R. (2004). Using visuals to communicate medicine information to patients with low literacy. *Adult Learning, 15*(1–2), 22.

Eagle, L., Bird, S., Spotswood, F., & Tapp, A. (2015). Ethical dimensions of social marketing does trying to do good equate to doing no harm? *Marketing in Transition: Scarcity, Globalism, and Sustainability* (pp. 431–436). Switzerland: Springer.

Eagle, L., Bulmer, S., De Bruin, A., & Kitchen, P. J. (2006). Advertising and children: Issues and policy options. *Journal of Promotion Management, 11*(2–3), 175–194.

Eagle, L., & Dahl, S. (2015). *Marketing ethics and society*. London: Sage Publications.

Eagle, L., & Dahl, S. (2016). Empowering or misleading? Online health information provision challenges. *Marketing Intelligence and Planning, 34*(7), 1000–1020.

Eagle, L., Dahl, S., Hill, S., Bird, S., Spotswood, F., & Tapp, A. (2013). *Social marketing*. Harlow: Pearson Education.

Eagle, L., Dahl, S., & Low, D. R. (2015). Ethics in social marketing. In L. Eagle & S. Dahl (Eds.), *Marketing ethics and society* (pp. 235–264). London: Sage Publications.

Eagle, L., Dahl, S., & Low, D. R. (2017). Ethical issues in social marketing. In J. French (Ed.), *Social marketing and public health: Theory and practice* (pp. 187–202). Oxford: Oxford University Press.

Eagle, L., Hay, R., & Farr, M. (2016). *Harnessing the science of social marketing and behaviour change for improved water quality in the GBR: Background Review of the Literature*. Retrieved from Townsville.

Eagle, L. C., Hawkins, J. C., Styles, E., & Reid, J. (2006). Breaking through the invisible barrier of low functional literacy: Implications for health communication. *Studies in Communication Sciences, 5*(2), 29–55.

Elbel, B., Kersh, R., Brescoll, V. L., & Dixon, L. B. (2009). Calorie labeling and food choices: A first look at the effects on low-income people in New York City. *Health affairs, 28*(6), W1110–W1121.

Esteves, I. (2017). *Vaccine-preventable outbreaks in Portugal: Hepatitis a and measles*. Paper presented at the European Academy of Paediatrics, EAP Spring Meeting, Faro.

Fairchild, A. L., Bayer, R., & Colgrove, J. (2014). The renormalization of smoking? E-cigarettes and the tobacco "endgame". *New England Journal of Medicine, 370*(4), 293–295.

Feenstra, R. A., & Esteban, E. G. (2017). Autocontrol: A critical study of achievements and challenges in the pursuit of ethical advertising through an advertising self-regulation system. *Journal of Business Ethics,* online edition (ahead of print), 1–14.

Fiksdal, A. S., Kumbamu, A., Jadhav, A. S., Cocos, C., Nelsen, L. A., Pathak, J., & McCormick, J. B. (2014). Evaluating the process of online health information searching: A qualitative approach to exploring consumer perspectives. *Journal of Medical Internet Research, 16*(10).

Forsyth, S. R., & Malone, R. E. (2010). "I'll be your cigarette – Light me up and get on with it": Examining smoking imagery on YouTube. *Nicotine and Tobacco Research, 12*(8), 810–816.

Freeman, B., & Chapman, S. (2009). Open source marketing: Camel cigarette brand marketing in the "Web 2.0" world. *Tobacco Control, 18*(3), 212–217.

French, J., & Blair-Stevens, C. (2007). *Big pocket guide: Social marketing*. London: National Social Marketing Centre.

French, J., & Gordon, R. (2015). *Strategic social marketing*. London: Sage Publications.

Gainforth, H. L., West, R., & Michie, S. (2015). Assessing connections between behaviour change theories using network analysis. *Annals of Behavioural Medicine, 49*(5), 754–761.

Giles, E. L., Sniehotta, F. F., McColl, E., & Adams, J. (2016). Acceptability of financial incentives for health behaviour change to public health policymakers: A qualitative study. *BMC Public Health, 16*(1), 989.

Glanz, K., & Bishop, D. B. (2010). The role of behavioural science theory in development and implementation of public health interventions. *Annual Review of Public Health, 31*, 399–418.

Goldenberg, M. J. (2016). Public misunderstanding of science? reframing the problem of vaccine hesitancy. *Perspectives on Science, 24*(5), 552–581.

Goodchild, M., Nargis, N., & d'Espaignet, E. T. (2017). Global economic cost of smoking-attributable diseases. *Tobacco Control, 27*(1), 58–64.

Gordon, R. (2013). Unlocking the potential of upstream social marketing. *European Journal of Marketing, 47*(9), 1525–1547.

Gordon, R., Dibb, S., Magee, C., Cooper, P., & Waitt, G. (2018). Empirically testing the concept of value-in-behaviour and its relevance for social marketing. *Journal of Business Research, 82*, 56–67.

Gordon, R., & Gurrieri, L. (2014). Towards a reflexive turn: Social marketing assemblages. *Journal of Social Marketing, 4*(3), 261–278.

Grier, S., & Bryant, C. A. (2005). Social marketing in public health. *Annual Review of Public Health, 26*, 319–339.

Hamby, A., Pierce, M., & Brinberg, D. (2017). Solving complex problems: Enduring solutions through social entrepreneurship, community action, and social marketing. *Journal of Macromarketing, 37*(4), 369–380.

Hamlin, R., & McNeill, L. (2016). Does the Australasian "health star rating" front of pack nutritional label system work? *Nutrients*, *8*(6), 327.

Hart, P. S., & Nisbet, E. C. (2012). Boomerang effects in science communication: How motivated reasoning and identity cues amplify opinion polarization about climate mitigation policies. *Communication Research*, *39*(6), 701–723.

Hastings, G. B., & Saren, M. (2003). The critical contribution of social marketing. *Marketing Theory*, *3*(3), 305–322.

Hay, R., & Eagle, L. (2016). *Harnessing the science of social marketing and behaviour change for improved water quality in the GBR: Documentary Analysis*. Townsville: James Cook University for National Environmental Science Programme Project 2.1.3.

Head, B. W., & Alford, J. (2015). Wicked problems implications for public policy and management. *Administration and Society*, *47*(6), 711–739.

Heise, L., Lutz, B., Ranganathan, M., & Watts, C. (2013). Cash transfers for HIV prevention: Considering their potential. *Journal of the International AIDS Society*, *16*(1), 1–5.

Herman, E. S., & Chomsky, N. (2010 (updated from1988 edition)). *Manufacturing consent*. New York, NY: Pantheon Press.

Hieke, S., & Harris, J. L. (2016). Nutrition information and front-of-pack labelling: Issues in effectiveness. *Public Health Nutrition*, *19*(12), 2103.

Hoek, J., Gifford, H., Pirikahu, G., Thomson, G., & Edwards, R. (2010). How do tobacco retail displays affect cessation attempts? Findings from a qualitative study. *Tobacco Control*, *19*(4), 334–337.

Hoek, J., & Jones, S. C. (2011). Regulation, public health and social marketing: A behaviour change trinity. *Journal of Social Marketing*, *1*(1), 32–44.

Hu, X., Bell, R. A., Kravitz, R. L., & Orrange, S. (2012). The prepared patient: Information seeking of online support group members before their medical appointments. *Journal of Health Communication*, *17*(8), 960–978.

Iyer, E. S., & Kashyap, R. K. (2007). Consumer recycling: Role of incentives, information, and social class. *Journal of Consumer Behaviour*, *6*(1), 32–47.

Jacobs, K. (2015). The 'politics' of Australian housing: The role of lobbyists and their influence in shaping policy. *Housing Studies*, *30*(5), 694–710.

Jessop, D. C., & Wade, J. (2008). Fear appeals and binge drinking: A terror management theory perspective. *British Journal of Health Psychology*, *13*(Pt 4), 773–788.

Jones, S. C., Wyatt, A., & Daube, M. (2016). Smokescreens and beer goggles: How alcohol industry CSM protects the industry. *Social Marketing Quarterly*, *22*(4), 264–279.

Julia, C., Kesse-Guyot, E., Ducrot, P., Péneau, S., Touvier, M., Méjean, C., & Hercberg, S. (2015). Performance of a five category front-of-pack labelling system – The 5-colour nutrition label – To differentiate nutritional quality of breakfast cereals in France. *BMC Public Health*, *15*(1), 179.

Kelly, M. P., & Barker, M. (2016). Why is changing health-related behaviour so difficult? *Public Health*, *136*, 109–116.

Kemper, J. A., & Ballantine, P. W. (2017). Socio-technical transitions and institutional change: Addressing obesity through macro-social marketing. *Journal of Macromarketing*, *37*(4), 381–392.

Kennedy, A-M., Kapitan, S., Bajaj, N., Bakonyi, A., & Sands, S. (2017). Uncovering wicked problem's system structure: Seeing the forest for the trees. *Journal of Social Marketing*, 7(1), 51–73.

Kennedy, A-M., Kemper, J. A., & Parsons, A. G. (2018). Upstream social marketing strategy. *Journal of Social Marketing*, 8(3), 258–279.

Key, T. M., & Czaplewski, A. J. (2017). Upstream social marketing strategy: An integrated marketing communications approach. *Business Horizons*, 60, 325–333.

Kraft, P. W., Lodge, M., & Taber, C. S. (2015). Why people "don't trust the evidence" motivated reasoning and scientific beliefs. *The ANNALS of the American Academy of Political and Social Science*, 658(1), 121–133.

Kubacki, K., Rundle-Thiele, S., Pang, B., & Buyucek, N. (2015). Minimizing alcohol harm: A systematic social marketing review (2000–2014). *Journal of Business Research*, 68(10), 2214–2222.

Langford, R., & Panter-Brick, C. (2013). A health equity critique of social marketing: Where interventions have impact but insufficient reach. *Social Science and Medicine*, 83, 133–141.

Lavack, A. M., Watson, L., & Markwart, J. (2007). Quit and win contests: A social marketing success story. *Social Marketing Quarterly*, 13(1), 31–52.

Lazard, A., & Atkinson, L. (2014). Putting environmental infographics center stage the role of visuals at the elaboration likelihood model's critical point of persuasion. *Science Communication*, 83, 726–735.

Lee, N. M., & VanDyke, M. S. (2015). Set it and forget it: The one-way use of social media by government agencies communicating science. *Science Communication*, 37(4), 533–541.

Lefebvre, R. C. (2011). An integrative model for social marketing. *Journal of Social Marketing*, 1(1), 54–72.

Lefebvre, R. C. (2013). *Social marketing and social change: Strategies and tools for improving health, well-being, and the environment*. New Jersey: John Wiley & Sons.

Lewandowsky, S., Ecker, U. K., Seifert, C. M., Schwarz, N., & Cook, J. (2012). Misinformation and its correction continued influence and successful debiasing. *Psychological Science in the Public Interest*, 13(3), 106–131.

Louise, J., Eliott, J., Olver, I., & Braunack-Mayer, A. (2015). Mandatory cancer risk warnings on alcoholic beverages: What are the ethical issues? *The American Journal of Bioethics*, 15(3), 3–11.

Low, D. R., & Eagle, L. (2017). *Marketing the contested belief system of science*. Paper presented at the Australia New Zealand Marketing Academy Conference (ANZMAC), Melbourne.

Lynagh, M. C., Sanson-Fisher, R. W., & Bonevski, B. (2013). What's good for the goose is good for the gander. Guiding principles for the use of financial incentives in health behaviour change. *International Journal of Behavioural Medicine*, 20(1), 114–120.

Manning, M., Smith, C., & Mazerolle, P. (2013, April). The societal costs of alcohol misuse in Australia. *Trends and Issues in Crime and Criminal Justice*, 454, 1–6.

Mart, S. M. (2011). Alcohol marketing in the 21st century: New methods, old problems. *Substance Use and Misuse*, 46(7), 889–892.

May, N., Eliott, J., & Crabb, S. (2017). 'Everything causes cancer': How Australians respond to the message that alcohol causes cancer. *Critical Public Health*, 27(4), 419–429.

Mikulak, A. (2011). Mismatches between 'scientific' and 'non-scientific' ways of knowing and their contributions to public understanding of science. *Integrative Psychological and Behavioural Science*, 45(2), 201–215.

Mortimer, D., Ghijben, P., Harris, A., & Hollingsworth, B. (2013). Incentive-based and non-incentive-based interventions for increasing blood donation. London: *The Cochrane Library*. https://www.cochranelibrary.com/cdsr/doi/10.1002/14651858.CD010295/abstract

Munafò, M. R., Roberts, N., Bauld, L., & Leonards, U. (2011). Plain packaging increases visual attention to health warnings on cigarette packs in non-smokers and weekly smokers but not daily smokers. *Addiction*, 106(8), 1505–1510.

Murphy, M., Koohsari, M. J., Badland, H., & Giles-Corti, B. (2017). Supermarket access, transport mode and BMI: The potential for urban design and planning policy across socio-economic areas. *Public Health Nutrition*, 20(18), 3304–3315.

Peattie, K., & Peattie, S. (2003). Ready to fly solo? Reducing social marketing's dependence on commercial marketing theory. *Marketing Theory*, 3(3), 365–385.

Peattie, K., Peattie, S., & Newcombe, R. (2016). Unintended consequences in demarketing antisocial behaviour: Project Bernie. *Journal of Marketing Management*, 32(17–18), 1588–1618.

Peeters, S., & Gilmore, A. B. (2015). Understanding the emergence of the tobacco industry's use of the term tobacco harm reduction in order to inform public health policy. *Tobacco Control*, 24(2), 182–189.

Peloza, J., Ye, C., & Montford, W. J. (2015). When companies do good, are their products good for you? How corporate social responsibility creates a health halo. *Journal of Public Policy and Marketing*, 34(1), 19–31.

Peters, E., Hibbard, J., Slovic, P., & Dieckmann, N. (2007). Numeracy skill and the communication, comprehension, and use of risk-benefit information. *Health Affairs*, 26(3), 741–748.

Polonsky, M. J. (2017). The role of corporate social marketing. *Journal of Social Marketing*, 7(3), 268–279.

Powell, L. M., & Chaloupka, F. J. (2009). Food prices and obesity: Evidence and policy implications for taxes and subsidies. *The Milbank Quarterly*, 87(1), 229–257.

Ricciardi, L., Mostashari, F., Murphy, J., Daniel, J. G., & Siminerio, E. P. (2013). A national action plan to support consumer engagement via e-health. *Health Affairs*, 32(2), 376–384.

Riley, K. E., Ulrich, M. R., Hamann, H. A., & Ostroff, J. S. (2017). Decreasing smoking but increasing stigma? Anti-tobacco campaigns, public health, and cancer care. *AMA Journal of Ethics*, 19(5), 475.

Rossi, J., & Yudell, M. (2012). Value-ladenness and rationality in health communication. *American Journal of Bioethics*, 12(2), 20–22.

Rothman, A. J., & Salovey, P. (1997). Shaping perceptions to motivate healthy behaviour: The role of message framing. *Psychological Bulletin*, 121(1), 3–19.

Rothschild, M. (1999). Carrots, sticks, and promises: A conceptual framework for the management of public health and social issue behaviours. *Journal of Marketing*, 63(4), 24–37.

Rucker, D. D., & Petty, R. E. (2006). Increasing the effectiveness of communications to consumers: Recommendations based on elaboration likelihood and attitude certainty perspectives. *Journal of Public Policy and Marketing, 25*(1), 39–52.

Sacks, G., Veerman, J. L., Moodie, M., & Swinburn, B. (2011). 'Traffic-light' nutrition labelling and 'junk-food' tax: A modelled comparison of cost-effectiveness for obesity prevention. *International Journal of Obesity, 35*(7), 1001.

Satterlund, T. D., Cassady, D., Treiber, J., & Lemp, C. (2011). Barriers to adopting and implementing local-level tobacco control policies. *Journal of Community Health, 36*(4), 616–623.

Schmidt, H., Asch, D. A., & Halpern, S. D. (2012). Fairness and wellness incentives: What is the relevance of the process-outcome distinction? *Preventive medicine, 55,* S118–S123.

Scholes-Balog, K. E., Heerde, J. A., & Hemphill, S. A. (2012). Alcohol warning labels: Unlikely to affect alcohol-related beliefs and behaviours in adolescents. *Australian and New Zealand Journal of Public Health, 36*(6), 524–529.

Schuster, L. (2015). Competition and its influence on consumer decision making in social marketing. *Journal of Marketing Management, 31*(11–12), 1333–1352.

Seiler, T-B., Engwall, M., & Hollert, H. (2013). Lost in translation? Ways for environmental sciences to communicate about risk and research. *Environmental Sciences Europe, 25*(1), 1–3.

Seo, K., Dillard, J. P., & Shen, F. (2013). The effects of message framing and visual image on persuasion. *Communication Quarterly, 61*(5), 564–583.

Siegrist, M., Leins-Hess, R., & Keller, C. (2015). Which front-of-pack nutrition label is the most efficient one? The results of an eye-tracker study. *Food Quality and Preference, 39,* 183–190.

Simis, M. J., Madden, H., Cacciatore, M. A., & Yeo, S. K. (2016). The lure of rationality: Why does the deficit model persist in science communication? *Public Understanding of Science, 25*(4), 400–414.

Smith, J. R., & Louis, W. R. (2009). Group norms and the attitude – Behaviour relationship. *Social and Personality Psychology Compass, 3*(1), 19–35.

Soraghan, C., Thomson, E., & Ensor, J. (2016). Using food labels to evaluate the practice of nudging in a social marketing context. *Social Business, 6*(3), 249–265.

Sörqvist, P., Haga, A., Langeborg, L., Holmgren, M., Wallinder, M., Nöstl, A., . . . Marsh, J. E. (2015). The green halo: Mechanisms and limits of the eco-label effect. *Food Quality and Preference, 43,* 1–9.

Stephens, C. (2014). Paying the piper: Additional considerations of the theoretical, ethical and moral basis of financial incentives for health behaviour change. *International Journal of Behavioural Medicine, 21*(1), 202–205.

Tengland, P.-A. (2016). Behaviour change or empowerment: On the ethics of health-promotion goals. *Health Care Analysis, 24*(1), 24–46.

Thomsen, D. C. (2015). Seeing is questioning: Prompting sustainability discourses through an evocative visual agenda. *Ecology and Society, 20*(4), 9.

VanEpps, E. M., Downs, J. S., & Loewenstein, G. (2016). Calorie label formats: Using numeric and traffic light calorie labels to reduce lunch calories. *Journal of Public Policy and Marketing, 35*(1), 26–36.

Vartanian, L. R., & Smyth, J. M. (2013). Primum non nocere: Obesity stigma and public health. *Journal of Bioethical Inquiry, 10*(1), 49–57.

Wakefield, M. A., Loken, B., & Hornik, R. C. (2010). Use of mass media campaigns to change health behaviour. *Lancet, 376*(9748), 1261–1271.

Walach, H., & Loef, M. (2014). The barriers and facilitators of health behaviour change: A comparative review of reviews. *The Journal of Alternative and Complementary Medicine, 20*(5), A107–A108.

Wettlaufer, A., Cukier, S., Giesbrecht, N., & Greenfield, T. K. (2012). The marketing of responsible drinking: Competing voices and interests. *Drug and Alcohol Review, 31*(2), 231–239.

Wettstein, D., & Suggs, L. S. (2016). Is it social marketing? The benchmarks meet the social marketing indicator. *Journal of Social Marketing, 6*(1), 2–17.

World Health Organisation. (2010). *Global strategy to reduce harmful use of alcohol.* Geneva: World Health Organisation Retrieved from www.who.int/substance_abuse/publications/global_strategy_reduce_harmful_use_alcohol/en/

12 Social Engineering and Social Marketing

Natalia Szablewska and Krzysztof Kubacki

Introduction

Social engineering often has negative connotations, as it is commonly perceived as being intrinsically 'bad' (Kennedy & Parsons, 2014), manipulative, or simply an oppressive activity. This is because we associate social engineering with totalitarian regimes, such as Nazi Germany, Stalinist Russia, Fascist Italy, Maoist China, or Khmer Rouge Cambodia (see also McMahon, 2001). However, it is not only totalitarian regimes that use social engineering; democratic governments also commonly employ social engineering tools to achieve socially desirable goals. The difference is that shared social values and ethical principles in any given democratic society undergo gradual evolution through social reforms and consensus, whereas ideologically driven totalitarian regimes attempt to change social values and systems more drastically through force and coercion. If we consider social engineering as an attempt to engender collective action,

> much of what goes on in every society's day-to-day operations qualifies as social engineering. One can view child rearing, schooling, military indoctrination and any other means of mobilizing bias as social engineering without doing violence to the concept.
>
> (Podgórecki, Alexander, & Shields, 1996, p. 9)

Further, there are many examples of the use of social engineering to achieve positive holistic systemic change in education, public health, urban planning, and transportation/communication systems (see Scott, 1998). This is why social engineering is not necessarily inherently 'bad,' but rather the value and ethicality of social engineering depends on a wide range of factors, including, for example, the context in which it is used, the rationale behind social change, the level of consensus in society, the aims of social engineering and its wider social impact on society as a whole, its nondiscriminatory character, the level of participation and inclusion offered to the general public, transparency of decision making processes, and accountability of decision makers.

In this chapter, we introduce the concept of social engineering and its origins as a form of applied and practical social science and an approach to planned holistic systemic change (see, e.g., Kennedy, 2017). Our discussion focuses on three classes of tools used by states at the macro level to manage social issue behaviours: education, law, and social marketing. After introducing the concept of social engineering, we consider several examples of negative social engineering and introduce a human rights-based approach as a practical guide to employing social engineering tools for the social good.

Social Engineering

Twentieth-century applications of social engineering, first in authoritarian states and later throughout western democratic societies, were shaped by ideas formulated in the nineteenth century. The term 'social engineering' is believed to have been coined by industrialist Jacob C. van Marken in the 1890s. He presented the idea of modern employers needing to draw on the expertise of 'social' engineers—in the same way as there is a need for technical expertise of 'ordinary' engineers—to address problems of the social world (van Marken, 1894). Since then, the term itself has been used to offer understanding of or tools for handling holistic systemic change, with applications ranging from theology (see, e.g., Earp, 1911) to eugenics (see, e.g., Galton, 1904).

One of the key ideas that shaped the practical application of social engineering was the concept of a nation state, with its focus on unification and standardisation of macrosystems such as markets, laws, and education across regions (e.g., the unifications of Italy and Germany in 1871). Although the rise of the nation state can be traced back to the Middle Ages, the early nation states were largely political entities with very limited political and cultural ties (Cobban, 1969). The rise of nation states in the nineteenth century was influenced by the emergence of two opposing perspectives on what constitutes a nation (Skinner & Kubacki, 2007). One perspective focused on the nation as a political entity regardless of the cultural and national identities of its citizens—for example, the Hungarian Law of Nationalities of 1868, which stated that *"all citizens of Hungary [. . .] form a single nation – the indivisible unitary Magyar nation – to which all citizens of the country, irrespective of nationality, belong"* (Cobban, 1969, p. 36). The opposing perspective prioritised the importance of cultural unity, as exemplified by the words of Ernest Gellner, who believed that *"two men are of the same nation if and only if they share the same culture, where culture in turn means a system of ideas and signs and associations and ways of behaving and communicating"* (Gellner, 1983, p. 6).

Although in practice understanding of the nation state since the second half of the nineteenth century has been by and large informed by the combination of both perspectives, the need to create homogenous nation states informed the development and application of twentieth-century social engineering. The idea that social engineering, as a branch of applied and practical social science, can transform societies at the macro level through state institutions and agencies, both top down and bottom up, found fertile ground among fragile nation states of the early twentieth century. The newly emerging European states, threatened by political, social, cultural, and economic instabilities, *"embarked on major interventions in the name of not only national interest and strategy, but in the name of social order and morality"* (Podgórecki et al., 1996, p. 2).

It is unsurprising that the theory and application of social engineering has also attracted considerable interest among academics. For example, in 1945, in his seminal work on the open society, Karl Popper (1945/2013; see also Avery, 2000) proposed the concept of 'piecemeal (or democratic) social engineering' (which he considered to be positive), as opposed to 'holistic (or Utopian) engineering' (which he viewed as negative). Through the prism of Popper's conception of 'piecemeal social engineering,' the practice of social engineering becomes an integral process of an open society where individual freedom is its basic value. If freedom is to be assumed to be intrinsic to social life (Ballard, 1978; Habermas, 1979), the very process of social planning is not at odds with, but is rather instrumental for, regulating social activities. According to Popper, and within the (neo)liberal political philosophy, the state and its institutions are to foster and safeguard the greatest possible freedom for all individuals who are to be protected from each other and the state.

More recently, Podgórecki and colleagues (1996) identified four types of social engineering. A legitimate form of social action and applied social science, referred to as 'sociotechnics proper,' focuses on goals based on universally accepted principles and values, as well as scientific knowledge, and introduces change with the knowledge and approval of those concerned (see also D'Souza, 1998). The remaining three types of social engineering violate at least one of the above assumptions: 'Self-made social engineering' relies on generalised professional experience rather than scientific knowledge; 'quackish social engineering' relies on myths and ideologies, and interprets them as scientific knowledge; and 'dark social engineering' implies the use of 'sociotechnics proper' to produce harm (Podgórecki et al., 1996).

Broadly speaking, all macrosystemic social change involves some form of social engineering understood as practices and agencies aiming to mould human behaviour and social relationships (Mannheim, 1940). Regarding the many different social engineering tools used by states to induce holistic social change at the macro level, Rothschild's (1999) three classes of strategic tools for the management of social issue behaviours remain some of the most widely recognised. According to Rothschild, education, law, and social marketing may be used by states to address wicked societal problems. Although each of the three classes of tools can be seen as a unique macrosystem, in practice they interact with each other, creating holistic social change (Kennedy, 2017). However, assuming that the three classes of strategic tools are value-free and ethically neutral, their use and outcomes should always be considered within a specific morality—i.e., a system of values. The systems of values and ethical principles inform the choice of societal problem that needs to be addressed, how the problem is conceptualised, what methodologies are used to understand the problem, and what framework(s) of analysis direct the social engineer's lens towards elements of the problem that are deemed important to the potential intervention (Cherns, 1975).

Thus, it can be further reasoned that social engineering at a macro level is a state action assisted by experts who claim to be able to better understand the perceived social problems, and provide empirically grounded solutions that can be implemented to allow individuals and societies to become better selves (Patel & Reichardt, 2016). Thus, 'social engineers' play a key role in the process, and thereby their own rationales and motivations cannot be underestimated, nor remain unchallenged. Podgórecki et al. (1996, p. 3) posited that:

> All social engineers are moralists. They behave as if they know good from bad in the social sphere. They also claim to have the technical knowledge necessary to attain what is good and eliminate what is bad. The latter holds priority; their first task is to eradicate evil.

In the next sections of this chapter we focus on the three classes of strategic tools used by states in the management of holistic systemic change to show that, despite their ethically neutral nature, there is imminent potential for evil when social engineers become ideologically driven "*servants of power*" who prioritise the effectiveness and efficiency of their tools (Podgórecki et al., 1996, p. 10) over commonly accepted systems of values and ethical principles. In particular, tools of social engineering may become tools of oppression when they are targeted at minorities, or at weak or vulnerable members of society, who often lack social, economic, and cultural capital, or are unwilling to perform the desired behaviours promoted by the state and its social engineers.

Education

Education is often considered an important social good to which all citizens are entitled. For the majority of adults, education provides them with at least basic literacy and numeracy skills, as well as knowledge required to fully participate in the cultural, economic, and social life of their society. The educational system is therefore critical for individuals to realise their potential. However, due to its common character, education is one of the most important agents of macro-level socialisation for both children and adults in all societies. Through education, broadly understood here as both formal schooling and all other forms of acquisition of knowledge and skills, we learn our common values and rules that shape the functioning of our society and prepare us to fulfill our roles in society. Although few would argue against education as an important social good, education has also long been recognised as one of the main tools of social engineering (Chern, 1975), and, as the following example shows, education has the capacity to produce harm when used to instill ideologies rather than commonly accepted values.

When discussing social engineering, reference is often made to Soviet or Stalinist Russia, quoting Stalin's description of Soviet writers as "*engineers of human souls*" (Zhdanov, 1934/1992, p. 45). But what hides behind this quote is a form of 'quackish social engineering' that relies on systemic use of arts and education to promote socialist realism ideologies and myths disguised as scientifically proven social philosophy (Podgórecki et al., 1996). The cultural ideologist behind socialist realism doctrine was Andrei Zhdanov, Stalin's cultural commissar and one of the Communist Party leaders in the first half of the twentieth century. Zhdanov's famous speech at the Soviet Writer's Congress in 1934 provided the ideological foundations for the doctrine and its explicitly macro-level educational character, demanding that writers become servants of political education and their work an educational tool in the promotion of politically correct art describing reality in its revolutionary spirit. In his speech, Zhdanov (1934/1992, p. 44) offered the following description of the role of socialist realism in political and ideological education of the people:

> it means knowing life so as to be able to depict it truthfully in works of art, not depict it in a dead, scholastic way, not simply as 'objective reality,' but to depict reality in its revolutionary development [. . .] the truthfulness and historical concreteness of the artistic portrayal should be combined with the ideological remoulding and education of the toiling people in the spirit of socialism.

The ideologically driven 'quackish social engineering' of Soviet socialism put the education of youth and reeducation of workers as its primary aim, to engineer a new society loyal to the Communist Party, its ideology, and myths. Soviet socialism's education efforts centred on school-based interventions, grassroots-level youth organisations, and the family as society's main institutions of socialisation (Podgórecki et al., 1996). For example, as Csaba (1996) illustrated, for over 50 years a fabricated myth of 13-year-old Pavlik Morozov—who denounced his father for what he believed was acting against the interest of the state, and was later murdered by his family—became one of the main educational tools used to instill new Communist morality, separating old bourgeois values from the 'New Soviet Man'. In the Pavlik Morozov myth, Pavlik's father represented undesirable behaviours and values that needed to be eradicated, while the story served to create new Soviet values, empower several generations of Soviet children, and validate the behaviours needed to engineer and inspire a better Soviet society. Pavlik-martyr became a role model, and his story a myth that perpetuated the Soviet psyche through social engineering, as originally intended by Zhdanov (1934/1992, p. 45): *"untiring work directed towards self-education and towards improving [. . .] ideological equipment in the spirit of socialism represents an indispensable condition without which Soviet writers cannot remould the mentality of their readers and thereby become engineers of human souls"*.

The myth of Pavlik Morozov exemplifies the harmful influence of Communist (or, indeed, any totalitarian regime) macro-level education and its 'quackish social engineering' aimed at dividing parents and children, and socially engineering a class of people that remains loyal to the state before and above anything or anyone else. It reminds us that when driven by ideologies, myths, and political indoctrination, education has the power to create social norms, attitudes, behaviours, and macrosystems of value that are oppressive and inhumane. When education is hijacked to serve the totalitarian state, its ideologies and interests, rather than the wellbeing of the people, its purpose becomes distorted and its outcomes destructive.

As 2015 Nobel Prize in Literature winner Svetlana Alexievich (2016) wrote in her *Secondhand Time: The Last of the Soviets*, Sovoks[1] survived the collapse of the Soviet Union to find themselves unprepared for the new macrosystem: an aggressive brand of Russian capitalism, with its disregard for the vulnerable and ubiquitous emphasis on competition in all spheres of life. Their life stories tell a tale of double tragedy of people who feel betrayed by their old Soviet world and abandoned by the new capitalist system. Their stories capture the human costs of ideologically driven social engineering. While socially engineered Soviet education left plenty of victims of the totalitarian regime, many of those who survived were left ill-prepared for the post-Soviet world. This exemplifies what a powerful tool social engineering education can be, due to both its short-term and long-term impact on societies at large. Consequently, it is routinely used for 'indoctrination' (aimed at engineering obedient citizens for the dominant macrosystem).

Law

As with education, law is a strategic tool through which human behaviour can be moulded (Rothschild, 1999), and thus it is considered an instrument of sociotechnical action (Massell, 1968). As Simpson and Field (1947, p. 145) contended: *"to control man's social environment is to control man. This is the main task of the law. This is a task of human engineering, with men in society as its raw material"*.

A resort to law can facilitate macro-social change, and thus law is neither apolitical nor free from ideological influences. In that sense, law—despite being ethically neutral as a tool—can be used as a method of oppression or to facilitate dominant discourses in a society, often to the detriment of the unprivileged or vulnerable groups. This is because law not only shapes society but is also shaped by societal values, scientific discovery, and contemporary scientific knowledge. Eugenics is a good case in point. The nineteenth century advances in genetics inspired many of the twentieth-century eugenics laws. Tracking the development of the concept and the different forms of its operationalisation is a good illustration of how law can become a form of 'dark social engineering' (Podgórecki et al., 1996), either by being misguided (by certain scientific discoveries) or simply used to support certain ideologies.

Coined by Francis Galton (1904), the initial idea behind eugenics called for 'improving' the characteristics of organisms and species by maximising desirable genes and minimising undesirable ones (see also Rifkin, 1998, p. 116). At one point, the idea was associated with social philosophy, with social implications that, at the time, were perceived as supporting the development of the science of population to assist in *"the distribution of socially valuable hereditary capacities"* (Osborn, 1937, p. 389). Osborne, arguing for 'positive' eugenics, emphasised the need to develop 'proper' population studies that would allow for addressing the *"danger that important matters of policy may be determined by the emotional bias of one group or another"*, which, in practice, would lead to better *"understanding of what changes are actually taking place and what forms of social control might be effectively employed to improve succeeding generations"* (p. 397).

Some of the claims posed by the early theories of heredity have been discredited since; nevertheless, they inspired various laws and policies, based on race and other biological or social identifiers, throughout the world in the early twentieth century, and these days are reflected in the various rationalised selective reproductive processes. Today, eugenics is most often associated with the policy of 'racial hygiene' (*Rassenhygiene*) and practices of Nazi Germany (see the incorporation of discriminatory eugenic ideas in Hitler's *Mein Kampf*, 1925). However, the Law for the Prevention of Hereditary Diseased Offspring (*Gesetz zur Verhütung erbkranken Nachwuchses*) of 1933 in Germany was inspired by the earlier eugenics laws in the U.S.

In the U.S., the first eugenics law was enacted in Indiana in 1907,[2] which provided for involuntary sterilisation of insitutionalised individuals perceived as 'unfit' to reproduce, including *"confirmed criminals, idiots, imbeciles and rapists"* (State of Indiana 1907, Chapter 215; see also Reilly, 1985). This was followed by another 26 states passing similar laws (Macklin & Gaylin, 1981, p. 65). It was only in the 1960s and 1970s that the civil rights movement started putting pressure on limiting government's interference in private reproductive decisions,[3] leading to many of the mandatory sterilisation statutes being repealed.

The idea of eugenics has evolved and taken on different forms but has not completely withered away. As observed by Black (2003, p. 411), "*after Hitler, eugenics did not disappear. It renamed itself. What had thrived loudly as eugenics for decades quietly took postwar refuge under the labels human genetics and genetic counselling*". To address the negative consequences relating to prior eugenics programmes, some bioethicists argued that if the decision making is transferred from governments to individuals exercising their free choice (i.e., 'liberal eugenics'), and done in a manner that does not infringe on individuals' (reproductive) rights, then it is not necessarily immoral, and should even be encouraged as it assists in addressing (genetic) inequality and supports public health (Buchanan, Brock, Daniels, & Wikler, 2000; see also Wilkinson, 2010; Wilkinson & Garrard, 2013). However, even framed as a preventive measure to "*help people make whatever voluntary decisions are best for them in the light of their own reproductive goals*" (Wertz et al., 1995, p. 3), it is still not without consequences. Prenatal or other types of genetic screening might be perceived as merely giving individuals 'information', on the basis of which they can freely choose to act, but in practice this also raises several ethical, and hence often legal, issues. Potential misuses of genetic information represent one of the main concerns, and some of the responses aim at preventing 'genetic discrimination' (see, e.g., a U.S. federal law to that effect, the Genetic Information Nondiscrimination Act, 2008) and protecting the 'right not to know' one's genetic makeup (see, e.g., Andorno, 2004).

The often-difficult balancing act (of the different needs and desires) is invoked in relation to most public health issues. The principles of autonomy and free choice underpin individuals' right to make personal decisions without interference. However, there are some bounds on individual *rights* imposed by *responsibilities* towards one's community or society at large (or, alternatively, seen as the *rights* of the community), raising the question of when one should end and the other begin. The public health model presupposes that certain systemic measures can be taken (such as vaccinations) to prevent spreading of infectious diseases, or that public communication campaigns are employed to encourage or discourage individuals from certain behaviours (such as healthy eating or smoking, respectively). Rationalised along similar utilitarian lines, some argue that the public health model should be applied to genetics (e.g., Shaw, 1989). For others, health responses used against communicable diseases can be justified on the basis of preventing harm to others, whereas genetic diseases affect people of different races differently, thus always leaving it open to racially discriminatory policies (Damme, 1982).

Unsurprisingly then, genetic screening programmes, like eugenics in the past, have spawned heated debates about their ethical, moral, and social implications (Blank, 1982), including suggestions that they might lead to stigmatisation and discrimination in the social context, restrict access to insurance or employment (see, e.g., Billings et al., 1992), or amount to an invasion of privacy, amongst other negative consequences.

The debate on the ethical and legal dimensions of 'eugenics' (understood here as deliberately altering humans' genetic makeup) or 'genetic screening' (whether mandatory or voluntary) continues to be an ethical and legal quagmire. Neither of them are necessarily 'bad' or 'good' per se; rather, this depends on how they are used and by whom, even if the popular discourses might give rise to controversy and often be associated with unpopular ethical positions based on certain prior programmes. Ultimately, human betterment through the maximisation of human genetic material (whether labelled as 'eugenics', 'genetic screening', or something else) will continue to occupy scientists, ethicists, and lawyers. However, this is not a straightforward exercise as the values of individuals and communities need to be weighted against such endeavours. In this regard, social engineering is facilitated by law, as it offers a form of *"regulatory or coercive action of politically organised society [that] touches the lives of individuals and of community"* (Simpson & Field, 1947, p. 145, ft. 1), which makes it a very effective tool for attaining macrosystemic social change.

Social Marketing

Along with education and law, social marketing is seen as the key strategic tool for holistic social change (Rothschild, 1999). The consensus definition of social marketing adopted by the leading social marketing organisations states that *"social marketing seeks to develop and integrate marketing concepts with other approaches to influence behaviours that benefit individuals and communities for the greater social good"* (AASM, ISMA, & ESMA, 2013). As Kennedy and Parsons (2012, p. 37–38) pointed out, *"macro-social marketing used in conjunction with other tools [e.g. education and law], forms part of a social engineering approach to societal change"*. Thus, macro-social marketing, if it is part of a long-term plan for social change, can be viewed as a positive social engineering intervention (Kennedy & Parsons, 2012). However, as we argued earlier, no systemic social change tool is inherently 'bad' or 'good', as it is merely used to achieve societal aims. Thus, when used for ideological, unethical, or reprehensible goals, they can be employed as means of oppression and to coerce certain attitudes, norms, and behaviours.

However, even 'positive' social engineering—that is 'sociotechnics proper'—when employed at a macro level, may lead to the emergence of 'self-made social engineering' (Podgórecki et al., 1996). This means that the systemic social change action originally instigated by the state can be embarked upon by individuals (e.g., social activists, self-proclaimed change agents) or institutions (e.g., commercial organisations, nonprofit organisations, research institutes) who lack the authority and/or legitimacy to intervene in the life and fabric of society, and who rely on generalised professional experience rather than scientific knowledge, or else on dubious scientific knowledge. The process of social change then becomes a bureaucratic exercise concerned more with the promotion of ideologies, and often what we may term the fallacy of effectiveness—i.e., with the effectiveness of the tools employed, rather than scientific validity of the intervention's aims, the ethicality of its tools, and its broader social impact on society as a whole.

We must, therefore, acknowledge that social marketing, as per all other tools of social engineering, is not inherently 'good,' even though its intended aim is to benefit society (see, e.g., Andreasen, 1994). Extensive literature has discussed a wide range of ethical challenges and unintended consequences faced by social marketers (see also Chapter 11, this volume). For example, social marketing has been criticised for being manipulative (Andreasen, 2002; Brenkert, 2002), paternalistic (Donovan & Henley, 2010), or a form of social control (Cherrier & Gurrieri, 2014), thereby infringing on the rights and freedoms of individuals (Holden & Cox, 2013). Social marketing campaigns have become one of the key macro-marketing measures to manage social issues, such as obesity (Witkowski, 2007). As Gurrieri and colleagues, (Gurrieri, Previte, & Brace-Govan, 2013; Gurrieri, Brace-Govan, & Previte, 2014) demonstrated through examples of weight management, physical activity, and breastfeeding social marketing campaigns, social marketing's simplified messages may harm those who are unable or do not want to comply with the dominant norms promoted by social marketing campaigns, leading, in the case of weight management campaigns, to stigmatisation, social exclusion, and other unintended psychological and physiological consequences of weight stigma, such as low self-esteem, poor body image, binge eating, and depression (Annis, Cash, & Hrabosky, 2004). The narrowly defined 'healthism', Gurrieri and colleagues argued, which over-relies on medical evidence and disregards social and cultural practices, reduces the government-instigated social action to a war on obesity with very limited focus on broader improvement of general health and wellbeing. In a spirit of self-made social engineering, macro-social marketing campaigns (and, increasingly, commercial marketing campaigns with social goals such as weight control, using pseudo-feminist language to create the illusion of female empowerment yet unequivocally designed to pursue profit—see, e.g. Stinson, 2001), employ limited scientific knowledge and selective use of promoted values, frequently reducing the scope of social change to a focus on market segments and consumer insights promising to deliver the highest return on investment in the shortest possible timeframe.

Preoccupation with effectiveness, disregard for the impact of interventions on society as a whole, social action without legitimacy and/or authority, and instrumental use of social science knowledge may bring social marketing dangerously close to self-made social engineering. Thus, just as social marketers must be prepared to probe their own biases and question the rationales for social interventions they have been enlisted to conduct, like social engineers they *"should be ready to investigate their epistemological assumptions, so that the limitations of those assumptions are rendered apparent, and new planning options are made manifest"* (Murphy, 1981, p. 16). Murphy (1981, p. 14) termed this an 'epistemological openness'; that is, a realisation that *"planning cannot be logically removed from interpretation"*, which he also perceived as necessary for ensuring non-repressive and rational social planning.

Human Rights Discourse

Viewing social engineering merely as a form of 'social planning' (Popper, 1945/1966a, p. 158) does not negate the criticism or rejection of totalitarianism. However, even if it is accepted that there is a significant difference in oppressive social planning and socially desirable social planning (often presented as scientifically motivated desire for social change), how do we ensure that the latter does not transform into the former? We propose that the human rights discourse—which in practice involves following a human rights-based approach—can offer guidance in assessing the ethicality of macro-level social interventions and provide direction to avoid negative forms of social engineering, including those described earlier in this chapter.

The human rights discourse is widely debated, and often disputed and criticised, but it continues to be one of the most influential discourses in modern history. It is beyond the scope of this chapter to engage fully in an overview of the complex system devised to promote and protect human rights. However, simply put, human rights are legal, political, and moral standards that claim to be of universal applicability (UDHR, 1948), even though some regional differences in their legal aspects remain. The philosophical underpinnings of human rights can be located in many different cultures and traditions (see, e.g., Robinson, 1998), with the primary focus on the need to protect individual liberties and freedoms from unwarranted intrusions of the state (De Schutter, 2014; Rehman, 2010; Turner, 1993).

Unsurprisingly then, the contemporary system of legally enforceable human rights crystallised following the Second World War and became entrenched in the Universal Declaration of Human Rights (UDHR) in 1948, which, while not legally binding, provided foundations for the so-called International Bill of Rights.[4] The atrocities committed during and following the aftermath of the Second World War prompted the international community to develop a global system of human rights standards that would protect individuals (citizens) from abuses of their governments, and to agree on minimum standards of justice, equality, and dignity afforded to all. In that sense, human rights standards (or in some cases actual human rights obligations) can provide a roadmap by which to assess the different forms of social engineering, i.e., education, law, and social marketing.

As a way to facilitate the interpretation of human rights as legal and moral concepts, a number of principles have been developed. Some of these principles are referred to as the 'content principles' (i.e., universality, inalienability, indivisibility, interdependence, and interrelatedness), and they sit alongside the 'process principles' (i.e., transparency and accountability; equality and non-discrimination; and participation and inclusion—UNDG, 2003, 2011). These principles (or normative standards) have achieved global legitimacy, and also inform analytical tools and offer operational guidance (Moser & Norton, 2001) in the development of frameworks that facilitate the implementation of human rights. In turn, a human rights framework has been shown to facilitate analysis of power relations and to identify and address the vulnerability of certain groups and individuals in different contexts. This can be achieved by applying a human rights perspective or following a human rights-based approach.[5]

Considering the earlier example of Soviet 'quackish social engineering' through education, such a form of social engineering would most likely be considered as noncompliant with human rights standards. The right to education is now recognised in the majority of international human rights treaties.[6] For example, the Convention on the Rights of the Child (1989) stipulates that public education should be directed to "*a wide range of values*" (CRC, 2001, p. 4). In addition to the right to education, international human rights law recognises the right to freedom of thought and the educational rights of parents, which in practice often means a balancing act between these different rights. Further, under the European human rights regime, the European Court of Human Rights has developed a 'prohibition of indoctrination' to ensure that the different religious and philosophical opinions can be respected in order for pupils to "*acquire knowledge about their respective thoughts and traditions*" (*Lautsi v. Italy*, paras. 47c–d). In that sense, the state is required to conduct public education in an "*objective, critical and pluralistic manner*" (*Kjeldsen, Busk Madsen and Pedersen v. Denmark*, para. 53). Even though the definition of 'indoctrination' is not particularly precise, it not only applies to the state-wide policies on education but also, as noted by the Inter-American Commission on Human Rights (1983, p. 39), political indoctrination (or the presence of "*numerous professions of doctrinal faith*"), which might also be seen as infringing human rights standards.

If we were to apply the proposed human rights-based approach to our earlier discussion on eugenics and genetic screening, some of these programmes would not stand up to human rights scrutiny either. For example, in the U.S., from the 1970s eugenics laws were replaced by mandatory genetic screening programmes, such as sickle cell disease (SCD) testing directed at the African American population. Even though a higher proportion of African Americans suffer from SCD compared to other population groups, the policy was perceived as a form of racial discrimination. The social implications of the policy were that members of the affected racial group were routinely denied access to education, employment, and health insurance on the basis of their *increased* likelihood of carrying SCD, even if they might have been healthy. In response to the public opposition, including on the part of the medical community, the U.S. Congress passed the National Sickle Cell Anaemia Control Act (1972) to end the discriminatory testing practices by making the screening voluntary.

The legal changes in this area have facilitated long-term social changes and enhanced public understanding of how various diseases might affect racial groups differently. However, SCD testing has also highlighted ethical and social questions surrounding genetic testing more generally. Thus, as shown in this example, state laws or policies, even when well meaning, must be closely monitored and reviewed in light of their wider social impact. Governments (whether at national or local levels) must systematically evaluate the law in terms of its compliance with human rights standards, not only to satisfy states' legal obligations but also to ensure best practice.

A Human Rights-Based Approach in Social Marketing

As highlighted in the earlier section on social marketing, as in education and law, macro-social marketing interventions have intrinsic ethical dimensions (see also Brenkert, 2002; Chapter 11, this volume). Therefore, reaching out to the human rights discourse offers some guidance regarding development of the theory and practice of social marketing. This goes into the very nature of the ethicality of social marketing, in that even though the purpose of social marketing is to advance social good (AASM et al., 2013, p. 1), in practice that requires social marketers to engage in the often complex and difficult considerations of what might constitute the socially responsible inducement of behaviour change.

As we argued elsewhere (Szablewska & Kubacki, 2019), a human rights-based approach offers a possible means by which to scrutinise social marketing interventions in terms of their processes (i.e., how well they align with human rights principles), as well as to evaluate their impact (intended or otherwise). Of the two types of human rights principles—'content' and 'process'—the latter are more relevant in the context of social marketing. The process principles (of *transparency* and *accountability; equality* and *nondiscrimination;* and *participation* and *inclusion*) are interwoven and mutually reinforcing, and thus must be consulted throughout the processes of development, implementation, and evaluation of social interventions.

Starting with decision making as to which macrosocietal issues or problems to focus on, social issues must be identified that would entail interventions (which might stem from states' legal obligations, such as in the realm of the right to health). Thus, those involved in the decision making need to be *accountable* for the decision making, and the processes of determination of those social issues need to be *transparent*. Further, it must be ensured that social interventions are *nondiscriminatory*, as all people have an *equal* right to protection and respect, which might require looking beyond the immediate origins of problems into the structural and systemic causes and their manifestations (see, e.g., Boesen & Martin, 2007). Finally, in the selection of methods and tools used to devise social programmes and interventions, as well as their assessment, individuals and target groups must be effectively *included* by gaining access to information, as well as opportunities that allow them to develop their capacity for *participation* to influence the decision making that affects their lives.

Breastfeeding social marketing campaigns (analysed by Gurrieri et al., 2013), for example, often do not meet these standards. It could be argued that many of these campaigns promote a particular ideology without acknowledging alternative motherhood discourses (thus lacking *transparency* and *accountability*), which leads to discrimination of mothers who make alternative choices about infant feeding (thus, they fail to ensure *equality* and *nondiscrimination*), and often do not provide mechanisms for participation and engagement in the promoted behaviour for mothers who, for personal or health reasons, do not want or are unable to breastfeed (resulting in falling short of facilitating *participation* and *inclusion*).

As a tool of social engineering, social marketing must ensure that the choice of marketing tools, the target audience(s), and how these groups are targeted, entail the application of a human rights-based approach to achieve socially responsible interventions. Aside from ethical arguments in favour of adopting such an approach, it also increases effectiveness, efficiency, and legitimacy of social marketing interventions. Employing a human rights-based approach helps to improve risk management and identify opportunities, as well as effectively dealing with wicked problems and challenging social issues. We argue, therefore, that the proposed approach offers a practical means by which to address some of the ethical issues and challenges identified in the theory and practice of social marketing (see Chapter 11, this volume).

Conclusions

In this chapter we have introduced the concept and origins of social engineering as a form of applied and practical social science. Through several examples, we have shown that the three classes of strategic tools for the management of social-issue behaviours at the macro level—i.e., education, law, and social marketing (Rothschild, 1999)—have been used as various forms of social engineering by totalitarian, as well as democratic, governments. Therefore, social marketing interventions should not be considered innocuous activities. Social marketing is a tool in the process of social engineering, as it is a way to affect social change. Thus, when social marketers engage in macro-level interventions, they need to consider the interventions' wider impact on the target group(s) and beyond, as well as acknowledge the rationales and motives for their interventions, and take all necessary steps to minimise potential negative and unintended consequences of their actions.

If social life is perceived to be in constant flux, then the very process of change in social relations and the engineering of social and individual behaviour are unavoidable. The question, then, is how to ensure that social engineering offers a *"synthesis of the possible and the permissible in pursuit of the desirable"* (Duff, 2005, p. 68). As similarly argued by Murphy (1981), (non-repressive) social planning is a social product, and can therefore be altered or abandoned altogether, suggesting that it is historically constituted and self-motivated. This gives rise to 'true' social engineering, *"in that a society monitors its own developmental progress, instead of merely attempting to invent methods which will insure that a society will be capable of adjusting to a set of social demands that are not necessarily relevant"* (Murphy, 1981, p. 14).

As highlighted earlier, social engineering is used by all governments, whether democratic or not, but the means though which the social change is instigated, and often the aims of such a change, differ. Government programmes aimed at discouraging smoking, drink-driving, or domestic violence are achieved not only through social marketing interventions, but also through law, education, and other socially driven programmes such as community mobilisation, training, and funding to aid societal change (Kennedy & Parsons, 2014). Thus, attempts to alter any social behaviour must aim to be socially 'desirable' across society (even if not necessarily by all), which legitimises such interventions in terms of falling within the remit of the government's duties to protect and safeguard society at large.

However, to ensure that governments (and those working on their behalf) engage in forms of social engineering that are indeed socially desirable, rather than serving their own agendas, more proactive steps than just faith in governments are needed to implement progressive policies. In the context of social marketing, we have argued that by following a human rights-based approach (and, in particular, the principles of *accountability* and *transparency, equality* and *nondiscrimination,* and *participation* and *inclusion*), social marketers will be better equipped to avoid the dangers of 'negative' social engineering, as well as the unintended consequences of 'positive' social engineering.

Notes

1. In Russian, a derogatory description of people who uncritically believe in Soviet values.
2. This was found to be unconstitutional by the Indiana Supreme Court in *Williams v. Smith, 131 NE 2 (Ind.), 1921.*
3. Upheld by the U.S. Supreme Court in *Griswold v. Connecticut, 381 U. S. 479 (1965); Roe v. Wade, 410, U. S. 113 (1973).*
4. Currently, there are nine core legally binding international human rights treaties: International Covenant on Civil and Political Rights, 1966; International Covenant on Economic, Social and Cultural Rights (ICESCR), 1966; Convention on the Elimination of All Forms of Discrimination Against Women (CEDAW), 1979; International Convention on the Elimination of All Forms of Racial Discrimination, 1965; Convention Against Torture and Other Cruel, Inhuman or Degrading Treatment or Punishment, 1984; Convention on the Rights of the Child (CRC), 1989; International Convention on the Protection of the Rights of All Migrant Workers and Members of Their Families, 1990; Convention on the Rights of Persons with Disabilities (CRPD), 2006; and International Convention for the Protection of All Persons from Enforced Disappearance, 2006.
5. It is beyond the scope of this chapter to provide a more detailed overview of human rights-based approaches, but in the field of development see, e.g., HRCA, 1995; UNDP, 2000, 2003; OHCHR & UNDP, 2005. In relation to reducing poverty see, e.g., OHCHR, 2002. In relation to access to justice see, e.g., UNDP, 2005.
6. ICESCR (Art 13); CEDAW (Art 10); CRC (Arts 28–29); CRPD (Art 24).

References

Alexievich, S. (2016). *Secondhand time: The last of the Soviets.* Melbourne: The Text Publishing Company.

Andorno, R. (2004). The right not to know: An autonomy based approach. *Journal of Medical Ethics, 30,* 435–440.

Andreasen, A. (1994). Social marketing: Its definition and domain. *Journal of Public Policy and Marketing, 13*(1), 108–114.

Andreasen, A. (2002). Marketing social marketing in the social change marketplace. *Journal of Public Policy and Marketing, 21*(1), 3–13.

Annis, N. M., Cash, T., & Hrabosky, I. I. (2004). Body image and psychosocial differences among stable average weight, currently overweight, and formerly overweight women: The role of stigmatizing experiences. *Body Image, 1*(2), 155–167.

Australian Association of Social Marketing, International Social Marketing Association, and European Social Marketing Association (AASM, ISMA, and ESMA). (2013). *Consensus definition of social marketing.* Retrieved

September 18, 2018, from www.i-socialmarketing.org/assets/social_marketing_definition.pdf

Avery, T. (2000). Popper on "social engineering": A classical liberal view. *Reason Papers, 26*, 29–38.

Ballard, E. C. (1978). *Man and technology: Toward a measurement of a culture.* Pittsburgh, PA: Duquesne University Press.

Billings, P. R., Kohn, M. A., de Cuevas, M., Beckwith, J., Alper, J. S., & Natowicz, M. R. (1992). Discrimination as a consequence of genetic testing. *American Journal of Human Genetics, 50*, 476–482.

Black, E. (2003). *War against the weak: Eugenics and America's campaign to create a master race.* New York, NY: Four Walls Eight Windows Publishers.

Blank, R. H. (1982). Public policy implications of human genetic technology: Genetic screening. *The Journal of Medicine and Philosophy, 7*, 355–374.

Boesen, K., & Martin, T. (2007). *Applying a rights-based approach: An inspirational guide for civil society.* Copenhagen: Danish Institute for Human Rights. Retrieved June 12, 2015, from www.acfid.asn.au/aid – issues/files/applying – a – rights – based – approach – 2013 – an – inspirational – guide – for – civil – society

Brenkert, G. G. (2002). Ethical challenges of social marketing. *Journal of Public Policy and Marketing, 21*(1), 14–25.

Buchanan, A., Brock, D. W, Daniels, N., & Wikler, D. (2000). *From chance to choice: Genetics and justice.* New York, NY: Cambridge University Press.

Cherns, A. B. (1975). Social engineering in Britain: The use of social sciences in social policy. *Current Sociology, 23*(1), 99–127.

Cherrier, H., & Gurrieri, L. (2014). Framing social marketing as a system of interaction: A neo-institutional approach to alcohol abstinence. *Journal of Marketing Management, 30*(7–8), 607–633.

Cobban, A. (1969). *The nation state and self-determination.* London: Fontana.

Committee on the Rights of the Child (CRC). (2001). *General comment no. 1: The aims of education* (article 29), CRC/GC/2001/1.

Csaba, K. (1996). Pavlik Morozov: A Soviet case study of "dark" social engineering. In A. Podgórecki, J. Alexander, & R. Shields (Eds.), *Social engineering* (pp. 113–130). Ottawa: Carleton University Press.

Damme, C. (1982). Controlling genetic disease through law. *University of California Davis Law Review, 15*, 801–807.

D'Souza, V. (1998). Review. *Sociological Bulletin, 47*(2), 265–270.

De Schutter, O. (2014). *International human rights law: Cases, materials, commentary* (2nd ed.). Cambridge: Cambridge University Press.

Donovan, R., & Henley, N. (2010). *Principles and practice of social marketing: An international perspective.* Cambridge: Cambridge University Press.

Duff, A. S. (2005). Social engineering in the information age. *The Information Society, 21*, 67–71.

Earp, E. L. (1911). *The social engineer.* New York, NY: Eaton and Mains.

European Court of Human Rights. (1976). Kjeldsen, *Busk Madsen and Pedersen v. Denmark*, no. 5926/72.

European Court of Human Rights. (2009). *Lautsi v. Italy*, no. 30814/06.

Galton, F. (1904). Eugenics: Its definition, scope, and aims. *The American Journal of Sociology, 10*(1), 1–25.

Gellner, E. (1983). *Nations and nationalism.* Ithaca, NY: Cornell University Press.

Gurrieri, L., Brace-Govan, J., & Previte, J. (2014). Neoliberalism and managed health: Fallacies, facades and inadvertent effects. *Journal of Macromarketing, 34*(4), 532–538.

Gurrieri, L., Previte, J., & Brace-Govan, J. (2013). Women's bodies as sites of control: Inadvertent stigma and exclusion in social marketing. *Journal of Macromarketing, 33*(2), 128–143.

Habermas, J. (1979). Historical materialism and the development of normative structures. In J. Habermas (Ed.), *Communication and the evolution of society* (pp. 95–129). Boston, MA: Beacon Press.

Holden, S. S., & Cox, D. (2013). Social marketing: Immunizing against unethical practice. In K. Kubacki & S. Rundle-Thiele (Eds.), *Contemporary issues in social marketing* (pp. 59–75). Newcastle Upon Tyne: Cambridge Scholars Publishing.

Human Rights Council of Australia (HRCA). (1995). *The rights way to development: A human rights approach to development assistance.* Marrickville: HRCA.

Inter-American Commission on Human Rights. (1983). Report on Cuba, OEA/Ser. L/V/II. 61, Doc. 29 rev. 1.

Kennedy, A. M. (2017). Macro-social marketing research: Philosophy, methodology and methods. *Journal of Macromarketing, 37*(4), 347–355.

Kennedy, A. M., & Parsons, A. (2012). Macro-social marketing and social engineering: A systems approach. *Journal of Social Marketing, 2*(1), 37–51.

Kennedy, A. M., & Parsons, A. (2014). Social engineering and social marketing: Why is one "good" and the other "bad"? *Journal of Social Marketing, 4*(3), 198–209.

Macklin, R., & Gaylin, W. (1981). *Mental retardation and sterilization: A problem of competency and paternalism.* New York, NY: Plenum.

Mannheim, K. (1940). *Man and society in an age of reconstruction: Studies in modern social structure.* New York, NY: Harcourt, Brace and Co.

Massell, G. J. (1968). Law as an instrument of revolutionary change in a traditional milieu. *Law and Society Review, 2*(2), 179–228.

McMahon, L. (2001). The impact of social marketing on social engineering in economic restructuring. *Journal of Nonprofit and Public Sector Marketing, 9*(4), 75–84.

Moser, C., & Norton, A. (2001). *To claim our rights: Livelihood security, human rights and sustainable development.* London: Overseas Development Institute.

Murphy, J. W. (1981). Applied sociology, social engineering, and human rationality. *The Journal of Sociology and Social Welfare, 8*(1), 10–18.

The Office of the United Nations High Commissioner for Human Rights (OHCHR). (2002). *Draft guidelines: A human rights approach to poverty reduction strategies.* Geneva: OHCHR.

The Office of the United Nations High Commissioner for Human Rights and United Nations Development Programme (OHCHR and UNDP). (2005). *Lessons learned from rights-based approaches in the Asia-Pacific region.* Bangkok: OHCRH.

Osborn, F. (1937). Development of a eugenic philosophy. *American Sociological Review, 2*(3), 389–397.

Patel, K. K., & Reichardt, S. (2016). The dark side of transnationalism social engineering and Nazism, 1930s – 40s. *Journal of Contemporary History*, *51*(1), 3–21.

Podgórecki, A., Alexander, J., & Shields, R. (1996). *Social engineering*. Ottawa: Carleton University Press.

Popper, K. R. (2013). *The open society and its enemies*, (One-volume ed.). Princeton, Oxford: Princeton University Press. (Original work published 1945).

Rehman, J. (2010). *International human rights law* (2nd ed.). Harlow: Pearson Education.

Reilly, P. (1985). Eugenic sterilization in the United States. In A. Milunsky & G. Annas (Eds.), *Genetics and the law III*. New York, NY: Plenum.

Rifkin, J. (1998). *The biotech century: Harnessing the gene and remaking the world*. New York, NY: Jeremy P. Tarcher.

Robinson, M. (1998, January 27). *Opening address on the occasion of the 50th anniversary of the universal declaration of human rights at the Symposium on human rights in the Asia-Pacific Region*. Retrieved September 18, 2018, from http://archive. unu. edu/unupress/Mrobinson. html

Rothschild, M. L. (1999). Carrots, sticks, and promises: A conceptual framework for the management of public health and social issue behaviours. *Journal of Marketing*, *63*(4), 24–37.

Scott, J. C. (1998). *Seeing like a state: How certain schemes to improve the human condition have failed*. New Haven, CT and London: Yale University Press.

Shaw, M. (1989). Conditional prospective rights of the fetus. *Journal of Legal Medicine*, *5*(1), 63–116.

Simpson, S. P., & Field, R. (1947). Social engineering through law: The need for a school of applied jurisprudence. *New York University Law Quarterly Review*, *22*(2), 145–193.

Skinner, H., & Kubacki, K. (2007). Unravelling the complex relationship between nationhood, cultural identity and place branding. *Place Branding and Public Diplomacy*, *3*(4), 305–316.

State of Indiana. (1907). Acts 1907–Laws of the state of Indiana, passed at sixty-fifth regular session of the General Assembly. Indianapolis: William B. Burford.

Stinson, K. (2001). *Women and dieting culture: Inside a commercial weight loss group*. New Brunswick, New Jersey, and London: Rutgers University Press.

Szablewska, N., & Kubacki, K. (2019). A human rights-based approach to the social good in social marketing. *Journal of Business Ethics*, *155*(3), 871–888.

Turner, B. S. (1993). Outline of a theory of human rights. *Sociology*, *27*(3), 489–512.

Universal Declaration of Human Rights (UDHR). (1948). U.N.G.A. Res. 217A (III). U.N. Doc A/810.

United Nations Development Group (UNDG). (2003). *The human rights-based approach to development cooperation: Towards a common understanding among the UN agencies*. Retrieved September 18, 2018, from http://hrbaportal.org/the – human – rights – based – approach – to – development – cooperation – towards – a – common – understanding – among – un – agencies

United Nations Development Group (UNDG). (2011). *UN common learning package on HRBA principles*. Retrieved September 18, 2018, from https://undg.org/home/undg – mechanisms/undg – hrm/knowledge – management/

about – the – un – practitioners – portal – on – hrba – programming – hrba – portal/english – learning – package/

United Nations Development Programme (UNDP). (2000). *Human develop-ment report 2000: Human rights and human development.* New York, NY: UNDP.

United Nations Development Programme (UNDP). (2003). *Human development report 2003: Millennium development goals: A compact among nations to end human poverty.* New York, NY: UNDP.

United Nations Development Programme (UNDP). (2005). *Programming for jus-tice: Access for all: A practitioner's guide to a human rights-based approach to access to justice.* Bangkok: UNDP.

van Marken, J. C. (1894). Sociale ingenieurs. In Delftsch Studenten Corps, *Delftsche Corps-Almanak.*

Wertz, D. C., Fletcher, J. C., Berg, K., & Boulyjenkov, V. (1995). *Guidelines on ethical issues in medical genetics and the provision of genetics services.* Geneva: World Health Organization.

Wilkinson, S. (2010). *Choosing tomorrow's children: The ethics of selective reproduction.* Oxford: Oxford University Press.

Wilkinson, S., & Garrard, E. (2013). *Eugenics and the ethics of selective repro-duction.* Keele: Keele University.

Witkowski, T. (2007). Food marketing and obesity in developing countries: Anal-ysis, ethics, and public policy. *Journal of Macromarketing, 27*(2), 126–137.

Zhdanov, A. (1992). Soviet writer's congress, 1934. In S. Sim (Ed.), *Art: Con-text and value.* Milton Keynes: The Open University. (Original work published 1934).

13 Warmth Rationing as a Macro-Social Problem

The Application of the Chrematistics Framework

Djavlonbek Kadirov

Warmth Rationing as a Wicked Problem

Comfortable warmth is a basic human need, and perhaps one of the fundamental human rights in countries with a cold climate. Warmth provisioning, the maintenance of comfortable indoor temperatures, is part of the generation and supply of the basics of life (e.g., food, water). Besides, it is morally and legally unacceptable to intentionally deprive people of warmth, since the exposure to sustained low temperatures may be life threatening. The need for warmth may vary depending on different circumstances and conditions. The World Health Organization's standard for warmth is 20°C for the sick, disabled, and vulnerable population, while it is 18°C for healthy people with adequate clothing. Consequently, warmth provisioning is a societal issue that needs to be thoroughly addressed. The market logic limits the consumption of warmth to those who can afford it, while most critics of the energy sector believe that people have the right to access an inclusive, reliable, and efficient supply of energy that guarantees comfortable warmth for all citizens.

In the last three decades, energy prices has seen a steady increase in New Zealand, while the energy supply industry reported healthy revenues. At the same time, rationing warmth, in some extreme cases, endangering the health of the self and dependants by limiting access to warmth, gradually unfolded into a new type of a wicked problem. Wicked problems are complex societal 'malaise' (Kennedy, 2016) that exhibit easily identifiable symptoms and extremely entangled causes. Wicked problems, especially those that are linked to marketing systems, are difficult to resolve as no single solution exists, although all parties may agree that the problem exists and that it needs to be addressed at a societal level.

Current societal discourse indicates that a dangerous institutional tendency is on the rise in New Zealand. That is, simply 'going cold' and rationing heating has become normal in New Zealand in recent years (Stuff, 2018a). This 'norm' proliferated not only among low-income and vulnerable groups, but also among medium-income households. The deficit of indoor household warmth often translates into excess winter mortality. Research estimates that New Zealand has a significant excess winter mortality attributed to low indoor temperatures, among other causes (Davie, Baker, Hales, & Carlin, 2007; Hales, 2012). It appears that New Zealanders, facing increasing prices for life necessities, are cutting on heating costs. The recent survey by Credit Simple involving over 1,300 households found that 53% of New Zealanders often switch off heating to save on the cost. This number was 69% in Otago, the coldest region in winter. Going cold is a difficult dilemma for most families, however, when it comes to a trade-off, it often wins over other discomforts (e.g., going hungry). Some families resorted to 'Kiwi ingenuity', adapting ovens, stoves, and barbeques for indoor heating purposes (The Spinoff, 2017).

Warmth rationing is not simply a matter of a single factor (e.g., energy prices). It is a complex, system-wide wicked problem that comprises many different factors. For instance, some might argue that it has deep historical roots. Historically, it was believed that warming a house is like burning money (BBC, 2011). In New Zealand, the norms of going cold may be related to house building standards, as until recently houses used to be built with no consideration for energy efficiency which made them draft-prone, cold, and damp (Howden-Chapman et al., 2009). Culturally, people still believe that heating more than one room of the house is irrational, which led to slow proliferation of central heating systems (Howden-Chapman et al., 2009). Moreover, industry factors such as innovation concerning solar panels, energy storage, alternative energy networks, and construction materials significantly impact the situation. Furthermore, government subsidies and initiatives also significantly influence people's behaviour. For example, the recently introduced Winter Energy Payment scheme subsidises heating costs for low-income and vulnerable households, but it may create yet another justification for the others to go cold just because they are not qualified for the subsidy. This problem relates to social marketing at the micro, meso, and macro levels. At the micro level, social marketing can focus on transforming individuals' behaviour, attitude, and emotions. In particular, this would involve modifying how people think about, deal with, and solve warmth rationing issues at an individual level. At the meso level social marketing would be concerned with raising awareness as well as promoting initiatives, best practices, and programmes related to workable solutions among corporations, businesses, industrial associations, households, and other stakeholders (Kennedy, 2016). At the macro level, social marketing could consider enrolling government support in tackling marketing system design issues in a way that warmth rationing turns into an irrational, unwarranted, and unjust 'macro-value' from the system actors' point of view (Kadirov, 2018).

In this chapter, I will argue that wicked problems related to marketing system design issues can be examined and analysed through the chrematistics framework (Kadirov, Varey, & Wolfenden, 2016). The framework is particularly useful in scrutinising the hidden structure of the problem. This analysis can potentially provide avenues for further action for public policy and macro-social marketing practice. Specifically, the use of chrematistics in macro-social marketing helps the social marketer to identify the power structures at the macro, meso, and micro levels perpetuating the wicked problem. By understanding the structure of the problem, system-wide interventions relating to the general societal drive for profit over societal wellbeing can be developed.

The Chrematistics Framework

Aristotle defined 'chrematistics' as the art of wealth generation and acquisition. Although wealth generation is a neutral process, the concept of chrematistics is mostly associated with its negative connotation. In this sense, chrematistics means obsession with money-making, where money is taken as an ultimate end. Chrematistics comes into play when money generation becomes the sole purpose of marketing system design rather than a means to attaining societal wellbeing. Another factor in the chrematistics equation is the use of market power. Taking this perspective, Kadirov et al. (2016) define chrematistics as the regulative impact of market action of actors with power on marketing system design and operations. If chrematistics is geared to wealth acquisition only, then its effect on society may be negative. For instance, it can be seen in the example of the energy marketing system in New Zealand driving wealth acquisition before social wellbeing through manipulating citizens' access to warmth in winter. The abridged framework for analysing chrematistics in marketing systems involves the following steps:

- Delineating and characterising focal marketing systems
- Analysing symptoms of chrematistics
- Identifying forgone alternatives
- Assessing collective self-deception and societal rhetoric

The subsequent sections of this chapter will focus on the application of the chrematistics framework to the analysis of the structure of the warmth rationing problem in New Zealand.

The Analysis of Chrematistics

Delineating the Marketing System

Warmth rationing is related to institutional conditions perpetuated by focal marketing systems. Here, the focal marketing system is the totality of market regulatory activities in the energy market effected by different system actors. These actors are:

- Power generating companies: Genesis Energy, Contact Energy, Meridian Energy, Mercury Energy, and TrustPower. This is an oligopolistic supply system, where five big companies control over 90% of the market.
- Retailers: about 30 brands, including the previous five big companies, supply electricity directly to consumers.
- National Transmission Network: Transpower, a state-owned company, operates high-voltage lines, which transport electricity from generating companies to local distribution networks.
- Local Distribution Networks: regional companies that operate medium/low-voltage lines and transport energy from the National Transmission Network to individual consumers.
- Consumers: residential, commercial, and industrial actors. New Zealand's Aluminium Smelter Ltd consumes 12% of electricity, while residential consumers account for just over 30% of electricity demand.
- Regulating Bodies: Electricity Authority is an independent entity that regulates the market.
- Other government actors: Commerce Commission, Ministry of Consumer Affairs, Electricity and Gas Complaints Commission, Energy Efficiency and Conservation Authority, Ministry for the Environment, Ministry of Business, Innovation and Employment.
- Other stakeholders: Consumer NZ, Business NZ Energy Council, Electricity Networks Association, Electricity Retailers' Association NZ, Major Electricity Users' Group.
- Societal stakeholders: researchers, investigators, commentators, media.

It is argued that a well-balanced energy system needs to solve 'the energy trilemma', that is, the energy supply must be affordable, reliable, and sustainable. In fact, electricity is a standard commodity and different system design configurations are possible. Since 1999, the reforms moved the NZ energy system from a public system of provisioning to a deformed 'market-like' institution. Although Electricity Authority NZ claims that the supply side of the system has become more efficient and reliable, arguably due to some 'competition' created through the wholesale spot market and the retailer-consumer market, many independent commentators maintain that the system is dysfunctional. The International Energy Agency's (IEA) review in 2016 found that the electricity price for residential customers in New Zealand saw a radical increase in the last several years which surpassed the IEA average. In the wake of this news, the New Zealand government has initiated a review of electricity prices (Ministry of Business, Innovation, & Employment, 2018). The purpose of the review was to find out whether the current energy system delivers a 'fair and equitable' price to consumers. Energy and Resources Minister Megan Woods commented: *"residential electricity prices have risen by around 50 per cent since 2000 but the price for business remained flat. We want to find out why that is"*. Such comments reflect a public consensus that there is a clearly visible symptom: Energy prices have become less affordable.

Investigating Symptoms

The investigation of the symptoms of a problem is the first step of the chrematistics analysis process. To locate a relevant symptom of warmth rationing, one needs to investigate whether myopia exists regarding the recognition of community priorities within the system. As it can be observed, there are several developments in the NZ energy sector that indicate possible myopia. First, it must be recognised that communities and households need a reliable and affordable supply of energy, while from the societal perspective the marketing system must be designed to provision this need. However, the current situation in the energy supply system is underscored by a growing warmth rationing tendency that is exacerbated by the system's irrational focus on profits. Here, we have to distinguish a marketing system from a specific actor operating within the system. A specific type of actor within the system, a 'for-profit' corporation, can be expected to act to maximise profits while ignoring the system-level health and long-term energy supply security. This can be seen in the case of Contact Energy Ltd., the runner-up in the award for the worst transitional corporation operating in New Zealand (i.e., 2004 Roger Award), which acted to the detriment of the majority of New Zealand stakeholders (Newberry & Rosenberg, 2005). Profit orientation is a normal characteristic of a specific type of marketing system actors (i.e., corporations), but not of the whole system. The generation of profits, i.e., the accumulation of huge sums of fiat currency in few accounts, is not the primary need which the system should be expected to satisfy. Neither should it be the provision of a reliable means for investing and multiplying money.

Second, it appears that the current situation in this system is underscored by the 'corporatisation' process where it is assumed that the maximisation of profits for shareholders is the sole responsibility of the system actors, while this process will somehow, perhaps indirectly, benefit consumers. The process started with the contentious 'deregulation' initiative, where the 1986 Commerce Act created favourable conditions for the removal of statutory monopolies, and then later, privatisation of the state owned enterprises (Newberry & Rosenberg, 2005). It was hoped that deregulation would lead to competition and allow consumers to enjoy the benefits of privatisation. However, the outcome appears to be less than positive. Wolak's (2009) report showed that in the NZ energy sector, the electricity generating companies were placed in a good position to exercise unilateral market power. The report argued that this power had in fact been fully exercised, which generated the customer overcharge of NZ$4.3 billion over a period of seven years. Dr. Geoff Bertram from Victoria University of Wellington estimated that the powerful players in the industry extracted over NZ$14 billion from the market in the form of pure capital gain over the period of 30 years. In relation to the Electricity Authority's belief that it is an effective system, one might argue: Yes, it is effective; but in terms of exploiting apparent vulnerabilities of the system and creating cash surpluses (Beder, 2013). However, the system is ineffective in terms of meeting the primary need of society for affordable energy.

Third, the case for myopia is reinforced if one evaluates the real cost society bears, that comes in the form of human suffering, child sickness, and winter mortality for the sake of accumulation and disbursement of excessive profits. Considering money being 'debt', i.e., the holder's claim on societal services in the future, I would call such a myopic situation the 'chrematistics craze', especially when system regulators and public policy makers make naïve decisions to uphold the interests of the investors, and thus end up doubly punishing citizens. The irony is that major investors are overseas investors. For example, Contact Energy is estimated to be 62% overseas owned (Newberry & Rosenberg, 2005). Deregulation seems to have created rent-seeking 'sharks' whose goal is "*to aggressively pursue business expansion to secure and enhance future earning capabilities*" (Newberry & Rosenberg, 2005, np). This approach puts the real interests of local consumers and foreign investors in direct conflict.

Finally, the myopic situation is exacerbated by the fact that it is assumed that the system serves 'consumers'. Since the consumer is someone who has specific needs as well as the ability to pay for the service, the system is, by design, expected to filter out many 'non-consumers' who will find the service unaffordable. First and foremost, consumers are to be seen as people. People should never be used as a 'means' for some other ends (Laczniak & Murphy, 2006). As the need for warmth is fundamental irrespective of whether a person qualifies as a consumer or not, it is very easy to highjack this fundamental need for other ulterior motives if government does not offer protection. Evidence shows that as the system became more commercialised, the number of network disconnections surged (RadioNZ, 2018). Society has become the victim of 'marketisation' and the illusory hope that workable competition is possible for electricity (Newberry & Rosenberg, 2005). However, in this case, a free market, where the consumer faces multiple alternatives, does not really exist. A 'market' is not less than a fantasy which some myopic system actors maintain. In fact, a free market in electricity is impossible, as the consumer is unable to choose 'non-consumption' (Easton, 1995; Newberry & Rosenberg, 2005).

Another symptom of the problem is the power of the key industry actors that enables them to manipulate the intensity and level of customer demand for the services they offer. In fact, the demand for electricity is extremely inelastic. This is due to the fact that the use value of electricity greatly exceeds its exchange value, often by multiple times. This is the seller's market, especially when the generators can artificially lower the output to create stronger willingness to pay for the commodity in deficit. Here, a surge in prices does not involve the risk of consumers switching to another commodity, except an illusory option for switching between retailers who offer nearly similar packages. Regarding this switching behaviour, it seems to be turning into a 'neurotic turbulence', as nearly half a million households (439,682) switched electricity companies just in 2017 (Electricity Authority, 2018). This number amounted to 1.11 million switches over the last five years. Easy switching between retailers creates a perception of consumer sovereignty, however, the benefits of such freedom seem to be illusory. Wolak (2009) shows that electricity is not a type of commodity that can be framed as a 'commercial product' in a 'free market'. Rather, it possesses all required characteristics that transform the supplier into a 'king' with unilateral market power.

Perhaps some might argue that electricity, or energy in general, is not a basic necessity of life. Such arguments mask the fact that warmth, which is generated through electricity, is, since in New Zealand the main means of maintaining warmth is electricity. If that's the case, why should electricity be left at the mercy of profit-making motives and foreign investors? As the experience of many developing countries indicates, commercialising a basic necessity of life is fraught with many dangers (Kadirov et al., 2016). Some critics oppose close public scrutiny as an undesired move towards 'communism', an idea that is strongly stigmatised. However, this argument detracts the attention from the real problem. Chrematistics, unhealthy money-making tendencies, have the same impact on both capitalist and socialist economies. If in socialist economies it leads to corruption, in capitalist economies it leads to rent-seeking.

Forgone Alternatives

To create a better understanding of the problematic situation, the chrematistics model redirects the focus onto forgone possibilities in the marketing system (Kadirov et al., 2016). From this perspective, warmth rationing is the direct result of misguided system design. The selection of a specific system design and reinforcing it through marginal policies means shunning other possible designs. Hence, other possible designs are the opportunity cost that needs to be taken into account. In the NZ energy market, the current deformed 'market-like' structures are not the only solution to the problem. Many critics proposed the move towards a single purchaser of electricity as an alternative design solution. Others opposed it, citing several disadvantages. Nevertheless, the weaknesses of the single-buyer proposal do not mean that the current design alternative must be the best one. There could be many other alternatives to the current system which need to be properly evaluated.

One of such alternatives is the introduction of options that guarantee the attainment of 'social maxima/minima' and minimisation of social costs (Kapp, 2015). The social maximum option would be that customers would be able to receive a 'no-frills' electricity/gas contract. Such a contract should involve a supply of a standard commodity at a set price (determined by the government as the fraction of the minimum wage rate taking into account the profitability of involved institutions), which does not involve any extra value-adding services. As all suppliers would offer the same standard commodity (here electricity or gas) at the same price as a no-frills package, the locus of competition would switch to the realm of extra 'frills', i.e., services which offer extra value for customers. It can be predicted that at the beginning the majority of households would switch to the standard 'no-frills' package. However, as new creative solutions proliferate, innovative businesses will grow on the basis of the new stable foundation. It is akin to building a foundation as a 'platform' (e.g., Facebook), through which services are provided free or at low cost. This societal business design would guarantee that all societal members have a balanced, uninhibited access to the commodity, where the price would reflect the real cost of operating the whole system in a sustainable way. Other businesses would compete in the market through offering services with added value (e.g., green electricity, smart metering, grid-interactive water heaters, energy storage, and peer-to-peer trading). This is a mix of macro- and meso-level macro-social intervention. Social marketers must work with government, regulators, industrial associations, and businesses to promote the idea that many healthy alternatives are being discarded due to myopic focus on futile attempts to enable 'competition' in electricity/gas provisioning. These actors should be helped to realise that the real arena for competition is the locus of high-tech services offered beyond and above the standard commodity delivery.

Collective Self-Deception and Societal Rhetoric

The chrematistics model calls for the analysis of collective self-deception as well as rhetorical mechanisms which support such societal deception (Kadirov et al., 2016). It can be argued that warmth rationing tendencies are reinforced via collective self-deception and associated rhetorical logics. In relation to this, it can be said that New Zealand society is being misled regarding the effectiveness of the energy sector. One of the most common statistics cited is the share of renewable resources in electricity generation which is currently 82%. The target is set at the 90% level, which is to be achieved by 2025. Although these facts are impressive and fit the country's 'clean and green' image, it does not mean that the system as a whole is responsive to the real needs of the country's population. Although the system can be made more sustainable, it might fail to cater to the needs of all members of society. Perhaps, further research is needed on *potentially sustainable but not just* marketing systems. For instance, even if New Zealand reaches the target of 90% renewable energy in the future, it would not mean that the warmth rationing problem would disappear. Social marketers must work to de-mystify such claims, perhaps through encouraging critical activity among citizens in online media, through exposing the misleading nature of government-set goals.

Another rhetorical 'trick' that is being used currently is the narrative of the 'death cycle' with regard to customers installing solar panels who are supposedly turning into a 'burden' on local networks. These customers, framed as 'wealthy' just because they can afford solar systems, are blamed for driving the prices up. It is believed that as these people minimise their usage of electricity and their cost, this would increase the 'cost' to be shared for all others. Such a narrative is being reiterated by the government as well. Energy and Resources Minister Megan Woods issued a warning: "*the Government is watching to make sure low-income consumers don't end up facing higher electricity costs caused by wealthier people installing solar power units*" (Stuff, 2018b, np). Some local distributors, for example, Unison in Hawkes Bay, introduced a solar charge for households installing solar panels. It appears that the logic of chrematistics dictates how sustainability should be framed. For the incumbents of the industry, it is not about attaining an optimal form of sustainability. It is about the correct form of 'sustainability', which should not hinder profit maximisation. Hence, the industry circulates rhetorical reports that are completely anti-solar in order to encourage public self-deception. This seems to be a paradoxical move, considering the world-wide trend of fast solar technology uptake. Nonetheless, it is not a surprising finding from the chrematistics framework's point of view. To combat this rhetoric, macro-social marketing campaigns can promote the ideology of Solar Commons (www.solarcommons.org), focusing on providing community trusts with solar technologies and using resulting income to finance energy assistance for low-income households. The case in point is the Solar Commons project in Tucson, Arizona (Hanson, 2017). In addition, social macro-markets can work towards society-wide acceptance of two important tweaks in the legal foundation: a law that prohibits local distributors from applying extra solar charges, and a law of 'net metering' and feed-in tariffs, crediting the customer's account for the amount of energy they have produced.

Last but not least, the societal debates over less or more deregulation and the need for nationalisation versus privatisation appear to be rhetorical diversion strategies that mask more fundamental problems (Beder, 2013). The real question is not whether society needs more/less privatisation, rather whether marketing systems are effectively designed to counter the damaging effects of narrow-minded chrematistics.

Concluding Remarks and Macro-Social Marketing Implications

Access to affordable energy may not be a human right per se, but access to warmth in cold climates is. Warmth rationing is increasingly emerging as a new wicked problem in New Zealand. Citizens, including children, are directly experiencing the consequences of some of the myopic policies perpetuated by powerful system actors related to energy system design. The societal need for affordable, reliable, and sustainable energy supply is not being met, while the energy marketing system is racking up billions of 'surplus' money. Although the government expressed concern over high prices, it is not prepared to take radical steps to rectify the problematic situation. For some marketing system actors who are under the 'spell' of chrematistics, warmth rationing may not even appear to be a problem. The satisfactory solution to the problem may require transformative system re-design, which should involve system actors' disenchantment with 'money-making'.

The energy marketing system should be redesigned with major emphasis being placed upon community energy provisioning (instead of attempting to engineer 'perfect' wholesale or retail exchange). Rather than only privileging large-scale producers and distributors, the doors of opportunity must be opened to small-to-medium scale community-level energy provisioning networks. In such distributed energy generation networks, every actor is an energy generator, a user, and an energy storage agent at the same time. In such networks, energy is not 'a product' to be exchanged, rather it is a common resource that is enabled, produced, shared, and consumed collectively (Martinez, 2017). Social macro-marketers can play an important role in such transformation. Possible macro-social interventions could include: a) facilitating the change of a societal mind-set, that is, to promote the urgency of the societal task of re-conceptualising energy as a commons and the energy marketing system as a system of custodianship over energy commons; b) creating a societal discourse on the perils of granting unbalanced power to specific groups (including foreign investors) who might employ this commons as a means of money-making; c) rallying public support for groups advancing community interests concerning distributed energy generation; and d) enhancing societal awareness of alternative energy-related laws and bylaws (e.g., energy price cap, feed-in-tariffs, net metering). At the meso level, macro- social marketers could employ the following interventions: a) training government agencies, public policy makers, and industry regulators to recognise ideological differences between community provisioning and chrematistics; b) collaborating with businesses and industrial associations to promote innovative ways of solving warmth rationing issues; c) ensuring the inclusion of warmth rationing into the corporate sustainability agenda and the discussion of warmth rationing mitigation in corporate sustainability and community reports; and d) partnering with regional and local councils in improving housing energy efficiency (e.g., assuring that every premise must have its energy efficiency rating and certificate like its seismic performance rating under the Building Act). The micro-level interventions should highlight the negative consequences of warmth rationing on health, wellbeing, and social dynamics. Another point is that the individual must be persuaded that the solution for warmth provisioning issues must be sought through engagement in community initiatives and projects rather than through an isolated consumerist activity (e.g., dreaming about or attempting to earn more money to make warmth affordable). Social marketing, through traditional and online media, should inculcate the idea that warmth rationing cannot be solved individually, one person at a time. Systems and community-level changes are necessary.

Macro-social marketing is defined as the use of social marketing techniques to effect a societal-level change which would involve changing the context of the behaviour under focus (Domegan, 2008; Kennedy & Parsons, 2012). Most often, it would need a re-design of marketing systems (Kennedy, 2016). Macro-social marketers, including public policy makers, should realise that warmth rationing is a different kind of beast. Unlike societal ills such as smoking or obesity, it is associated with unhealthy decrease rather than increase in consumption. Although micro-social marketing can be used to discourage warmth-rationing and encourage effective energy consumption at an individual level by stressing negative health consequences, a rather fundamental approach to re-configure how citizens see themselves as well as society is needed. For the vital commodities such as energy, macro-social marketing should re-focus system design from the logic of 'exchange in markets' to 'provisioning in society'. The societal understanding of the situation should be shifted beyond a micro-managerial logic that energy provisioning is akin to a chocolate bar business. Energy provisioning pertains to the domain of invaluable resources (i.e., a resource beyond market valuation) which is related to human dignity (Jagadale, Kadirov, & Chakraborty, 2018).

Specifically, Kennedy (2016) suggests that macro-social marketers should aim to change economic-task norms and cultural-moral institutional norms. In the energy marketing system, the current economic-task norms are formed around social mechanisms such as deregulation, privatisation, and competition. These are seen to be positive forces that would 'magically' entail low-cost, reliable, and effective services for consumers while ensuring reliable earnings for investors. In reality, the former is never realised, while consumers cornered to be exploited as 'cash cows' are thrown at the altar of chrematistics. Some may call this smart business, but macro-social marketers must expose such chrematistics rhetoric to initiate a nation-wide norm shift. Humorous social marketing campaigns may work best in such situations. For example, the intervention could borrow from HPA's innovative approach to tackle excessive alcohol consumption through the provision of a fun 'language', such as 'Say Yeah, Nah'. The target market for such campaigns could be the population of low socio-economic status, for whom the concepts such as 'deregulation' might sound like a positive mystery. The social marketing campaign may provide this population with a new language that would signify the concepts such as 'deregulation' using connotations such as 'daylight robbery' or 'rent-seeking'. Moreover, a new cultural-moral institutional norm that needs to be inculcated in all levels of society is the notion that warmth is a human right. Perhaps the first step would be to prepare a legal foundation for such shift. For example, in Canada, the U.S., and Europe, city bylaws require minimum indoor temperature of 20–22°C to be maintained in a sustainable way in residential homes, rented buildings, and public spaces. Macro-social marketers should promote this view, which needs to gain society-wide acceptance, that there should be a legal minimum warmth requirement stipulated by bylaws in New Zealand. Social marketers could employ guerrilla marketing techniques to highlight the importance of this issue. For example, a social marketing campaign can replicate Duracell's Moments of Warmth campaign first introduced in Canada. This campaign targeted frequent travellers using public transport. The social marketers employed bus shelters equipped with heaters which would provide warmth only if people cooperated with each other to activate them.

Furthermore, macro-social marketers must work towards weakening the one-system-design-fits-all logic. The system should be broadened to include multiple regimes, technologies, networks, and arrangements. This concept is represented by societal movements for energy democracy (Burke & Stephens, 2017). It is even possible to employ processes such as privatisation, corporatisation, and competition to the advantage of the nation, without letting foreign investors dictate their chrematistics-oriented conditions. For instance, creating workable competition within the system is not impossible in energy markets, as some economists argued. It would simply require a cap on the price for the key commodities only (e.g., electricity, gas), while the prices for other related services would be left to float. Consequently, the domain of competition would shift to the supply of added value. Moreover, the idea of local energy-generating, prosumer community networks must be empowered, where these networks would be based on the use of locally sourced renewable energy (e.g., solar), distributed generation, and innovative energy storage technologies. Macro-social marketers can use the community-based social marketing approach (McKenzie-Mohr, 2011) to promote energy democracy (Burke & Stephens, 2017; Morris & Jungjohann, 2016). The community-based social marketing approach emphasises direct contact with community members and the removal of barriers that impede the desired change. At a macro level, the social marketing activity must focus on removing legal and structural barriers and introducing solutions that would motivate the change. At a meso level, the work would involve securing commitment from the energy marketing system actors to work towards energy democracy and tackling institutional barriers for implementation. At a micro level, social marketing campaigns could focus on promoting the future vision of distributed generation and gradually transforming individuals by instilling in them the social identity of a responsible prosumer.

References

BBC. (2011). *How warm is your home?* [Online] Retrieved July 30, 2018, from www.bbc.com/news/ magazine-12606943

Beder, S. (2013). The real cause of electricity price rises. *Australian Options*, 72, 14–16.

Burke, M. J., & Stephens, J. C. (2017). Energy democracy: Goals and policy instruments for sociotechnical transitions. *Energy Research and Social Science*, *33*, 35–48.

Davie, G. S., Baker, M. G., Hales, S., & Carlin, J. B. (2007). Trends and determinants of excess winter mortality in New Zealand: 1980 to 2000. *BMC Public Health*, *7*(1), 263–272.

Domegan, C. T. (2008). Social marketing: Implications for contemporary marketing practices classification scheme. *Journal of Business and Industrial Marketing*, *23*(2), 135–141.

Easton, B., (1995, July 8). Competitive electricity: Whatever the equation, power prices will rise. *Listener*, 56.

Electricity Authority. (2018). *Retail category: Dashboards: Annual switching activity summary*. [Online] Retrieved July 29, 2018, from www.emi.ea.govt. nz/Retail/Dashboards/

Hales, S., Blakely, T., Foster, R. H., Baker, M. G., & Howden-Chapman, P. (2012). Seasonal patterns of mortality in relation to social factors. *Journal of Epidemiology and Community Health*, *66*(4), 379–384.

Hanson, F. (2017). The sun shines for everyone: Creating community solar business models that include culturally and geographically diverse low-income Americans. *Lindmark Fellowship in Ethics*, *3* [Online] Retrieved July 29, 2018, from https://digitalcommons. csbsju.edu

Howden-Chapman, P., Viggers, H., Chapman, R., O'Dea, D., Free, S., & O'Sullivan, K. (2009). Warm homes: Drivers of the demand for heating in the residential sector in New Zealand. *Energy Policy*, *37*(9), 3387–3399.

Jagadale, S. R., Kadirov, D., & Chakraborty, D. (2018). Tackling the subaltern quandary: Marketing systems of dignity. *Journal of Macromarketing*, *38*(1), 91–111.

Kadirov, D. (2018). Towards a theory of marketing systems as the public good. *Journal of Macromarketing*, *38*(3), 278–297.

Kadirov, D., Varey, R. J., & Wolfenden, S. (2016). Investigating chrematistics in marketing systems: A research framework. *Journal of Macromarketing, 36*(1), 54–67.

Kapp, K. W. (2015). *The heterodox theory of social costs.* London: Routledge.

Kennedy, A. M. (2016). Macro-social marketing. *Journal of Macromarketing, 36*(3), 354–365.

Kennedy, A. M., & Parsons, A. (2012). Macro-social marketing and social engineering: A systems approach. *Journal of Social Marketing, 2*(1), 37–51.

Laczniak, G. R., & Murphy, P. E. (2006). Normative perspectives for ethical and socially responsible marketing. *Journal of Macromarketing, 26*(2), 154–177.

Martinez, C. (2017). From commodification to the commons: Charting the pathway for energy democracy. In D. Fairchild & Al Weinrub (Eds.), *Energy democracy* (pp. 21–36). Washington, DC: Island Press.

McKenzie-Mohr, D. (2011). *Fostering sustainable behavior: An introduction to community-based social marketing.* Gabriola Island, Canada: New Society Publishers.

Ministry of Business, Innovation, and Employment. (2018). *Electricity price review* [Online] Retrieved July 29, 2018, from www.mbie.govt.nz/info-services/sectors-industries/energy/current-reviews-consultations/electricity-price-review

Morris, C., & Jungjohann, A. (2016). *Energy democracy: Germany's Energiewende to renewables.* London: Palgrave Macmillan.

Newberry, S., & Rosenberg, B. (2005). *Electricity reforms and contact energy ltd* [Online] Retrieved July 28, 2018, from www.converge.org.nz/watchdog/08/06.htm

RadioNZ. (2018). *Surge in electricity disconnections over unpaid bills* [Online] Retrieved July 28, 2018, from www.radionz.co.nz/news/national/359094/surge-in-electricity-disconnections-over-unpaid-bills

The Spinoff. (2017). *'It wasn't supposed to be like this': Starting life from scratch in industrial West Auckland* [Online] Retrieved July 25, 2018, from https://thespinoff.co.nz/auckland/22-03-2017/it-wasnt-supposed-to-be-like-this-starting-life-from-scratch-in-industrial-west-auckland/

Stuff. (2018a). *Being cold and rationing heating is now 'normal' in New Zealand* [Online] Retrieved July 27, 2018, from www.stuff.co.nz/business/money/104100512/being-cold-and-rationing-heating-is-now-normal-in-new-zealand

Stuff. (2018b). *Way to be cleared for big electricity players to prey on low-income households.* [Online] Retrieved July 25, 2018, from www.stuff.co.nz/national/politics/opinion/102708888/way-to-be-cleared-for-big-electricity-players-to-prey-on-lowincome-households

Wolak, F. (2009). *An assessment of the performance of the New Zealand wholesale electricity market.* Wellington, New Zealand: Report for the New Zealand Commerce Commission.

Contributors

Paul Ballantine

Paul W. Ballantine is a Professor of Marketing and Head of the Business School at the University of Canterbury in Christchurch, New Zealand. His research interests include retailing, consumption behaviour (particularly the negative aspects of consumption), and social and ethical issues in marketing. His recent publications have appeared in outlets including the *Journal of Retailing and Consumer Services, Journal of Marketing Management, Journal of Brand Management*, and the *Journal of Consumer Behaviour*.

Stephan Dahl

Stephan Dahl is the founder of the The Quinta Project Social Enterprise in Portugal and Adjunct Associate Professor at James Cook University. His research interests include social media, marketing ethics, and social marketing, and he has published in national and international journals, including the *Journal of Advertising Research* and *Journal of Marketing Management*. He is an editorial board member of the *International Journal of Advertising* and the *Journal of Consumer Affairs*. He published the books *Social Media Marketing: Theories of Digital Communications* and *Marketing Ethics & Society* (both Sage) and is also the co-author of *Social Marketing* (Pearson) and *Integrated Marketing Communications* (Taylor and Francis).

Kim Daniloski

Dr. Daniloski is an Associate Collegiate Professor of Marketing at Virginia Tech. Daniloski has published journal articles on her research in social marketing, social influence, and analytic methods and has presented her work at national conferences in consumer behaviour and marketing and public policy. Dr. Daniloski is also the co-director of several study abroad programmes based in Switzerland and East African Nations.

Christine Domegan

Dr. Christine Domegan is an applied systems thinking researcher with over 20 years' experience and a Senior Lecturer in Marketing at the National University of Ireland, Galway; Visiting Professor, Florida Prevention Research Center; and Fellow and Associate of the World Health Organization Collaborating Center on Social Marketing and Social Change at the University of South Florida; Adjunct Professor, Griffith University; and Honorary Associate Professor, Institute of Social Marketing (ISM), Scotland. Christine is the European editor for the *Journal of Social Marketing* and co-author of *Social Marketing: Rebels with a Cause*, 2018, which draws upon her work as lead social innovation methodologist on a number of European Union (EU)-funded projects, including Sea for Society, Sea Change, and Seas, Oceans in Public Health in Europe.

Lynne Eagle

Professor Lynne Eagle's research interests centre on trans-disciplinary approaches to sustained behaviour change in social marketing/health promotion/environmental protection. She researches marketing communication effects and effectiveness, including the impact of persuasive communication and the challenges of communicating effectively with population sectors that face specific challenges. She has published widely and is on the editorial board of several journals. Her work has been cited extensively by academics and industry spokespeople. She has served on national advisory committees and consulted with the health service, local authorities, and councils on a range of social marketing/behaviour change issues.

Jeff French

Professor Jeff French is a global thought leader in the fields of behavioural influence, social marketing, social communication, and citizen focused programme planning and evaluation.

Jeff has published over 100 academic papers and five books plus numerous guides and tool kits on these subjects, including the European Centre for Disease Control first technical guidance on social marketing. Jeff is a visiting Professor at Brighton University and a Fellow at Kings College London University and teaches at four other universities on a regular basis. Previously, he was Director of Policy and Communication at the UK Health Development Agency and a senior civil servant in the UK Department of Health. In 2004, Jeff led the UK government review of social marketing and set up the National Social Marketing Centre in 2005. In 2009 Jeff became the CEO of Strategic Social Marketing.

Jeff has worked in over 30 countries with NGOs, private sector companies, government departments, and agencies on behavioural programmes related to: health, transport, road safety, fire safety, drug and alcohol misuse, sexual health, gambling, forestry, environmental issues, public sector responsiveness, sustainable fishing, financial literacy, public sector recruitment, volunteer recruitment, obesity prevention, smoking school health, animal health, and public service reconfiguration.

Maja Golf-Papez

Dr. Golf-Papez is a Lecturer in Marketing at the University of Sussex, UK. She completed her PhD in Marketing at the University of Canterbury, New Zealand. Her research interests lie in exploring the consumption of technology; specifically, Maja's thesis research sought to understand online trolling as a form of consumer misbehaviour. Maja's work has been published in *Journal of Marketing Management* and *Advances in Consumer Research* and has been presented at several international conferences. Prior to her doctoral studies, Maja worked as the Chief Marketing Officer for a charity dedicated to alleviating child poverty in Slovenia.

Anne Hamby

Dr. Hamby is an Assistant Professor in Marketing and International Business at Hofstra University. Her research interests fall in the areas of consumer psychology and narrative processing, or how consumers understand and are persuaded by narrative messages.

Dr. Hamby has international experience working in several African countries developing adolescent risk-behaviour reduction programmes, including a year living in South Africa as a research associate on a Kellogg foundation funded project. She has taught marketing courses for several semesters in Lugano, Switzerland and has also worked with international, heath-focused professional associations in Switzerland on multiple marketing-related projects.

Djavlonbek Kadirov

Djavlonbek Kadirov (Ph.D., University of Waikato) is a marketing lecturer at the School of Marketing and International Business, Victoria University of Wellington, New Zealand. Djavlonbek's research interests include marketing systems theory, symbolism in marketing systems, sustainable marketing, and marketing morality. His research has appeared in journals such as *Journal of Macromarketing, Journal of Marketing Management, Journal of Business Research, Journal of Brand Management, Consumption Markets & Culture,* and *Journal of Customer Behaviour.*

Sommer Kapitan

Sommer Kapitan is a senior lecturer in marketing at Auckland University of Technology. In her research and teaching, she focuses on sustainability, advertising effectiveness, and consumer wellbeing.

Joya Kemper

Dr. Joya Kemper is a Lecturer in Marketing at the University of Auckland Business School. Her research focuses on how to transition to a sustainable and healthy society through individual and institutional change. Joya's interests include the broad areas of sustainability marketing, healthy and sustainable eating, social marketing, ethical and sustainable issues surrounding business activities, and marketing education. She has published in outlets such as the *Journal of Macromarketing, Journal of Marketing Management, Journal of Social Marketing*, and *Tobacco Control.*

Ann-Marie Kennedy

Dr. Ann-Marie Kennedy is a senior lecturer in marketing at the University of Canterbury. She specialises in macro-social marketing and sustainability. Her research has been published in the *European Journal of Marketing, Journal of Marketing Management, Journal of Social Marketing*, and *Journal of Macromarketing*, among others. She has worked with the New Zealand Transport Agency, Catholic Church of New Zealand, Canterbury Clinical Network, and the Cancer Society on their social marketing.

Matthias Koch

Matthias Koch worked as lecturer at the University of Melbourne, Australia. His publications have appeared in *Industrial Marketing Management* and *Journal of Business-to-Business Marketing*. He held general management positions in the industry and now works as CMO in Germany.

Krzysztof Kubacki

Dr. Krzysztof Kubacki is Associate Professor in Marketing at Social Marketing@Griffith, Griffith Business School. After working for several years as a musician for the Helena Modrzejewska Theatre and Wrocław Opera House in Poland, he became a full-time academic in 2003 when he joined the University of Glamorgan, moving to Keele University in 2006. Krzysztof's research focuses on identification, trial, evaluation, and critique of behaviour change programmes. Recently he spent five years (2013–2018) working as VicHealth's Social Marketing Research

Practice Fellow. The findings and frameworks emanating from his VicHealth Fellowship have directly informed state and nationwide behaviour change programmes. His research has been published in over 100 books, book chapters, journal articles, and industry and government reports.

David Low

Professor David Low has been the Dean of the College of Business and Law at Charles Darwin University since July 2018. He was previously the Dean of the College of Business, Law and Governance at James Cook University, 2014 to 2018; Head of School–Business JCU, 2011 to 2014; and Head of School–UWS School of Marketing, 2006 to 2011.

David holds a Doctorate in Marketing and Management and is a Graduate Member of the Australian Institute of Company Directors as well as a Fellow of the Institute of Public Accountants and a CPA. He has held a wide variety of both industry and academic management and boardroom positions and spent the first half of his working life in industry.

David's research interests include social marketing, cross cultural issues, country of origin Studies, ethnicity, market orientation, firm performance, e-marketing, innovation, SMEs, and the use of technology in business value chains.

Patricia McHugh

Dr. Patricia McHugh is a Lecturer in Marketing at the National University of Ireland, Galway. Patricia's passion for achieving change and societal impact has led her to spend the last 10 years designing and implementing a Co-Creation Toolkit and an Impact Assessment Framework for Environmental Behaviour Change and Engagement. Patricia's roles on European Funded Projects SOPHIE, Sea Change, and Sea for Society involve designing and implementing Applied Systems Thinking for Change. Patricia has published her work in the *Journal of Social Marketing, Social Marketing Quarterly, Journal of Marketing Management, Social Indicators Research* and *Marine Policy.*

Davide C. Orazi

Davide C. Orazi is Assistant Professor of Marketing at Monash Business School, Australia. His research is mainly in consumer psychology applied to consumer wellbeing and narrative consumption, with a keen interest on the application of psycho-physiological research methods. He has published in *International Journal of Research in Marketing, Journal of Business Research, Journal of Business*

Ethics, *European Journal of Marketing*, and *Journal of Macromarketing*, among others.

Meghan Pierce

Meghan Pierce is an Assistant Professor of Marketing at La Salle University. She received her B.S. in Marketing, B.A. in Foreign Languages and Literatures, M.S. in Marketing Research, and Ph.D. in Marketing from Virginia Tech, with several years spent working with the Health Communication Lab and Center for Organizational Research at the University of Lugano, in Switzerland. Prior to La Salle, she was an Assistant Professor of Marketing at the Catholic University of Chile. She teaches Consumer Behaviour, Principles of Marketing, and Marketing Research. Her research is focused in two areas: how people understand and interpret social information and international social development. Her work has been published in *Journal of Macromarketing*, *Journal of Services Marketing*, *Group Processes and Intergroup Relations*, *Social Marketing Quarterly*, and the *International Marketing Review* and presented at international conferences such as the Association for Consumer Research, Marketing Science, Society for Consumer Psychology, and Public Policy and Marketing.

Liam Pomfret

Dr. Liam Pomfret is an Associate Lecturer in Marketing in the UQ Business School. His research relates to consumer privacy, with a focus on consumer decision making and behaviour for privacy protection, and disclosure of personal information. He has a particular interest in the application of systems thinking to the understanding of firms' ethical responsibilities in marketing, and to understanding complex social problems to which marketing activities have contributed. He holds positions on the boards of the Australian Privacy Foundation and Electronic Frontiers Australia.

Josephine Previte

Dr. Josephine Previte is a Senior Lecturer in Marketing in the UQ Business School whose research focuses on the socio-cultural aspects of consumer behaviour, market systems, transformative service, and social change. She is particularly interested in applying alternative research approaches such as Q methodology and interpretive textual and visual research methods to study social problems, gender, and social technologies. She has worked on a broad range of social marketing projects, including alcohol consumption, breastfeeding, breast screening, blood donation, and new technology use to deliver social marketing services. Her scholarship has appeared in the *Journal of*

Macromarketing, Journal of Marketing Management, European Journal of Marketing, Journal of Social Marketing, Australian Feminist Studies, and *Journal of Sociology.*

Natalia Szablewska

Dr. Natalia Szablewska is Senior Lecturer at the School of Law and Justice, Southern Cross University (Australia) and Adjunct Professor at the Royal University of Law and Economics (Cambodia). She has over 15 years of experience spanning across the public sector, governmental and non-governmental organisations, and academia in five countries. Natalia is a social scientist and lawyer specialising in human rights (law) and transformative justice processes. Her research centres on themes at the intersection of law, public policy, and ethics, and she employs gender and human rights approaches to examine issues relating to vulnerable populations and social and legal (in-)equalities. Natalia has published widely for academic and non-academic audiences, and her academic work has appeared in leading law and social sciences journals.

Srishti Varma

Srishti Varma is currently pursuing her marketing graduate degree at Monash University. In the future, she intends to be involved in researching and innovating solutions related to educational opportunities in developing communities.

Ekant Veer

Dr. Veer is an Associate Professor of Marketing at the University of Canterbury Business School, New Zealand. His primary areas of interest include the use of marketing technologies and advertising to encourage social change and the role that online consumption patterns play in developing consumer identity. His work has been published in a number of international journals, including *Journal of Public Policy and Marketing, European Journal of Marketing, Journal of Consumer Behaviour,* and *Journal of Marketing Management.*

Ben Wooliscroft

Ben Wooliscroft is Professor of Macromarketing at Auckland University of Technology, New Zealand. He has published widely in marketing journals and is an associate editor of the *Journal of Macromarketing,* where much of his research is published. His research focuses on sustainable business, ethical consumption, and the transitions that society requires to become more sustainable.

Kseniia Zahrai

Ms. Zahrai is a doctoral student at the University of Canterbury, New Zealand. Her doctoral thesis investigates the impact social media and wider influencing factors play on consumer wellbeing and welfare. Prior to starting her doctoral studies, Kseniia worked as a consultant with over 10 years of marketing, communications, and advertising experience with some of Ukraine's most popular brands.

Index

Note: page numbers in *italics* indicate figures; page numbers in **bold** indicate tables.